WHAT ARE PEOPLE SAYING ABOUT *ELEVEN 22?*

You will laugh; you will cry; you will sing praises. You will live firsthand, utter devastation . . . yet be amazed at the strength of faith, the character, and joy in the heart of a courageous young fighter. Jenna faced the giants of death and darkness with only the bright shining light of her amazing soul, and a family of saints. Her goodness was too much for this world. Her power, though only internal, moved mountains and people around her. The best book I have read in years.

— **J. Thompson Cravens,**
Esquire, Cravens & Noll
Former Captain, U.S. Army
Former U.S. Army Judge Advocate General's Corp. (JAG)

Jenna's story is hard—hard to believe the unending pain she went through, hard for the reader to agonize with her, and best of all, hard to put down. This is a story of resilience and faith, of love and triumph. What is missing is complaining and self-pity. Instead, we see an optimism even in the setbacks and darkest hours. When I met Jenna, she had endured many of the trials you are about to read. I can assure the reader the person I met and the person you are about to meet in this piece of work are the genuine article—both worth your time. This book will introduce you to the kind of person we'd all like to be.

— **Dr. William Gribbin**
Former Dean and Professor of English, Liberty University

Jenna's story is amazing and truly one that leaves the reader in awe and amazement. I cried as I read about Jenna's journey, as J. A. Sailsbury's words brought back so many fears and hopes I once faced. It is inspirational and emotional and leaves you questioning how much one body can endure before shutting down.

— **Michelle Crocker**
Mother
Cellmate

Glorious story of extraordinary courage demonstrated throughout an excruciating journey. Jenna, a battle-tested soldier, worthy of the struggle. God picked this young girl for a journey, a journey delivering a compelling message because He knew she would see it through to the end, whenever her end may be. She was surrounded by family, friends, thousands of everyday people, and professionals who rose to the occasion—with many Esther's in this story who showed up *for such a time as this*. I believed God would deliver Jenna. What I did not know until now, was why, how, or what she would have to endure. I am humbled and shamed to know the extent of the suffering she endured to run her race—few, if any, could have.

— **Joe Amadee III**
Former, Senior Advisor to the Assistant Secretary of the
Army for Acquisition, Logistics and Technology
Senior Vice President International Business True Velocity Ammunition and Weapons
Executive Consultant for Defense Contractors, Defense
Industrial Base and United States Army

Jenna – a name I only prayed for until I had the privilege to call her my friend. Words cannot express how her life has blessed mine and anyone who has ever met her. Jenna's life has taught me despite whatever happens in my life, there is a purposeful plan in it.

— **Sharon J. Hartless**
Retired Vice President for Administration,
Liberty University

ELEVEN 22 is an amazing book recounting many potentially fatal circumstances beyond Jenna's control. Her journey was a long and arduous one continuing for over a decade. Along the way, she was courageous, matured beyond her years, and developed a perspective on life containing many lessons for the readers of this book. These lessons will focus on the most important things in life, and when taken to heart, will have a lasting impact on the reader. Jenna is my hero!

— **Joanne Kurtzberg, MD**
Jerome Harris Distinguished Professor of Pediatrics and Professor of Pathology
Director, Marcus Center for Cellular Cures
Director, Pediatric Blood and Marrow Transplant Program
Director, Carolinas Cord Blood Bank
Co-Director, Stem Cell Transplant Laboratory Duke University Medical Center

---

Suffering—it is a point even the greatest authors and poets have grappled with over the course of the millennia, attempting to justify its reality and provide an escape. It may be absurd to think when challenged by this immense adversity, we have a choice, even if relief is only for a moment. Few stories throughout human history enlighten the internal warfare with suffering and how to live with it. This is one of them.

— **Alex Lemieux**
Automotive Journalist
Freelance Writer

We all need constant reminders of how amazing God really is. Jenna's life is one of those reminders. With shocking vulnerability, the author shares not only Jenna's physical struggles but also her struggles with faith and fear. As I watched Jenna suffer for many years, I learned to lean in and listen to how she was wrestling with hard questions. I saw how every hardship in her life was serving God's purposes for her life. I'm overjoyed others now get to read Jenna's story. As you read this book, your heart will experience the gospel in new ways, even embracing trials and grief with joy.

— **Ryan Doherty**
Pastor of Mobilization, Apex Campus,
The Summit Church, Durham, NC

ELEVEN 22

J.A. SAILSBURY

[signature]

11/19/23

To everyone who prayed . . . all over the world.

CONTENTS

AUTHOR'S NOTE

Everything in this story is based on real experiences and actual events. It's shared with you through the memories and journals of friends, family, and others mentioned in this work of non-fiction. Please understand there are tragic, heart-wrenching stories within, but the resilience of the human spirit will illuminate hope throughout the book.

FOREWORD

It's been many years since the event which brought Jenna and I together, and while some details are shaky, the feelings, impressions, and impact of that day remain with me still. My life at the time was extremely full and as busy as I've ever been. I was shooting a television show called *JAG*, which at the time was in full swing and a big show for CBS. The demands on me were tremendous. I worked on average, 15–18-hour days, five days a week, and would then often be tasked with attending events, photo shoots, talk shows, and interviews on the weekends. It was during one of those busy days that my publicist called me on the set of *JAG* and said a request had come in for me to visit a young girl. While I had been a part of many charitable events in the past involving children in need, there was no way I could prepare myself for this one.

As a father of a beautiful 6-year-old little girl at the time, meeting Jenna that day in 1999 really hit home for me. It was a moment that changed my life forever. What Jenna endured in her lifespan would make anyone cry, "surrender." Her story is filled with moments of absolute heartbreak and moments of triumph. Most of the stories that grab me as a reader are these kinds of stories. Stories of triumph over adversity, and adventures gone awry. War stories. Stories where people pit themselves against the odds and rise to the challenges, overcoming obstacles and finding the courage to stare death in the eye and say, "not today!" Tales to help build my confidence by knowing others have faced far worse than I may be facing and through their courage, I'm able to endure the same or certainly hang tough through a lesser challenge. Or as Shakespeare said, "And in this thought they find a kind of ease, bearing their own misfortunes on the back of such as have before endured the like."[1] Jenna's story is one such story that takes the reader through life and death challenges, a battle with forces so terrible and powerful, challenges that could only be faced alone, while her family could only watch and pray. I believe Jenna found her strength through God and, though she chose to fight with every part of her being, withstanding the withering pain and seemingly endless letdowns, Jenna found peace with her struggle and her journey is all the more fascinating because of it. To watch a young child stand as tall as she did in the face of adversity gave me hope that I too could face my own life's tests with more grace.

Now we all have problems. We would hardly be human if we didn't. Be they physical, financial, or spiritual, we all have challenges to face but how we go about dealing with or solving them is where our road's part. What Jenna and her family showed me was how a life lived in faith can overcome even the worst life can throw at you. While our beliefs may differ somewhat, we maintain a spiritual practice and an acceptance in the mysterious ways God works. What an inspiring book and one I feel honored to have witnessed from such a close proximity as Jenna's friend. As I helplessly witnessed her struggle, she made me view my life in a far more grateful manner. I'm better for having known Jenna, and her story will always be an inspiration to me. It is a story that has so eloquently been put to a page and will help so many others to soldier through whatever hardships they encounter in life. J. A. Sailsbury is a born storyteller, with a great narrative touch. This beautiful book will have you turning page after page right through until the end, I simply couldn't put it down!

— **David James Elliott**
Actor, Director, Writer, Producer
Star of CBS Television Series JAG

Dying to live . . .

ELEVEN
22

PROLOGUE

"I have to get this door open," was all Hannah could think to herself as she shouldered every ounce of her body weight against the steel-framed, wooden hallway door of her college dorm. With each movement of the screeching door, she knew she was only inches away from the inevitable fate piled on the other side. She could feel the frigid air of the winter storm begin to send chills throughout her body as she finally created a small clearing, just large enough to squeeze through the opening.

With her body wedged against the door, she took one look down at the ground and saw the mounds of freshly fallen, powdery snow that had barricaded the door shut. The snow had been falling since early morning that January day in 2010 in Lynchburg, Virginia. Now with the sun setting, and the storm only becoming more treacherous, Hannah knew time was running out.

She took a deep breath, pulled her knitted beanie down over her head, and took one giant step into the snow to begin her journey across Liberty's campus towards the chapel.

Bam!

A gush of wind slammed the door behind her as if only to solidify there was no turning back.

Slowly, Hannah began trudging through the knee-high snow that had covered the iced-over sidewalks. There were so many apprehensive thoughts racing through her head. "There is no way anyone will be there. There is just too much snow!" It had now covered the three-acre-wide LU monogram on the mountain overlooking the campus. All Hannah could think was, "This winter blizzard is going to stand in the way of a miracle." Then she paused. "Maybe, just maybe, this is one puzzle piece of the miracle."

Head down, trying to avoid the icy, white pellets angling towards her face, Hannah slogged through the snow and up the last hill. With only about a hundred feet to go, she looked up and saw tiny black specks through the hazy, white snow that had draped over the landscape like a curtain after the final scene of a play. As Hannah shuffled closer, she began to see a line of students outside the chapel huddled closely, trying to avoid the winds blowing in from the surrounding mountains. Standing there frozen in amazement, now partly due to the melted snow seeping through the layers of clothes she had on, Hannah could not believe what she saw. They had made it!

She began to make her way through the crowd, only to hear the sound of muffled voices slowly becoming melodious roars as she inched closer and closer to the entrance. She placed both of her gloved hands on the antique polished brass door handles of the small white prayer chapel and swung open the double doors.

The radiant sounds of singing bellowed as the doors opened widely.

"Oh, happy day! Oh, happy day! When Jesus washed my sins away. He taught me how to watch, fight, and pray. Oh, happy day!"

Hannah began to scan the small sanctuary only to see raised hands and swaying bodies dancing to the rhythm of the heartfelt praises of the people all around her. As the line of friends and fellow classmates began to crowd inside the already packed chapel, Hannah anxiously made her way towards the front. With pure desperation in her voice, she explained the dire need for prayer. Hannah didn't have to say much. With no hesitation, the once singing crowd joined in with the students who had come to pray.

She stood there motionless in utter wonder at the incredible vision of 100 students surrounding her. "I am looking at a scene straight out of a war movie," she thought. The troops had been gathered. They were all headed into battle. Each was given their orders, every brigade sent to carry out their mission. Some knelt, and some shouted victoriously as they charged towards the gates of heaven, pleading to their Almighty God. Each unit was sent to pray. Their mission: a miracle.

Tears began to flood Hannah's eyes, as she could not help but have moments of déjà vu pierce through her mind as memories began to flow from the story that started 11 years ago.

1

IT'S THE MOST WONDERFUL
TIME OF THE YEAR

It was just past noon, and the scene outside the frost-cornered windows of their black-shuttered, white Cape Cod-style home was a picture-perfect postcard of a winter wonderland. Excitement welled up inside as the anticipation of incoming snow filled the air on that chilly December day in Chesterfield, Virginia. The hustle and bustle of the holiday season was just now dying down as Christmas had come and gone a few days before. However, Hannah's family had not gotten their complete fill of the Christmas season, as later that afternoon they would have one more family gathering.

Kay, Hannah's mom, was in the kitchen cooking food while Hannah cleaned the house, preparing for about 35 of Kay's family members from Pennsylvania, West Virginia, and around the local area who would soon be arriving. Her dad and brothers did what they could to avoid any of the *womanly* chores, so they scooted to the basement to battle each other in a cut-throat game of nine-ball on

1

the pool table. But there was someone missing from all the pre-party chaos that surrounded them, Hannah's older sister, Jenna. Feeling a bit under the weather, Jenna had been stretched out on the couch most of the day. Yet, she wanted nothing more than to be a part of the festivities later in the evening as she lay there, daydreaming about the most wonderful time of the year.

For her, there was just something about beeping car horns in store parking lots with eager drivers trying to get to their next big shopping deal of the day; the long lines at all the popular stores; and the smells of cinnamon rolls, peppermints, and the crisp, evergreen scent of freshly-fallen pine needles. There was nothing like curling up on the couch wrapped in Christmas-colored blankets next to the wood-burning fireplace while watching old Christmas movies. Faint sounds of bells would become louder and louder as carolers would ride by in a hay-lined trailer hitched to an old tractor, hoping to bring a little more Christmas cheer to neighbors sipping hot cocoa inside their houses on those frosty December nights.

Like clockwork, Hannah, and her older brothers, Zachary and Gabriel, and Jenna would wake up early on Christmas morning. Well, everyone except for Gabriel. They had to drag him out of bed, often adding a little extra force by placing an ice-cold rag on his face.

Before making their way downstairs, the four kids would sit at the top of the staircase. With bright eyes, they would talk about how they had heard the hooves of Santa's reindeer on their rooftop the night before. Just as they started to run down the stairs in anticipation of what was piled beneath the Christmas tree, their mom would stick out her hand and say, "Stop, stop, stop! I'm not ready!" Rolling their eyes, they knew she had not gotten the camcorder ready.

Once the red light flashed on, they were off. Rounding the corner to the den, they would see the freshly cut Christmas tree shimmering with the sparkles of thousands of tiny, multi-colored lights, accented with a red and green plaid tree skirt, covered in gifts that Santa had brought for them.

After watching each other open presents, it was time for their mom's infamous Christmas breakfast. The table was filled with hot biscuits and sausage gravy, scrambled eggs, crispy bacon, fresh fruit, and buttered grits. The kitchen smelled of sweet sugary treats as her piping hot cinnamon roll Bundt cake had just come out of the oven. Nothing made that morning more memorable than their mom's Christmas breakfast.

The rest of the afternoon, they would all sit around the den enjoying Christmas movies, visiting with Mema and Papa, their grandparents on their mom's side, or go outside and play with their new toys before heading to their other grandparent's house for Christmas dinner with their dad's side of the family.

As soon as they walked into Grandma and Grandpa's house, the smells and noises just screamed Christmas. The aroma of fluffy, melt-in-your-mouth homemade rolls, something they only ate at Grandma's, filled the air. Their grandpa's collectible trains chugging around the tracks beneath the Christmas tree, resounded throughout the house. It was a real-life Hallmark Christmas movie.

After dinner, they would open more presents. Each of the cousins had handpicked one person's name out of a bowl during Thanksgiving, and they would buy a gift for them. Part of the fun was finding out who had picked their name the month before, with all the cousins secretly hoping it was either cousin David or Michael, as Aunt Vonnie always bought the best presents for them to give. The rest of the night, all the cousins would play games together on the floor as their aunts, uncles, and grandparents talked and watched along.

Christmas traditions around their house probably looked and smelled much like most perhaps, spending time with loved ones, surrounded by good food and cheer. And just like every Christmas leading up to that one, 1998 was no different.

Moments before Kay's family began to arrive on December 28, everything was just about ready for the party to begin. Jenna had begun to make her way off the couch as the food was prepared and the floors were vacuumed. It was Jenna's perfect picture of Christmas, the innocent storybook view of a child.

And then it happened—the instance when the excitement of their holidays, just stopped . . .

The phone rang.

The family pediatrician was calling with blood test results they had ordered for Jenna earlier in the week. She had strep throat. The family was already aware of this because of previous tests, and quite frankly, the news of sickness was nothing new in their household. Usually, without fail, one of the four kids would be sick over the holidays. That year, Jenna had taken a big one for the team and covered both Thanksgiving and Christmas, as it was actually her second round of strep. After the first round of antibiotics, the strep subsided, but just a few weeks later, it had reared its ugly head again, just in time for Christmas.

Jenna's spleen was enlarged earlier in the week when she went in for the checkup, so the pediatrician decided blood tests were warranted. After inconclusive results at the pediatrician's office—the doctors actually thinking their machines were broken because the results were so unusual—Jenna was sent to a local hospital to have more blood tests completed. Now, on the other end of the receiver, the pediatrician had the results in his hand.

With hesitation in his voice, he told Kay she needed to take Jenna to a different hospital for more testing. After one trip to the pediatrician's office, another to a local hospital, and now the news of a second hospital needed, fear overcame Kay. But she tried to convince herself it was just a bad case of mono, something Jenna had once before when she was only three years old.

Kay began explaining to the doctor they had many family members coming over shortly. "Do I need to take her in today?" she questioned.

There was a brief moment of silence on the other end of the phone. The family pediatrician, a man who usually carried a jolly, Santa-like smile on his face while cracking jokes as the four children barreled in the office door, exclaiming, "The Wrecking Crew is here!" had a solemn tone in his voice. He softly said, "Let her spend time with her family."

So, that was what they did. They celebrated Christmas just like every year before, letting all the cousins spend the night, sleeping bags covering the bedroom floors. Then, two days later, Jenna, her dad, Ray, Kay, and her 15-year-old cousin, Natalie, headed to the hospital upon the pediatrician's orders.

2

ELEVEN

As Jenna walked through the revolving hospital doors for the first time, the experience was not what she had anticipated. Yes, she knew getting stuck with needles wouldn't be the most enjoyable activity, but what she was not prepared for was the royal treatment bestowed upon her.

Jenna and Natalie were brought into a large white room, strangely resembling a castle's lofty steeple ceilings. Placed all around them were a large array of toys and games. They were not the typical doctor's office games like the hundreds of varieties of bead mazes, but rather hands-on games neither she nor Natalie had ever played before.

As the morning proceeded, the nurses began placing various colorful, plush-stuffed animals at the feet of Natalie and Jenna. Jenna could not believe her ears when the nurses told her she would get to take home the mound of cuddly toys beginning to gather at her feet like a large crowd of commoners adoringly surrounding a newly crowned king and queen. Little did she know, those stuffed animals were just tools used for a specific purpose, to get her mind off the heaviness looming around her like dark, billowing storm clouds.

While the games and fuzzy bears at Jenna's feet were new accommodations for her, everything else seemed too familiar that day. Over the past few years, she had become accustomed to doctor's offices and what to expect when entering them. Though the hospital was quite a bit larger, the familiar smells of rubbing alcohol and latex gloves filled the air just like all the other doctor's offices she had been to before.

Since the second grade, Jenna had dealt with being in pain, pain of which no doctor could pinpoint the source. At times, the aches would become so intense the mere pressure of walking would send throbbing sensations through the bottoms of her feet, leaving her butt as the only means to get up and down the stairs in their home. Her hands would become very sore, imitating elderly hands stricken with severe arthritis, leaving the tips of her fingernails as the only option to press the buttons on the TV changer. Just the tiny bit of pressure it took to push the channel button would send pulsating pains throughout her hands. She never really thought about how much she used her hands until the aching had become so overwhelming even the idea of pushing a button, let alone trying to grip the TV changer in her clenched fists, was painfully agonizing.

Jenna never had perfect attendance in school because of the pain she suffered through, and the school nurse had come to know her very well. So well, she would take her temperature when entering the clinic, a customary practice for them to do, and then ask her, "Do you want me to call your mom, or do you want to try and wait it out?" Jenna, never wanting to leave school or the normal life, waited out the pain to avoid going home.

The other kids in school never knew Jenna's pain because in class and on the playground, Jenna was skilled at hiding it, putting the pain aside, running around playing hopscotch and four square like any other active child.

In fifth grade, the doctors finally diagnosed her with fibromyalgia, a disorder which causes widespread musculoskeletal pain and fatigue, sleep, memory, and mood issues.

So, for Jenna, walking through those revolving doors after Christmas was just another diagnosis day. The pokes, the prods, and all the random tests were just ordinary steps to figure out how to get rid of her strep throat.

As stomachs began growling, and the sun reached its peak of the day, they all desperately needed a change in scenery and a meal, so Kay and Ray took the two girls to a McDonald's across the street to get some lunch. With four kids, they didn't get fast food too often, and if there were any perks to being sick, that was one of them.

After the food had been ordered and they nestled into the red, polyester-lined booth, it didn't take long for Jenna to realize that day's fast-food experience was vastly different from those she had enjoyed in the past. As she looked at her parents' faces sitting across the booth from her, their glazed-over eyes gave her a glimpse of the story that was about to unfold.

This was not the beginning of a fairytale or the happily ever after part. No, it was definitely not that. It was more like the part where Belle runs away from the Beast's castle into the haunted, dark woods, winds blowing, owls hooting, wolves howling, and the only hint of light was cast by a full moon in the pitch-black skies above her. Then, out of nowhere, a pack of wolves would circle her. Terror and defeat gripped every part of Jenna as her face reflected the fear. That was the story beginning to unfold. No fairytale, just real life.

The Happy Meal in front of Jenna couldn't distract her from the fact that her parents had been crying. She was completely unaware of the conversations in the hospital before lunch, but their bloodshot eyes couldn't hide the evidence they had already been given preliminary results in the minutes before walking under the Golden Arches. Trying not to reveal anything to her, they did their best to hide the rising emotions whirling inside them like a tornado obliterating Midwestern crop fields.

No matter how much Jenna's parents wished they could have frozen time and sat there in the red, polyester-lined booth for the rest of the day, they couldn't. They had to face the harsh certainty their reality would change forever when they stepped back through those automatic doors after finishing their hamburgers and fries.

Hours later, the confirmation results were in, and the doctors had the diagnosis. It had been a long day, now almost 3:00 p.m., and quite frankly, the mounds of stuffed animals posing as adoring commoners were not doing the trick anymore. Jenna was restless and ready to go home.

Her parents were sent back first to speak with the doctor, leaving Natalie and Jenna playing in the waiting area. Moments later, a nurse came to bring Jenna back to be with her parents. Jenna sat for what seemed like hours in a cramped, white-walled room containing the examining table she was sitting on, a sink for the doctors to wash their hands in before beginning the examination process, and a cabinet filled with all sorts of medical tools. She could not help but feel the anxiety within her fluttering like a butterfly's wings when she saw the large, wooden door slowly open as the doctor walked in.

She watched his face closely, then she looked over at her parents' faces. Something was dreadfully wrong. It was one of those moments when you don't remember the exact words spoken, a moment when you know you should probably be paying closer attention, but the world seems to fade away slowly. It was in between all the medical mumbo jumbo coming out of the doctor's mouth that he said it. He spoke the word, that ugly word no one ever wants to hear . . .

Cancer.

Jenna's heart dropped, and the room began to spin. It was as if she had fallen into a tunnel, staring through a small pinhole, unable to hear anything going on, watching the world around her in slow motion. Panic mode set in. She was petrified. She wasn't scared of what the doctor had just said, because, honestly, she had no idea what that word even meant. But her parents' faces said everything. They did their best to hold back their tears, but she could tell. She could tell it wasn't something they could protect her from. Her dad could not ride up on a white horse as a knight in shining armor, pick her up from the jaws of a fire-breathing dragon, and ride off into the sunset back towards her castle. No, it was different. Tears began flowing from Jenna's once youthful eyes as she saw the tears streaming down her parents' faces. As the news began to set in, she should have become more frightened, but the only fear she saw was the looks on the faces of her mom and dad.

Jenna thought, "Okay, so I have another disorder with a weird name like fibromyalgia." Honestly, she was just waiting for the part where they gave her stickers for being a good patient and sent her home with an antibiotic. Devastatingly, that would not be the case.

The blood test concluded Jenna had acute lymphoblastic leukemia (ALL). No one in their immediate family had ever experienced cancer, so it was completely foreign territory. The word cancer didn't even exist in their vocabulary.

Natalie, her 15-year-old-cousin, who had been anxiously waiting by herself for quite some time, was frustratingly arguing with a nurse who tried explaining Jenna had leukemia. "She does not have leukemia!" Natalie forcibly insisted as the nurse tried to offer her as much comfort as possible. "I was specifically just told by another nurse she had cancer," she exclaimed, completely unaware the two words were one and the same.

Natalie and Jenna were still so blissfully innocent, utterly clueless of the magnitude of the situation. They were just two young girls who had spent the last few hours playing with stuffed animals. No one ever told them there would be more to go through than the fun and games they had experienced earlier in the day.

Jenna didn't really know what to ask or say. She was diagnosed and immediately ushered into another room to start chemotherapy treatments. With no time to process anything, Jenna had no clue once the IV was placed in her arm, there was no going back, no do over; that was it.

She wasn't told she would be unable to complete her sixth-grade year at Bailey Bridge Middle School. There would be no more end-of-the-day locker meets with her second-grade elementary school sweetheart. He would no longer walk her to the bus, barely making eye contact, as their child-like innocence was still very much the glue that held together their indescribable bond.

Jenna didn't know her best friend, Rhonda, was coached to control her emotions so Jenna wouldn't know the severity of what was happening around her. Rhonda's only devastating knowledge of cancer came from the books that she would no longer be able to muster up the courage to read. This wasn't one of her fiction books; it was real life. She was now playing the role of the friend who couldn't show how scared she was because her fear would only alert Jenna's suspicions of that whole new world.

But Jenna figured it out anyway. It didn't matter who cried or what the doctors said, she began to know something was horribly wrong. Just the number of visitors she had seen her first night in the hospital following her diagnosis revealed that. There was no escaping it. Her new life started at that moment, that day, that very minute. Admitted into the hospital immediately, she would not receive her typical friendly send-off comment, "We will see you in a week." The nurses simply took her to a larger room in the hospital with nothing but cheap, green pleather reclining chairs lining old, white cinderblock walls.

An IV was placed in Jenna's arm, marking the beginning of her treatment. A nurse with her hands covered in a particular pair of latex gloves walked over. Those gloves were a precautionary measure used to protect her skin from any leakage of the chemotherapy which could potentially burn a hole in her hand. Those same burn-inducing toxins would flood Jenna's veins like a tsunami devouring a poor, innocent town in the blink of an eye.

An 11-year-old girl's life changed forever that day. There was no more reminiscing of sitting around packed, Christmas feast-filled tables at Grandma and Grandpa's house. The enchanted scene surrounding her was gone. Right there, in a room filled with white lab coats, nurses, her parents, and funny-looking machines that were attached to aluminum poles with wheels at the bottom, Jenna's life turned upside down.

In that weathered, green recliner, Jenna sat there and stared at everyone around her. The voices soon faded to silence, and people began to disappear. Only Jenna and her mom remained. Kay watched her 11-year-old daughter, hooked up to a machine, with only grim thoughts of what was about to come.

Only For a Moment:

JOURNALING

In an unexpected and unplanned moment, Jenna's family was given a horrible diagnosis leaving their lives forever changed. It's those moments that can make you hit rock bottom. The reality is life is hard. Trials come. They seem to hit when you least expect it, whether big or small. So, what can you do?

On that day, in the middle of plush stuffed animals piling up around Jenna, amidst all the bottled-up emotions, she had to find a way to get through the trauma coming in the days ahead. So she began searching for moments, moments of relief to express her feelings, anger, hurt, and fears. Maybe you need an outlet from life right now. Feel free to journal. Sometimes it helps to take a moment.

_____

_____

_____

_____

_____

_____

_____

Always remember . . . take a deep breath,
keep breathing, and keep going.

3

PERCENTAGES

Daunting storm clouds began to hover over Ray and Kay's heads as the doctors started throwing many percentages their way. It started the moment they said the word cancer, and it would not stop until the whole nightmare was behind them. Much like an anxious batter in the World Series stepping up to bat with two outs in the bottom of the ninth, the troubling numbers began to whiz past her parents. Dangerously, they drew closer and closer to strike three.

The doctors would matter-of-factly say, "Patients may react to this drug with a headache, nausea, or chills. This surgery may totally fix the problem, but it also could cause another." The doctors weren't there for a few strikeouts that would only minimize the effects those life-altering treatments could have on Jenna. They were there to win the game. They were there to beat the cancer, whatever the cost.

However, it wouldn't take long to realize those percentages meant absolutely nothing, and none of them would really ever apply to Jenna as the first pitch was thrown.

The tests had begun. Within the first week, Jenna was at-bat facing her first minor surgery, a Port-a-Cath (port) placement. A port is a small medical device placed just below the skin in the upper chest, bulging outward, resembling a fireball candy lodged on the inside of a young child's cheek. It is connected to a large vein, allowing multiple drugs and blood samples to be taken without a high percentage of the vein collapsing. Designed to decrease the discomfort of being constantly stuck by a needle, the device sounded like a godsend, and it would have been, if her name wasn't Jenna. Nonetheless, after surgery, she was discharged from the hospital and sent home for recovery, seemingly without any complications.

Before leaving the hospital, the doctors gave all the necessary precautions, much like the signals a third base coach gives as he instructs the batter on his next move. The doctors could not stress enough how important it was for Jenna to exercise. It had only been one week, but the combination of lying in bed, the new medicines, procedures, and surgery had been quite a shock to her body, and it was slowly beginning to weaken. So, just like any new patient, her parents heeded the doctor's orders and headed home with Jenna.

As soon as Kay stepped into the house, she took on her new role of nurse mom. Fifteen years prior, when her eldest son, Zachary, was born, Kay excitedly stepped into her new role as a stay-at-home mom. Kay wore many hats in their household, not out of obligation, but because she truly loved it. Her kids were her joy, and being a mom was her gift—her passion in life. Grandma would always tell Kay, "Your kids are your play toys, because you're always playing with them."

In Jenna's eyes, her mom was *Supermom*. Standing at five-foot-five with beautiful, short, curly, sandy-brown hair, her mom was a knockout, or at least that was what all the boys in the church youth group called her, as they all proudly proclaimed they would gladly take her off Ray's hands anytime. Kay was her kid's taxi driver to ball practices and piano lessons, their teacher when they needed help with English, their friend, their disciplinarian, their playmate, and perhaps most importantly, their example of Christ's selfless love.

Although she had not worn a trauma nurse hat before, Kay learned quickly to push Jenna into doing exactly what the doctors ordered. There was no way she was going to let Jenna just sit in her dad's recliner and waste away to nothing. No way, not on her watch.

It was day one of recovery. Every hour, Kay made Jenna get up and walk laps around the downstairs of their home. Much like getting Gabriel out of bed on Christmas morning, Jenna wasn't amused. She did her best to resist, but she knew if she wanted her strength back, the laps were her only means to get it. So, Jenna walked. She walked through the kitchen, around the corner to the dining room, circled the dining room table, turned the corner to make the last leg of the journey down the six-foot hallway to the den, then rounded back through the kitchen for lap number two, touching each corner as if she were rounding the bases after hitting the softball to the fences. With each turn of the corner, Jenna would gasp for air like a seasonal asthmatic who had just run a marathon inhaling pollen with each breath.

She pushed herself hard, knowing the doctors insisted so her body could begin to heal. As she placed one foot in front of the other, her deep gasps, now weakened, resembled a tiny kitten struggling to meow for the first time. Her body slowly leaned forward like a Jenga tower beginning to lose its pieces as her energy withered away. The same corners she had rounded at near-Olympic caliber speeds just a couple of weeks earlier, dying to see what Santa had left beneath the tree, were now just leaning posts, as she could barely catch a breath long enough to make it from one corner to the next. The doctors had said, the more walking she did, the stronger she would become. So, her mom pushed her to walk and walk some more, hoping to refuel the little Energizer Bunny inside her.

But the struggle continued. As the hours passed, Jenna's breaths became so faint her mom would place her hand on her chest to ensure it was still moving up and down. After movement confirmation, Kay continued with her nursing duties as she crept up with a cup of water in one hand and a napkin in the other filled with Jenna's daily dose of pills.

But by that point, Jenna could barely whisper. With her voice weakening in the attempts to catch her breath, she resorted to her only means of communication, her hands. With motions and gestures, she signed to her mom that she could not swallow the pills. Kay brought her a mug filled to the brim with water, but Jenna couldn't even muster up enough breath to take a drink. It never even occurred to her it took a breath to suck water out of a cup until she had to swallow those pills.

As she took a tiny swig of water, the thumbnail-sized pill never made its way down her throat. Gagging and grabbing her neck, Jenna tried alerting her mom that the pill had lodged itself in her throat. She gasped for air. After a few more desperate sips of water, the medication slid its way down her throat. Jenna could hardly swallow her own spit, let alone a capsule.

With growing concern, Kay called Jenna's aunt, Vonnie, a nurse, to come over and listen to her breathing. Upon arrival, she placed a cold stethoscope against Jenna's back, and without any uncertainty, Aunt Vonnie insisted, "We have to go to the hospital right now!"

Kay hurriedly got Jenna dressed as she sat limply in the recliner. With Aunt Vonnie on one side and her mom on the other, Jenna leaned against them as they frantically rushed her to the car. Aunt Vonnie jumped into the driver's seat and Kay into the back with Jenna, knowing she could no longer hold herself up as she fell over in complete exhaustion. With her right foot to the floor, Aunt Vonnie sped towards the emergency room.

Suddenly, going about 80 miles per hour, a loud noise sounded from under the car.

Pop!

Rattled, Aunt Vonnie slowly eased on the breaks and pulled over. She hastily stepped out of the car, only to discover a tire had blown. They were stranded on the side of the highway with no means of communication.

Jenna's breaths were becoming shallower by the second. Time was running out. Jenna needed help, and she needed it fast. But just as suddenly as the tire had blown, an angel appeared in bright lights— literally. Blue lights were flashing behind them as a police car slowly veered off the side of the road to offer assistance. Not realizing the desperation they were in, the police officer calmly but firmly stepped out of the car. As the officer strolled up to the car, it was as if trumpets sounded an anthem song. The officer standing there in bright lights, just so happened to be a family friend. After a few frantic words from Kay, without hesitation, the officer flipped on her siren and speedily escorted them to the hospital.

As they pulled up to the hospital doors amidst a commanding scene of blazing sirens, the officer ran inside to grab a vacant wheelchair. Kay and Aunt Vonnie pulled Jenna from the backseat and placed her into the wheelchair, and the three of them rushed her into the emergency room.

Triage doctors ran tests as quickly as possible with time ticking down, knowing Jenna struggled more and more desperately for breath. After only one X-ray, it became clear. Jenna was suffering from a pneumothorax, or in layman's terms, a collapsed lung. She was rushed into surgery. Slowly, the waiting room began filling with friends and family, but one person was missing from the crowd, her dad.

The house was empty when Aunt Vonnie, Kay, and Jenna were forced to race to the hospital. Basketball season was in full swing, and Ray was with Zachary at his game.

As friends and family sat waiting for Jenna to come safely out of surgery, there was no doubt they wondered why Ray was not there to hold and comfort Kay as she sat hunched over in tearful prayer. But there were no more easy choices. Emotions were high for the entire family. Ray needed to be with Zachary to try and maintain some normalcy during such a chaotic time. The truth was, it would be the first of many decisions they would have to make. Their life as they knew it was changing, and the percentages were only a small reminder.

But the percentages had become real. Before placing the port, a percentage was given to Jenna. A ratio of less than one percent of patients had ever experienced a collapsed lung from that surgery, but it had happened. A medical resident had placed the port so deep they punctured her lung, thus beginning the legend of *A Jenna Thing*.

4

DADDIES ON DUTY

Jenna was rolled up to her hospital room immediately following surgery, lying completely still, dozing in and out of consciousness as she tapered off the anesthesia. She would spend the next two weeks in recovery with a chest tube protruding from an open puncture wound between two of the ribs on the left side of her body. As if a foreign object bulging from her body wasn't tricky enough to deal with, to make matters worse, her mom had come down with the flu, and left her dad and Aunt Jeannie, who was also a nurse, on hospital duty. Ray would bend over backwards for Jenna, but there is just something unavoidable that happens when daddies are on babysitting detail. And at their house, it was inevitable something uncanny was bound to happen when Ray babysat. Someway, somehow, one of the four kids, or Ray himself, would end up in the ER. In fact, it happened so often the receptionists at the check-in counter knew them by name.

One time, Zachary and Gabriel had a few friends hanging out at the house. Trying to find ways to keep themselves occupied, what better way than to play good-ole hide-and-seek? After all, the large field and expansive woods surrounding their house offered many places to hide. As each boy scattered around the house trying to find the best hiding spot, Zachary began counting, "One, two, three, ready or not, here I come!"

Zachary ran into the woods, down the beaten path the kids had made, leading to a grassy field with an old raggedy barn.

"There has to be someone in that barn," he thought. Edging closer to the paint-chipped ladder leading to the barn's loft, Zachary climbed up and began rummaging around. Tossing old pieces of wood off to the side, Zachary cleared a path to the hayloft doors to get a better view of the vast hiding places in the adjacent field. As he reached the opening, his body barreling forward, he kicked off a rotted piece of wood out of the hayloft opening. Completely ignorant of what was coming down above him, Gabriel, who was hiding just below the opening, did not even have time to react.

Wham!

The board ripped down the back of his arm near the shoulder, and a rusty nail protruding from it sliced it open. Bleeding profusely, Gabriel stomped through the woods towards the house as mad as a hornet, yelling, "I need a towel! Zachary kicked a piece of wood down on top of me!"

Massive amounts of stitches were required inside and out. The doctors later explained if the nail had landed just an inch to the left, he might not have had regular, everyday use of his arm.

A nail to Gabriel's shoulder, a snakebite to his foot as he stepped on it running through the woods, and a dog bite to Hannah's face were not the only instances of ER trips while their mom was away. Another time, their dad couldn't get them all wrangled for bed before an avalanche of four excitable children would soon come tumbling down on him. Being a daddy's girl, Jenna hopped on her dad's back for one last horsey ride before bed. But what fun would a typical horsey ride be without Zachary?

Zachary had a lay-it-all-on-the-line personality. Go big or go home was his motto. He was the type no one could play catch with because his Division I pitching arm only had one speed, rocket. Why throw a ball if you don't throw it fast, was his mentality. If there were a task at hand, he would put all his might into it, and that night there was a task at hand—knock Jenna off the horsey.

Not even a minute into her pony ride, Zachary did a piledriver maneuver straight out of a scene from WrestleMania. He carefully climbed onto the sofa seats, wedged his feet into the cracks of the cushions as if to get a solid jumping base, and leaped off in a diving motion with his arms opened wide, wrapping his arms around Jenna in midair.

Smash!

Jenna tumbled to the floor.

Pop!

Both Jenna and her dad heard the sound from her neck. She screamed, Ray called 911, and Kay pulled up just in time to hitch a ride on the ambulance to the hospital.

Mishaps and pranks were typical for the boys, Jenna, and Hannah, and their dad was often on the receiving end. One day at Lowe's, Zachary reached up and pulled down his dad's shorts as he stretched to grab a tool high on the shelf, leaving Ray standing there in the middle of a crowded store in nothing but his whitey-tighties. Those times were just another reason they were called *The Wrecking Crew*. So, although Jenna was thankful to have her dad with her in the hospital, there was no wonder why the many whoopsie-daisy moments floated through her head as she looked down to see the massive object piercing out of her side.

Unable to avoid discomfort if she moved, Jenna lay still in excruciating pain as the chest tube would tug at her side with any slight change in her position. So, Jenna waited until the last second when those IV fluids had flushed through her. "I need to go to the bathroom," she insisted. And just like the pit crew at Talladega, her dad and Aunt Jeannie jumped out of their seats and commanded their posts knowing there was not much time as Jenna had held it as long as she could.

Ray raced to the bathroom where a portable toilet was stored and carried it over to Jenna's bedside. She peeked over to observe her angle of approach. Trying to get on that thing became a strategically thought-out process in and of itself, one her dad carefully coached Aunt Jeannie through, as he did not want to cause Jenna any more unnecessary pain. Her aunt tactically maneuvered the IV lines coming out of Jenna's chest from the port while pushing the IV pole and holding up her fashionable hospital gown. Her dad carefully held the chest tube steady. The task had to be done precisely one way, or the pain would be unbearable. If the chest tube dropped or lifted in any way, it felt as though it, along with Jenna's lung, would come barreling out of her side.

After two grueling weeks had passed, the tube was finally ready to come out. However, the excitement soon ended as Jenna realized just how they were going to pull *out* the plastic hose. Unlike the actual tube placement surgery, the doctors would not put Jenna to sleep for the removal. While she lay helpless in her bed, the doctor would yank the tube right out of the side of her torso. To an 11-year-old girl, it was the same as pulling out the suctioned end of the vacuum from the wall outlet her dad had installed when he built their house just a few years prior, except it was coming out of her.

In that moment, Jenna began to realize her body was no longer her own. When a procedure needed to be done, her fears did not matter; neither did the pain nor her embarrassment. She had to endure it. Despite everything, there was no escape into a different reality. Still uncertain of what she would face on the long road to recovery, those two weeks taught Jenna her old life was slowly coming to an end. There would be no more softball games, standing on the pitcher's mound with the whole team cheering around her, waiting to pitch the last strikeout to win the game, no more all-night youth group activities, and no more middle school.

The first inch of her dignity was stripped as her dad stood over her while she used the bathroom because she couldn't go by herself. Unable to juggle all the tubes coming out of her body, all the while holding up her hospital gown to sit on the toilet, Jenna needed help.

Aunt Jeannie had to sponge bathe her, something Jenna wanted no part of. But for the first time in her life, she couldn't step into a bathtub and turn on the faucet. She could only lie there in bed while her aunt wiped her down with a prickly, soap-filled sponge, cleaned her bruise-covered body, and scrubbed her in places she could no longer call private.

Those moments of complete helplessness were just the beginning, and the percentages were only starting to become a factor. Doctors told Jenna the treatment protocol to rid her body of cancer was two and a half years. Two and a half years was a lifetime to an 11-year-old child, but if anyone could do it, Jenna could. There was at least an end to this part of her life. She just had to beat the percentages. Once those years were over, she would be healed and finished with that place for good. She just had to survive.

Only for a Moment:

IT'S GAME TIME

Percentages are tricky. Some are logical facts, some just merely guesses, and others are strictly fun-filled. Sometimes there are ways to help, and sometimes you just have to hope the percentages come out in your favor. Jenna found comfort in numbers but in a completely different way. She learned about Sudoku puzzles and passed the time away by plugging in numbers.

Take a deep breath, keep breathing, and keep going.

	5			1	3		7	9
8		9	4				5	
4	7					8		6
			6			9	4	
	2			4	5		3	
9					7	6		
3	6		5			7		1
	8	2	3					
		1			4		6	

5

FALSE START

The chemotherapy was nothing to sneer at. Everything Hollywood movies portrayed it to be was pure fantasy. Treatment was brutal and began to take a toll on Jenna's body. Slowly, it was doing its job, eating away at the cancer cells, along with what seemed to be every muscle and bone in her body. The doctors had said they would have Jenna in remission, showing no signs of cancer, within 30 days, and they were taking whatever means possible to get her there.

Jenna had very little energy, and what remained she mustered up to get herself to the bathroom where her head and the toilet became new best friends. Her body was slowly withering away before her parents' eyes, and all they could do was sit there and watch as their little girl began to show signs of defeat. As if the physical pain was not hard enough, the emotional pain was about to hit full throttle.

It had only been a month into chemotherapy, and more testing revealed Jenna had a specific chromosome. Completely unaware the doctors were even running tests to determine if Jenna had a chromosomal abnormity, Ray and Kay were totally blindsided.

The doctors explained further, "Only two or three percent of people diagnosed with acute lymphoblastic leukemia have this specific Philadelphia chromosome, and our hospital has seen only one case of it." Jenna now made two. She was diagnosed with Philadelphia chromosome-positive acute lymphoblastic leukemia (Ph+ ALL). Simply put, the newly-found Philadelphia chromosome meant Jenna had a rare form of leukemia. As if the news of two and a half years of chemotherapy wasn't hard enough to hear, the doctors proceeded to say, "This cancer is so rare and aggressive, the normal chemotherapy regimen she is on will not cure it."

Jenna continued in those small percentages. The only positive at that point was she had moved up in the brackets, now in the two or three percent, and no longer in the less than one percent for a collapsed lung after the port placement.

All Ray and Kay could see was their frail little girl lying in bed, beginning to grasp that all the misery she had endured thus far meant nothing in the grand scheme of things. The current treatment would not cure her. Her only option now was a bone marrow transplant, and time was their enemy.

It was as if she was back at school at the starting line of a 400M race; the pistol sounded, she pushed off the starting blocks down the track, and then the buzzer sounded.

Bbbzzzz!

False start; back to the blocks.

The nerves started to kick in as the false start penalty zapped her waning strength. One more, and she would get disqualified.

That was Jenna. She was back at the starting line again, more percentages thrown her way, and only one more chance to get it right.

The doctors explained Jenna had a 33 percent chance of survival with the transplant. To her parents, 33 percent was like hearing zero.

However, an even lower percentage was given if she didn't have the transplant. Her odds decreased to a grim five percent chance to live. In life, options are nice, and there are often many options, but that time, Jenna only had one. Regardless, with her heart in her stomach, she placed her feet on the starting blocks once again, and the doctors started prepping her body for a transplant.

As time crept on, Jenna entered into remission, a stage she had to remain in to receive the transplant. For the months to come, doctors designed the treatment protocol for her to undergo the most aggressive chemotherapy regimen. If she relapsed and the cancer returned, the fight was over, and the option of a transplant may no longer be on the table.

A transplant, well, it was a whole new world for Jenna. She wished she was Disney's Jasmine, soaring over shining, shimmering, splendid cities, flying over the treatments, and on her way to life as a normal 11-year-old again. But that would not be Jenna's magical, Persian-carpet ride. Much like the Cave of Wonders in *Aladdin*, Jenna would be flying at warped speeds towards the collapsing mouth of the tiger, bobbing and weaving, trying desperately to miss the mounds of magma that were falling around her.

Jenna's mom began to learn more about that new world in the coming weeks, and it did not take long for her to realize it would be nothing like those two and a half years of the original protocol. She would be devastatingly reminded as a group of ladies entered Jenna's hospital room one somber afternoon.

"Hi, Kay," one of the ladies said as she introduced herself. Kay led them outside Jenna's door into the hallway, and they began sharing their stories as each of them had come to offer support. Each mom had a son or daughter who all rode that same petrifying carpet ride through the crumbling walls of a transplant Jenna was just about to embark on.

While giving insight on what was to come in treatment, Kay grew even more leery about the days ahead. Scared to death by what she was learning, she naively asked, "How are your children doing now?" With blank stares on their faces, all but one of them sadly explained their children had not survived their transplants.

Kay's stomach began churning. She felt sick with emotion because of the ominous foreshadowing the group had presented her. In her confusion, she deflatingly thought to herself, "You mean you're here to offer support, but only one of your kids made it through?" She needed hope, and that was just not it. The truth was though, those were just more statistics, more battles with percentages being thrown her way. But, no one knew what was to come.

As Kay stepped back into Jenna's room, she looked over at Jenna as she lay, her youth withering away like shriveled grapes fallen from a vine as the toxic chemotherapy spread throughout her body. Meanwhile, the doctors continued to do their part, desperately searching for a bone marrow match.

It did not take long for friends and family to join in on the search. But to start, the word had to get out, and what better way to begin than being on TV.

6

NO AVERAGE JOE

A local news station came to their house to interview Jenna's family and broadcast her story to the public. She sat propped up in her dad's recliner, and although Jenna didn't say much, her weakened demeanor served as a heart-wrenching picture for those watching from their homes. Viewers were urged to donate their blood in hopes someone would be a bone marrow match for Jenna. Kay was not particularly thrilled about being on TV, as she feared speaking in public, but Kay would have gone to the moon and back if it meant saving her daughter's life.

Following the interview, a picture of Jenna went up on a local billboard. It read, "Call . . . Help save a life." Jenna's Aunt Cindy had begun to organize a bone marrow drive in honor of Jenna. Her hope was that one of the hundreds, and even thousands of people who rode by the billboard every day, would be a match for Jenna. But as more precious time slipped by, Aunt Cindy knew she needed help, so she picked up the phone and called the first person she could think of. His name was Joe, and he was anything but average.

As a friend of their family, Joe could not sit idly in the pew each Sunday morning as updates and prayers for Jenna swarmed their local church; it was just not in his nature. He knew Jenna's chance of survival without a transplant decreased daily. Joe had to do something. So, he, along with Aunt Cindy, other family, and dear friends, continued organizing a bone marrow drive that would be held at their church—putting hours upon hours of their time into this mission.

On a beautiful sunny day in March, people from all over Virginia and nearby states came to Chesterfield to give blood in hopes they would be the ones to save Jenna's life. Police came to direct traffic, and a local fire station came with their trucks. Baked goods sales were raised for the donor search. A race car, face painting, and other activities to kept donors occupied while waiting in line. The Chick-fil-A cow had even come to entertain the children tagging along with parents.

Before the drive, Joe informed the Virginia Blood Services marrow coordinator they would need to bring at least 4,000 test kits. She smiled and chuckled, knowing how many people typically showed up at those events. "We'll bring 400," she said. Joe tried convincing her there would indeed be thousands of people in attendance, but she laughed it off as if it were not possible.

Well, everyone soon learned when Joe was on a mission, nothing was impossible. Joe, a dark-haired, 5'7" Italian stallion was a force to be reckoned with. He had faith like David as he faced Goliath, and he would not accept no for an answer. Joe believed he was witnessing a miracle. God would save Jenna, and there was no way he would not be a part of it. He emphasized, "You can either be a part of a miracle or be looking in the window from the outside and wishing you were a part of it."

People started flooding the church grounds as the bone marrow drive started. Within the first 30 minutes, the 400 test kits were gone. A local politician in attendance was tasked to keep the crowd occupied with a motivational speech, something only he was equipped for during that time. The marrow coordinator, the one who said they would not need 4,000 test kits, was being escorted by the police to the local blood bank to retrieve thousands more.

After keeping the crowd engaged until the convoy could retrieve enough blood testing kits, the politician, a father who had never missed ten years' worth of his son's baseball games until that day, asked Joe if there was anything more he could do. Without hesitation, Joe, who had helped organize what would be the largest bone marrow drive the state of Virginia had ever seen, said, "Yes, I need to get a hold of Dr. Jerry Falwell Sr., the president of Liberty University. I want to do this same thing at Liberty." The politician smiled at Joe, looked through his phone, and dialed the number. With very little formalities, the politician introduced Joe to Dr. Falwell Sr., and handed over his phone. Joe urgently asked for another bone marrow drive to be held at Liberty's campus. He knew Jenna's best hope for a match would be found in a young person, and what better place to find gold than at a gold mine—a college campus.

Within a week, Joe and Ray met with Dr. Falwell Sr. and about six or seven of Liberty's school administrators. Falwell asked Joe what he needed. After a detailed description, Dr. Falwell Sr. looked at the other administrators in the room and told them, "Joe is to receive whatever he needs." So, that is what the Liberty leadership did. They turned the entire campus over to Joe and Ray. The staff, the campus police, the facilities, everything was given to them—this was love put into action; the heart of Liberty.

Joe knew, just like everyone else, the more people who gave blood, the better chance Jenna had at surviving. With four kids of his own, he felt compelled to do whatever he could for her. He said, "We're praying for a miracle, and we're working like the miracle is up to us."

Joe was adamant Kay, being Jenna's mom, be the one who spoke at Liberty, but Jenna was too sick and there was no way Kay was leaving her side. So, Joe took the reins and spoke at convocation, a chapel-like service that happened three times a week at Liberty. Standing at the podium like a general addressing an army of soldiers, he spoke of Mordecai's plea to Queen Esther to save the Jewish people from destruction, ending his charge to the students with the phrase encapsulating a series of unusual and foretold events, *for such a time as this.*

But the biblical heroine was not the only woman in Joe's plea. He spoke of another named Mary. Mary was a fellow church-goer who befriended Joe and his wife. Nearing the time of the birth of their youngest daughter, Mary had implored Joe to call her as soon as his wife went into labor, as she was a nurse at the hospital where Joe's wife would give birth.

When the day came, it was time for Joe to make that call. Mary walked into the room to greet Joe and his wife, as the two were waiting patiently for doctors to come to deliver the child who would complete their family of six. Seconds later, after looking at the monitors hanging above the hospital bed, Mary ran out the door, frantically urging nearby doctors and nurses to deliver the baby immediately. Mary had seen the umbilical cord was wrapped around the baby's neck, cutting off oxygen to the brain. Had it not been for Mary being there for such a time as that, Joe's daughter and wife may not have survived.

So, Joe pleaded with the crowd. "Maybe, just maybe, you have been put here on this earth for such a time as this." Maybe someone at Liberty would help rescue Jenna from a most certain death.

After the convocation service, two young men walked up to Joe. With little formalities exchanged, they smiled at him and said, "We are Mary's sons." Joe had not heard from Mary in years, and there standing before him were her sons. He knew then. God was going to perform a miracle. Out of the millions of people who could have been there, God had placed Mary's sons there for such a time as that, a time which merged two peculiar medical fates. Jenna's dad, Ray, ended the service with a prayer and a plea. "Please help save my daughter's life."

A few local businesses had offered to cover the costs for anyone who volunteered to give blood at Liberty's donor drive. Ray went on a local Christian radio station, WRVL, urging people to come out; he needed someone to save his daughter's life. But just as life sometimes takes turns for the worse, another curveball was thrown.

At the last minute, those businesses backed out. Any student who volunteered to give blood would have to pay a fee, and paying to give blood was not an option for broke college students. But just like Joe proclaimed, a miracle was going to happen. An anonymous donor paid for the entire student body and anyone else who would give blood. Although Liberty's drive was not as big as the one in their hometown church, Liberty University now held the record for the second-largest bone marrow drive in Virginia.

Only for a Moment:

VOLUNTEERING

"If you keep quiet at a time like this, deliverance and relief
for the Jews will arise from some other place...Who knows if
perhaps you were made queen for just such a time as this?"
(Esther 4:14 NLT).

There are times when everything and everyone around you are doing well. Find delight in the good times, and do not squander them. Joe realized he was born for such a time as this. His mission was to help a little girl who was too weak to help herself. He was there to save a life, and he was not going to let it pass by him. While Joe was not Jenna's match, he did end up being the match for someone else. Just think, if he had given up his Esther opportunity, he would have never gotten the chance to save someone else's life.

Over 120 volunteers and almost ten thousand people gave blood in Chesterfield and Lynchburg at Liberty University. It is because of you, Jenna and other people diagnosed with cancer had, and still have, the option of life. Thank you for taking the time out of your busy schedules to put someone else's life above your own. One can only imagine what our world would look like if we all did this a little more. If you have not been placed on a bone marrow registry, go sign up. You never know; you just may be someone's only chance at life.

7

A BAG FULL OF
SAUSAGE BISCUITS

As the quest to find a bone marrow match continued outside the hospital walls, Jenna continued the fight on the inside. While she lay on a plastic-covered mattress, hidden by the 100-thread count cotton bed sheets, she stared at the sunlight reflected on the plain white walls of her room. Everything was so routinely mundane in the hospital, something vastly different from her life prior to leukemia. She couldn't help but reflect on her childhood before the word cancer entered her vocabulary.

To put it mildly, Jenna was an active child. As a family with four rambunctious children, there was never a dull moment in their household.

One time, Zachary, at only five years old, knocked their parked car out of gear. His only vision as he peeped above the steering wheel was his mom flailing her arms while running after the vehicle as she watched Zachary and her two other little ones in the car drift back towards a group of pine trees.

Gabriel made his adventurous debut a little earlier. At only two years old, he climbed a ladder to stand on the roof of their 12-foot high shed. But Kay didn't run towards him that time; rather, she ran into the house to grab the camera, making sure not to miss that Kodak moment.

Jenna and Hannah could be caught pretending to be school bus drivers who created make-believe bus routes while riding their bikes all over their yard. Whether running after cars, grabbing cameras, or searching for her toddlers, only to find them stripped down to their diapers and every inch of their bodies covered in mud, those kids never ceased to make life more eventful for Ray and Kay.

They were all active in sports, riding go-karts and four-wheelers in the field next to their house, rarely caught playing indoors. With the four of them close in age, there was always a sporting event or extracurricular activity. Therefore, coping with lying on a crinkly hospital bed watching television all day was new for Jenna, and she needed to find ways to manage it. On the rare occasion she felt somewhat normal, Jenna tried doing normal activities, or as normal as they existed in the hospital.

The treatment unit would often host some type of activity in the game room. It had been a few months into Jenna's treatment, and she had never visited that room. Jenna rarely had the energy to walk down the hallway, much less participate in any activity. One morning, she woke up with minimal pain in her weakened body and felt well enough to leave her hospital room sidekick, Chuck, as in chuck bucket, and headed to the game room.

Jenna's nurse followed her into the room, the only room on the floor with walls painted in a color other than white, filled with board games and painting stations. The nurse had a new bag of chemotherapy drugs to hook into Jenna's port and administered the first dose as Jenna sat down to enjoy her first activities outside her room.

As she took her seat, Jenna reached over to grab the sparkly sequins scattered across the table. They reflected light onto the walls like a prism painting a beautiful rainbow of colors. But before her hand could even touch the tiny, shiny charm of normalcy, Jenna's breakfast spewed from her mouth.

Tiny red dots began to scatter over every inch of her ivory skin. Her face started to swell quickly and turned shades of bright red, resembling the large vinyl balloons seen down the street at a local car dealership. Moments later, barely able to catch her breath, the nurse realized Jenna was having an allergic reaction. As panic began to set in, the nurse administered Benadryl just as quickly as she had pushed the toxic concoction of drugs into Jenna's veins. Benadryl saved her life that day as the probability she would have survived that reaction without it was slim to none.

Later in the day, the nurse assured everyone not to worry about Jenna being unable to take that specific chemotherapy to finish her regimen. Nonchalantly, she reassured Ray and Kay she hated that drug anyway because it had resulted in too many long-term side effects for other children. Speaking those words, offered absolutely no comfort at all.

As an 11-year-old, Jenna couldn't understand how a nurse could administer something into her body, knowing the potential harm it could later bring to her. But they administered those drugs hoping they would heal her, even though it may come with a cost. Those drugs were not like the antibiotics the family doctor prescribed Jenna to take in the past, and that near-death experience quickly taught her that.

As the weeks progressed, the intensity of the chemotherapy drugs only magnified. Quite frankly, *A Jenna Thing* was about to happen as she would leave one whale of a legacy in that hospital as the next drug, methotrexate, was administered to her.

The word *intense* could not even begin to describe the power of this drug's effects, not just on the cancerous cells streaming through Jenna's blood, but on her entire body. Doctors warned Jenna and her parents about the side effects each drug could cause—many times, explaining those debilitating facts *after* administering the medication. So, Jenna heeded the doctors' orders and swished the mouthwash they had prescribed, hoping just like a pebble thrown across the water, she would skip over the side effects and prevent potential mouth sores many patients endured with methotrexate.

Regardless of the swishing, one by one, they came. At first, the sores were small and manageable, but they soon spread like wildfire, not stopping until they had burned down Jenna's esophagus and into her stomach. The sores bled, and they bled a lot. They bled so much and so quickly the blood dried up before nurses could wipe it away; not that Jenna wanted anyone to wipe away the blood from her skewered lips. Her lips were cracked open and excruciatingly tender to touch, so it was less painful to let the blood dry rather than wipe the waterfall of blood flowing from them.

Soon after the sores developed, Jenna's lips molded shut by the dried blood, much like a bear trap clamped down on its innocent prey, unable for two human hands to pry it open, literally. At one point, she had seven doctors at the foot of her bed, all staring at the lesions on her lips, trying to figure out how they were going to detach them from one another.

She couldn't breathe through her mouth. She couldn't swallow. A piercing, burning sensation occurred any time saliva made its way down her ulcer-peppered throat. The doctors had never seen mouth sores get so bad. They had no idea what to do. Jenna's only option was to wait it out, so she did. For two weeks, she was placed on high-powered pain medicines, lying in the hospital bed, looking like some monster out of a children's storybook, or at least that was how her mom described her.

Jenna had friends and family visit her those weeks, but she would just lay there, unable to speak as her lips were welded together with dried blood. Her family from Pennsylvania was unprepared to see the toll chemotherapy had taken on Jenna's body. Stepping outside Jenna's room after a brief time, her aunt made a call back home to a friend who was helping her co-produce their church's Easter play.

"Can you handle production for a few more days?" she asked. After receiving confirmation, she hung up the phone and looked straight into Jenna's uncle's eyes. They both knew what the other was thinking. Emptiness filled them as they fully expected it would be the last time they would see Jenna.

A month later, same feelings of death anxiety entered her aunt's mind as Jenna sat up and said, "I want a sausage biscuit from McDonald's." Knowing how quickly her niece's appetite dissipated, her aunt gladly volunteered, "I'll go get it!"

Walking up to the register inside the McDonald's, she politely asked, "May I have a sausage biscuit, please?" Without hesitation, the young boy behind the counter said, "Ma'am, we are not serving breakfast at this time." Completely frazzled, she firmly stated, "You don't understand. I need a sausage biscuit." He again kindly confirmed they were no longer serving breakfast. With much more concern in her voice, she asked for a manager. As the manager made his way to the front, he explained, "Ma'am, my employee isn't mistaken. We are no longer serving breakfast."

Now, with tears streaming down her cheeks, she begged, "You don't understand. My niece is dying from cancer. She's barely eating. All she wants is a sausage biscuit from McDonald's. I cannot go back without it. I just can't."

Feeling her desperation, he said, "Wait right here." It didn't take long for him to walk back up with a bag full of sausage biscuits and hash browns in his hands. His words were simple, "Don't worry about the cost, and tell your niece we are praying for her."

That was how life continued for those months while searching for a donor match. Many people who would visit Jenna, all leaving with the same thoughts, "This is probably the last time we will ever see her."

8

BEHIND THE CURTAIN

Day after day, Jenna endured pain and suffering, and could only pray for momentary breaks between miseries. When doctors gave their approval for Jenna to rest at home in between treatments, it usually lasted only a couple of days, often resulting in a trip back to the hospital where she would stay for weeks. Jenna urgently needed the change in scenery to uplift her spirits, but it often felt like a cruel tease.

On many occasions, Jenna's blood counts would drop to dangerously low levels. This would only make her more susceptible to infection, leaving Kay to rush her back to safety at the hospital and Jenna to live more days on the crinkly bed in a stuffy hospital room. As the nurses began checking her levels, she spoke just long enough to ask her most critical question when entering the hospital, "Do I get a single room?"

Jenna did not concentrate on her counts being too low or that she was in a life-or-death situation; her only concern was if she had sole possession of the tv changer with a little bit of peace and quiet.

However, a state of solitude and serenity would not be in the cards for her on one particular stay.

While she lay in bed listening to the muffled sounds of the girl coughing in the bed next to her, Jenna would think. As annoying as it was not to get any sleep, nothing could change the fact she had a mom who rarely left her side. If Kay could not be there, which was extremely uncommon, she made sure a replacement was sitting in the hospital with her daughter. Even Jenna's friends, too young to be granted permission to be on the unit, pretended to be her family members to pull fast ones on hospital staff in order to sneak in a visit. There were also people outside the hospital raising money and awareness solely for her. Yet, the little girl lying in bed behind the curtain next to Jenna had no one. She did not have a mom taking care of her or visitors to check in on her. She was alone, and Jenna was not.

But that little girl wasn't the only child whose hospital stay involved more than just sickness. Instead of no one coming to visit, one boy had family in and out of his room for an entire night, one of Jenna's aunts remembered. The problem was this family was loud and completely oblivious to the fact that often the remedy to healing was rest. This was obvious when the mom of the young boy had all his younger brothers and sisters stay the night with him, climbing over his bed as if it were a jungle gym.

One night while Aunt Cindy stayed with Jenna, there was a baby across the hall who wailed the entire night. The mama in Aunt Cindy just wanted to comfort the baby who must have been in excruciating pain as the tormenting sounds of cries couldn't be subdued. She asked a nearby nurse if she could just sit and hold the baby. With a crooked smile, the nurse said, "Her mom should be getting off work soon." It was after midnight.

Jenna did not understand the importance of someone staying by her side until those moments. The support a friend or family member brought her when they came to visit was just what she needed to escape from the harsh reality she was living in. It would be Aunt Cindy who would give Jenna just what she needed to drown out the extra noise in her room.

As Aunt Cindy peeked into the room, she was shocked to see Jenna sitting up and awake. Slowly, she began unpacking her oversized purse, emptying books onto the bed in a pile. Jenna quietly smiled when she saw rather than books she could only read, they were drawing and coloring books. Thrilled to see a half-smile from Jenna, and with a beaming expression, Aunt Cindy exclaimed, "I thought we could draw together!"

Just a few weeks prior, when Jenna was suffering through the monstrous mouth sores, Aunt Cindy had come and stayed with her a couple of times. It was typical when coming to visit Jenna not to expect lots of conversation or interaction. The most family and friends could hope for was a hand or two of card games. Not only was the chemotherapy evaporating the energy from Jenna's body, it was taking her spirit along with it. Much like a note inside a glass bottle being cast out to sea, Jenna was slowly beginning to contain all her thoughts and emotions about this foreign world around her. Visitors had to get inventive if they did not want to just sit in silence, which was what Aunt Cindy did.

She pulled out a pen and a piece of paper and began doodling. Lying in bed, Jenna could see Aunt Cindy out of the corner of her eye. She could not talk as her lips had swollen shut; the dried blood had suctioned them together like super glue. So, she began motioning to Aunt Cindy she wanted a pen and a piece of paper too. Aunt Cindy's eyes slowly widened in bewilderment as Jenna began to doodle herself, realizing her niece had immense talent. With a common bond found between the two of them, Aunt Cindy decided to expand the reach of her talent by bringing Jenna actual drawing books on her next visit.

With the rhythm of raspy coughing from the girl behind the curtain, Jenna learned to draw cars, horses, and what would become her signature flower. The drawing was therapeutic. There was something about a completed picture that made her feel relief. It was peaceful to draw; it was healing.

However, Jenna wasn't the only one who had to find ways of coping with this new normal life; her whole family would have to.

Only for a Moment:

THE *ART* OF WAR

Jenna's body had taken some pretty hard blows, but it wasn't always the physical pain causing her body to shut down. The emotional battle was taking a toll on her as well. An outlet was needed. For Jenna, one of those was art. She coped with her feelings through drawing, painting, crafting, and sewing. She did so she could heal, so she could escape the pain if only for a moment. It was fun to color with someone in a paint-by-number competition. There was nothing like throwing darts at a paint-filled balloon wall if only to add a smile for a short while. So, if this is what you need, do it. But most of all, just breathe, keep breathing, and keep going.

You have just drawn Jenna's infamous flower.

9

BETTING MAN

Since Jenna was a minor, the surgeons would let Ray come back to the operating room to ease her anxiety. He had seen many of her procedures, but there was one spinal tap he would never forget.

Before every surgery or procedure, Jenna got a little something she liked to call "sleepy medicine," more commonly known as anesthesia. She would find herself coming up with silly little games to pass the time away in the hospital and fighting off the effects of sleepy medicine was one of them. Before each surgery, she would try her hardest to resist the anesthesia from putting her to sleep, much like someone on a diet fighting off the urge to devour a delicious piece of chocolate cake.

Her little game sometimes worked, as her stubborn self could fight off the effects. Jenna may have been small at 4'11", but her willpower was mighty. She fought off the sleepy medicine the best she could that day until her eyes slowly shut, and the doctors began the procedure. Standing alongside her as he usually did, Ray observed and waited while the doctor worked on Jenna.

Without warning, in the middle of the spinal tap, Jenna ended up defeating the anesthesia after all and woke up. She could feel the surgeon digging and thrusting instruments inside her lower back. Although she was dazed and slightly confused, she knew she was not supposed to be feeling anything. Between all the buzzing sounds of the drills and the doctors having a conversation about how their weekend went, it took everything in her to say, "I need more sleepy medicine." They must have obliged because she did not remember anything after she spoke those words.

As Jenna regained consciousness following the procedure, her dad casually asked her, "Do you remember waking up during surgery?" Jenna hazily looked at him as she slowly dozed in and out, still fighting the effects of the increased levels of anesthesia the team had given her. She whispered, "Yes, I asked for more sleepy medicine." He chuckled, and with a devilish grin on his face, proudly boasted, "Well, I just won a six-pack of Coke." Little did Jenna know when she had asked the doctors for more sleepy medicine, her dad reiterated the request. The doctor assuredly looked at him and stated, "She won't remember any of this." Ray said, "Do you want to bet?" Foolishly, the doctor took the bet and now owed Ray a six-pack of Coke.

As Jenna's days continued to teeter-totter from being in the hospital to short stays at home, she would just continue on with the silent attitude of I can do this. Maybe it was because the doctors, nurses, and her family spared her from being told what lay ahead, or perhaps she was just so sick she did not think about it. Whatever the reason, Jenna knew she could beat her disease.

However, that was not what her future held. The doctors were just about to drop another bomb of bad news lodging shrapnel into every part of Jenna and her family's hearts.

10

THE WALLS COME CRUMBLING DOWN

It was like time froze while Jenna was in the hospital. There were no special dates on the calendar, no plans to pencil in, and no news about the outside world. Jenna's parents did their best to shelter her from the horrific details of her leukemia and rarely told her what her friends and siblings were doing outside the hospital walls. In their minds, protecting her from what she was missing shielded her from any unnecessary, and unchangeable pain.

But Jenna knew. She knew softball season was right around the corner, and she would not be standing on the mound. Instead of beginning her pitching motions, a leather glove covering her left hand and clenching a softball in her right, she would be lying in a hospital bed with an IV in her left hand and a TV changer in her right.

No one could deny the toll the chemotherapy was taking on Jenna's body. The scales sat at barely 65 pounds when she placed her frail, twig-like legs on them. Her spiral strands of hair now constantly fell to the floor of their home.

Jenna would sit in a fold-up chair in the bathtub to be bathed by her mom because she could not get her port wet when it was accessed. It did not matter anyway; she was now too weak to even stand for a shower. Kay would slowly pour warm water over Jenna's matted bun of wispy strands resembling the style of the hair-netted cafeteria ladies she used to know. With each drop of water hitting her head, what remained of her locks were slowly stripped from her scalp.

Holding back tears, Kay walked Jenna down the stairs to the recliner in their den, preparing herself for what would happen as she placed a comb against her daughter's head. One stroke began the agonizing pain as she watched clumps of Jenna's once long, shiny black curls begin to shed from her scalp. Sitting across the room from Natalie, Kay motioned to her to grab a Ukrop's paper bag and bring it to her, both doing their best to keep it out of Jenna's view. Everyone knew the day was inevitable, but the actual sight of Jenna with only a few patches of long, thin black hair remaining on her head only made the cancer more real. Jenna would never let her mom cut her hair; patches were better than nothing in her mind. So, she waited it out as each strand fell slowly from her head. But one strand, one lone survivor hair follicle, stayed latched to her scalp for months.

Surprisingly, while the process of losing her hair was emotionally devastating to Jenna, once it fell out completely, it did not bother her so much. In some ways, it was kind of a relief. She tried wearing smiley face hats Joe's daughter had hand-sewn for her, but Jenna would get the worst hot flashes as a side effect from her treatment drugs. In a way, losing her hair was a blessing in disguise, just an easier way to deal with the heat pouring from her head.

Life for Jenna could have stopped as she was sitting there watching her hair float to the floor, but it didn't. Life never stopped. And thankfully during those moments, while everything inside her was dwindling, the urgency outside their family's house was in full stride. Along with family and friends, the doctors were still frantically searching for a donor match.

In some cases, an immediate family member, especially a sibling, would most likely be a match. Her family discovered early in the process that no one, neither her mom, dad, brothers, or sister, was a match for Jenna, making the bone marrow drives even more imperative for her recovery.

The doctors searched nationwide for a bone marrow donor during the first few months. After no match was found in the United States, the doctors requested a large sum of money from her parents to begin an international search for a viable match. While their family was by no means wealthy, Ray cashed in his retirement and used all their life savings. All of it was spent in hopes that it would mean more life for their daughter. So, with the stroke of the pen, her dad wrote a $10,000 check, one of many he would write, kicking off the international search that started and ended all in just 24 hours.

The next day, doctors confirmed it. Just like the hunt for that last puzzle piece, the one missing piece that always seems to get lost, the donor who would save Jenna's life would never be found.

Jenna not only had a rare leukemia, one only two to three percent of people were diagnosed with, but she also had a rare DNA. No donor's DNA would ever match hers. Truly, Jenna was one of a kind.

A bone marrow transplant was no longer in the cards for her. Jenna's 33 percent chance of survival was gone. The planned two and half years of chemotherapy were gone. She had no options, no hope of survival.

Doctors told her parents they could opt for a transplant with a two-out-of-six match, but the chances of survival were slim, and the side effects would be catastrophic. When Ray asked the doctors about the side effects, they began listing horrible, life-shattering consequences. A liver transplant, kidney transplant, and a feeding tube were just a few of the many terrible complications listed as a result of that bone marrow transplant. In complete disbelief, Ray remarked to the doctor, "My daughter is only 11. What kind of life would that be giving her?"

The doctor's only response, "She would be living."

Ray and Kay's hearts were shattered. If they were to proceed down that route, they felt like they were putting their child through a dangerous transplant only to be used as an experiment. It was not an option.

How do you tell your child the plan has changed? She would not get to experience the seventh grade, play in another softball game, have a first date or a first kiss, let alone get married and have children. The only thing she would be looking forward to was seeing Jesus sooner than expected.

As the days passed, Jenna's parents wrestled with the decision of whether to walk Jenna and their family down an unknown path. Quite possibly, they couldn't find the words to say or couldn't face the reality themselves. But maybe, just maybe, they were waiting on the miracle Joe kept insisting would happen.

Kay and a few of Jenna's aunts struggled with who would talk to her about death. They wanted to make sure she had made that most important decision and knew without a shadow of a doubt she would go to heaven. It was a conversation no one wanted to have, but time was precious, and where she would spend eternity was no longer just a Sunday morning call to the altar.

With the news all options were off the table, the word *defeated* did not seem adequate to describe the emotions flooding in. The agony her parents felt after watching Jenna suffer for months just to hear their daughter's fight would soon be over, was inconceivable. There was nothing else they could do. They could pay all the money in the world, but it would not give her an extra day of life. There was simply no cure for their little girl.

In moments where there seems to be no hope, and you are at the end of your rope, what do you do? What can you do?

Their family did the only thing they knew how to; they lived life. They spent the beginning of the summer swimming with friends, playing putt-putt, and going to the park as a family. Jenna desired to reenter middle school, even if only as a spectator. Most of all, though, they prayed and pleaded for others to pray. Everyone prayed for a miracle.

11

MOMENTS

It was now June 1999, a long six months after the original diagnosis, and Jenna was trying to live life as normally as she could. Her sixth-grade class was having their end-of-the-year awards ceremony in the coming week, and even though she had technically only completed half the year, she still wanted to participate with all her friends. Her immune system was low, so she put on a mask to protect her from catching germs, and headed out for the big day.

Kay had organized a surprise for Jenna, knowing how much she needed to enjoy just being a child. Jenna was invited into the teacher's lounge on the morning of the ceremony. When she entered the room, she saw many of her softball teammates and close girlfriends standing around waiting for her to join in on a pizza party. The slices of cheese, pepperoni, and sausage looked appetizing, but the best part about the surprise lunch date was Jenna could just be her old self. She could be one of the girls. It was nice to feel somewhat normal as she sat around watching them talk and laugh while they ate.

As they headed over to the auditorium for the beginning of the awards ceremony, she soon realized just how abnormal her life was. She walked past kids with full heads of hair, and their stares could not hide the fact they were living in two different worlds.

The awards ceremony concluded. Jenna's brothers and Hannah walked out of class on the last day of school, and it was time to start planning what could be their final summer together.

A family friend had heard Jenna's favorite racecar driver was Jeff Gordon. Truthfully, she was not really into racing, but her dad watched it every Sunday afternoon after church, so she learned to tolerate it. His favorite driver was Jeff Gordon, so Jenna just followed suit.

It was a beautiful sunny day, and family friends organized a helicopter ride to fly Jenna and her parents over to Richmond International Raceway.

Kay was a nervous wreck. Her fear of heights became a reality when she stepped into the helicopter's backseat. Jenna was a ball of excitement. She opted to sit right up front with the pilot to see the trees beneath her feet in the enclosed glass cockpit. Jenna relished in the fame, picturing herself as a movie star personally escorted to the Oscars.

Upon landing, Ray, Kay, and Jenna were ushered into the raceway complex on a golf cart towards the center of the track where all the driver's RVs were parked.

Jeff Gordon took the time to sign hats and T-shirts for Jenna and her parents. As Jenna sat in the golf cart watching Jeff talk to his adoring fans, she couldn't help but watch her dad. For one minute, he got to take a breather. He did not have to put in hours of overtime to support their family while all the medical bills began forming a paper Eiffel Tower on their dining room table. He was not spending his Saturdays at the hospital with Jenna wishing with everything in him he could take her place. Jenna could not help but smile, not because she had just met a famous racecar driver but because her dad was getting to enjoy life.

As Jeff went on to prepare for the upcoming race, Jenna, now completely worn out from all the excitement, figured watching the race from the comfort of her couch seemed like a better idea than hard, metal bleachers. So, they boarded the helicopter one last time before heading home.

It was nice to have special things done for her. Giving Jenna something to look forward to when her days typically revolved around hospital beds and the occasional card game with whoever came to visit, were the moments Jenna needed to make it through to the next day. But one thing more than anything else was Jenna's calm amidst the storm; the one thing that made coming home that much more enjoyable was her dog, Maggie.

Maggie, the family dog, was a Shetland Sheepdog who had a curious love for adventure, which made her an ideal fit as the sable-colored mascot for the Wrecking Crew. Her playful personality made her the perfect sidekick for Jenna and her brothers and sister as they ventured off on their childhood escapades. Rarely caught inside during the day, Maggie lived up to her breed as a herder. She wrangled up Jenna and Hannah as they rode their bikes around the front yard, herded Jenna's cat, Sugar, as if she were just another sheep in the flock, barked at Gabriel and Zachary as they aimed their BB guns towards the squirrels eating their dad's freshly grown tomatoes, and ran circles around Ray as he rode the lawnmower.

People had to drive slowly leaving their family's driveway as Maggie would attempt to herd traffic, barking at the wheels of their cars. Jenna and the rest of her siblings would all wave their hands at the drivers, motioning for them to go on as Maggie would always move out of the way, her lightning speed and agile movements offering her a quick escape from the car's front tires.

But as Jenna began her journey into the unknown chapters of cancer treatment, Maggie's personality changed. While her herding instincts and love for the outdoors remained, her priorities switched. Maggie now never left Jenna's side.

Whenever Kay and Jenna came home from the hospital, Maggie now used her immense speed to race to the back door to greet Jenna first with as much love and affection as possible through a wet nose and scratchy tongue. Maggie no longer lay on the cool, wood floor, trying to relieve herself from the heat pouring from her long, beautiful coat of hair. She now took her rightful place on the couch beside Jenna, knowing Jenna seemed to be more at peace as she rubbed her fingers through Maggie's silky mane. Even though chemotherapy had made Jenna's skin unbearably sensitive, her pain and fears seemed to vanish whenever she spread her fingers through Maggie's fur.

Jenna missed her deeply while she was undergoing testing and treatments at the hospital. It was nice when the therapy dogs were brought to the hospital and Jenna could sit with them. Not only did they bring her temporary relief from the pain, fear, and sadness, but they also encouraged Jenna to fight harder to recover so she could get home to her own bed, with Maggie lying at her feet.

Only for a Moment:

A MAN'S BEST FRIEND

Get out there and go get yourself a pet—dogs, cats, birds, you can even throw in a fish. Whichever animal you prefer, get it; they do wonders for the spirit! Animals sit and listen to your woes. They don't even bother you with what's going wrong in their lives! They just let you continuously pet them—well, maybe not fish.

In Jenna's experience, people couldn't offer the same type of comfort. Maggie brought Jenna a sense of relief and affection only she could give. When Maggie was by her side or lying at the foot of her bed, Jenna's pain and feelings of loneliness seemed to melt away. It was one of those indescribable bonds, but Maggie knew her role in the harsh world surrounding Jenna.

Take a breath, play with your pet, and keep going.

12

THE PHONE CALL

Kay's 40th birthday was just around the corner, and family friends had offered their house and pool as a place to celebrate. Zachary, Gabriel, Jenna, and Hannah didn't know at the time, but they were not just going to celebrate their mom's birthday. The pool party was another distraction, another moment to eliminate the anxiety surrounding a critical phone call Jenna's parents were expecting. But really, the word *critical* does not seem to be enough to describe that phone call. That life-altering phone call would change Jenna's life forever, for better or worse.

A couple months earlier, their family had gathered over at Aunt Cindy's house on Easter Sunday. While the kids were outside playing in the front yard, Jenna's dad and uncles gathered in the living room to talk about sports and work while all the aunts, including Kay, settled into the den. As the women chatted over magazines and sweet tea, Aunt Cindy leaned over and reached for a *Better Homes and Gardens* magazine. She flipped casually through the pages admiring the beautiful home decor and ideas for summer floral arrangements.

But as she turned over a page, her heart stopped in complete disbelief at the sight in front of her. In bold, shiny letters lighting up the page like the Las Vegas Strip lights seen from outer space, an article entitled, *Cord Blood versus Bone Marrow*, headlined the page. She began reading to herself, learning about new cancer treatments involving stem cells pioneered by Dr. Joanne Kurtzberg. As Aunt Cindy continued, she began reading aloud to Kay and her sisters about umbilical cord blood (UCB) transplants at Duke University Medical Center. With a simple nod of confirmation from Kay, there was no question; she needed more information.

Knowing Kay had been managing tough battles inside and outside the hospital, she was exhausted in the fight. So, Kay gave her sister the go-ahead to call Duke to see if this would be a chance to provide Jenna with one more summer, maybe even save her life. However, gaining information was no easy task as the Internet was not readily accessible in those days. Research by any means other than in a library was nearly impossible.

Nervous and fearing she was not up for the task, Aunt Cindy dialed zero and asked her first question to the phone operator, "May I have Raleigh-Durham, North Carolina?" Next, she said, "Give me Duke University Medical Center." Then, "I need the Children's Oncology Unit." When she reached someone on the unit, Aunt Cindy explained who she was and what her niece was going through. Her last plea ended with, "We were told we have no other options."

The lady on the other end of the receiver said, "Wait, you need to talk to Joanne." A little confused, Aunt Cindy thought, "Who is Joanne?"

After speaking with two operators and a receptionist, a doctor came on the line. "Hi, this is Joanne Kurtzberg," the doctor said.

A bit taken back by the fact she was now speaking to the same doctor she read about in the magazine, Aunt Cindy explained Jenna's story to her. After a 40-minute conversation, Dr. Kurtzberg calmly but confidently said, "We can help you." So, all of Jenna's medical records were sent to Duke for a second opinion of her total diagnosis, and her family waited for the call, still praying for a miracle.

At the pool party, friends and family did their best to make the event as fun filled as possible, knowing what news awaited Jenna's parents. Ray and Kay were praying for a misdiagnosis of the Philadelphia chromosome-positive, a snafu in the blood work, something besides the life-ending news doctors had given their daughter. They clung to the tiny ounce of hope that the coming news would be something different; there would be anything other than death.

Just as everyone began to pile hotdogs and hamburgers on their plates, the phone rang. It was unlike the naive moment right before their family's previous Christmas party. This time, Jenna's parents knew there would be significant news on the other end of the line. Kay, so shaken by what it may mean, could not bring herself to answer the phone.

Ring-ring-ring-ring-ring-ring-ring!

The phone on the wall rang continuously until, with a trembling hand, Ray walked over and answered the call.

Doctors at Duke University confirmed the Philadelphia chromosome-positive acute lymphoblastic leukemia. Jenna needed a cord blood transplant, and there was no time to waste. Her leukemia was aggressive, and she could relapse at any time. The intense treatment Jenna went through before the phone call had placed her cancer in remission, but it was only temporary. If she relapsed and the cancer returned, the option for a transplant to save her life would be off the table.

Those same pale faces and red glassy eyes, the ones they had when they learned Jenna had leukemia, resurfaced again as Ray and Kay imagined the brutal days ahead. It was a double-edged sword. There was hope, but with what her parents knew about a transplant, it was the last option anyone would choose for their child. And it was Jenna's last option, her only option.

The miracle, the miracle Ray and Kay prayed for to save Jenna's life, well, it had come, not as they had hoped, but in the most peculiar way.

13

A PAGE AND A HALF
OF CHANCES

Days after the call, Ray, Kay, Aunt Cindy, and Aunt Vonnie drove down to Duke University Medical Center to meet with Dr. Kurtzberg and the transplant team. As they entered the newly-built, modern glass building, the same anxious feelings of fluttering butterflies reemerged in their stomachs, like when Jenna received her original cancer diagnosis. The receptionist led them into a large conference room where they sat at a long-wooden, oval conference table, knees knocking together like clanging symbols in a marching band, waiting for the team to arrive. Doctors and nurses began entering the room one by one.

Sue, a nurse practitioner, was one of the first people to introduce herself. Her calm, sweet, and caring demeanor gave Ray and Kay the peace they needed to prepare themselves for what was to come. Unknown at the time, God was carefully beginning to place the exact people in their paths as Sue walked through those doors. She was like an angel sent from heaven.

Jenna was about to embark on one of the most challenging and treacherous journeys a human body can endure. God knew not only would she need someone with a servant's heart, but also someone who knew Him and had a relationship with Him in the same way she did. He knew Jenna would need a fiery redhead, a former lieutenant colonel in the United States Army, to push her on the days she did not feel like moving. She would be one of Jenna's driving forces as they all took that long and bumpy journey ahead.

As more of the team entered the room, a petite woman wearing bibbed overalls, florescent yellow running shoes, and topped with short, dark, curly hair stepped out from behind the taller doctors in front. As she reached out to shake Ray's hand to introduce herself, he stood and thought, "Who in the world is this woman?"

"Hi, I'm Dr. Kurtzberg. It's nice to meet you." Completely dumbfounded, Ray took a seat alongside Kay, and the meeting began.

Jenna's parents began showing Dr. Kurtzberg the chemotherapy protocol she was currently on.

In a soft and non-boasting manner, Dr. Kurtzberg said, "Oh, yes, I wrote the protocol for this case."

With hope in their eyes, hope they had yet to feel since they heard the word cancer, they felt a sense of peace. For the first time during the entire process, Kay and Ray felt like they were in the right place.

Whether Jenna was just another case to Dr. Kurtzberg or she was simply doing her job, Jenna's parents had just come from a hospital with no more options, leaving their daughter with no hope of survival. Sitting there inside a futuristic-looking medical building at a large conference room table in front of a team of nearly a dozen medical staff, it was as if King Arthur's knights had gathered to discuss their strategy before going into battle. Dr. Kurtzberg wielded her Excalibur. That miracle Jenna's parents so desperately needed had come as she leaned over the table and handed them a page and a half full of possible cord blood matches for Jenna. Dr. Kurtzberg assured them there would be a match for her.

"How is this even possible?" they thought. In one day, Jenna had gone from zero chances of survival to a page and a half full of opportunities to live. Dr. Kurtzberg gave hope to a family on the brink of losing their daughter.

Ray and Kay were in complete shock at what was unfolding in front of them. They had just been told Jenna's DNA was so rare there would not be a bone marrow match for her, but they weren't there to hear about a bone marrow transplant. They were there for a cord blood transplant.

There is a difference between the two transplant options. The cells in a cord blood transplant come from a newborn's umbilical cord. These cells are more immature and just beginning to grow and understand their role in the immune system. There are special proteins on the cells that are inherited and help regulate the immune system. They tell the body which cells belong, and which are *invaders*.

With a cord blood transplant, a 4, 5, or 6/6 match is possible because the cells are less mature, making units more readily available and easier to match. The typical reason why a cord blood transplant can fail is there are not enough cells, even though there is a recommendation for a minimum number of cells per weight for the best chance of success. Cord blood can also take longer to engraft which sometimes allows for complications. Ways to improve both the number of cells and promote the timing of the graft continue to be studied.

In a bone marrow transplant, the matching requirement for those special proteins is much higher, preferably a 9/10 or 10/10. The collection of cells from an unrelated bone marrow donor can be a lengthy process, which is risky with the possibility of a relapse. A body can reject a bone marrow transplant when those new cells are recognized as *invaders* and not as the recipients. This happens more with unrelated transplants. It is amazing to think how wonderfully created we are!

There had only been 1,400 unrelated, not sibling or parent, cord blood transplants completed in the world at that point in time. The process began in 1993, and Duke had only performed 300 of the procedures in the six short years before Jenna arrived. Dr. Kurtzberg, the leader of Jenna's medical team, was the first doctor in the world to perform one.

"Genius!" Jenna's parents thought. Dr. Kurtzberg was one of the most unassuming people Ray and Kay had ever met, often simply referred to as Dr. K. One look at her in those neon yellow tennis shoes, she seemed so normal, but she was one of the most brilliant people God had created. It was no accident that March 1999 issue of *Better Homes and Gardens* had landed in Aunt Cindy's hands.

A young man was visiting the clinic at Duke the same day Jenna's parents received the news she would undergo a cord blood transplant. He was the first person ever to successfully receive a related cord blood match. It happened in Paris in 1988, 11 years before Jenna was to have hers. This radical procedure was still new, but it was Jenna's last option. It did not matter if she was ready or not; she was heading into the experimental world.

Later that night, Jenna's aunts and parents returned home to explain more to their daughter. However, they did not tell her the experience she was heading into would not be like the intense chemotherapy, near-death experiences, allergic reactions, or the roommate coughing her lungs up on the other side of the curtain. It would not be like that at all; it would be 1,000 times harder.

The medical team gave Jenna's parents mounds of paperwork to look through to prepare them for the transplant. As Kay flipped through the pages, she suddenly came to a halt. Her heart stopped for a moment, and the world around her went silent. She could not read any further. She felt like she was leading Jenna into hell for the slim chance she would make it out alive. But the decision was not just for her parents because it was not solely their choice. Jenna had to make one too.

Dr. Kurtzberg told Ray and Kay it was up to Jenna whether she wanted to go through the treatment. She could only explain the facts about treatment so much and the progression through it, but ultimately, it would depend on Jenna if she was willing to do what it took to go through the transplant.

As an 11-year-old girl, Jenna didn't really look at something like that and weigh the options. It was an alien world even to adults, let alone a sixth-grader who was just now learning about teenage social skills and why boys were becoming attracted to girls. For Jenna, there was never really an option to quit or not to quit. In a way, she was just along for the ride. Her parents told her they were going to Duke, so she went. Jenna said her piece about things, but the option of saying no to a possible life after all that torture never even crossed her mind. Maybe it was because her parents never told her what was to come, but either way, it was time, time for her to start the transplant process.

The first step in the process was letting their home hospital know the news they had just received. Ironically, when told where Jenna was going, the doctors at her home hospital knew all about cord blood transplants at Duke but never told Ray and Kay. Their hospital had only done one cord blood transplant, and it had failed. They knew Jenna's family would not have stayed once they heard that statistic. Choosing money, the revenue it would have given their hospital for Jenna to spend the rest of her days there was worth more than her life, or at least, that was how Jenna's family saw it. So they left their home hospital, with no hesitation.

Only for a Moment:

ACTS OF SERVICE

There is so much more to life than what is just beneath your fingertips. There is a whole other world out there that needs hope. You can be that hope.

Although it is more known now than 20 years ago, cord blood donation is needed. For all the pregnant moms out there, find a hospital that will save your baby's umbilical cord. Those tiny cells inside the umbilical cord can save a life. You can choose to keep the cord blood for you and your family, or you can donate it so anyone can use it. Either way, do it. Life depends on it!

Take a breath, keep breathing, and keep going.

14

KNIGHT IN PURPLE

Only a few weeks separated the phone call and the beginning of Jenna's inevitable journey at Duke. Her future was not promised, so their family needed as many moments together that summer as they could cram in, moments that would last a lifetime. Everyone knew there was a high probability Jenna may not make it to her 12th birthday, and after they had been given those dreaded percentages once again by the doctors at Duke, they knew all the more Jenna's time on earth was precious.

Their family needed a getaway. Jenna needed to prepare, to ready herself before she entered Duke, and there was no better way to put a smile on Jenna's face than to take her to her favorite place to be: the beach.

Aunt Vonnie joined in with their family. With beach towels, folding chairs, and as many ham and tuna fish sandwiches Kay could make, they belted down Interstate 95 to Myrtle Beach, South Carolina, for a week their family would remember for the rest of their lives.

Early morning ribbons of sunshine bathed the beachfront town. Sounds of seabirds filled the salty air, greeting Jenna with warmth and comfort as she rose the first morning. There were no tubes, no IVs protruding from her body. The beeps and alarms of monitors indicating her frail body's lack of strength were now gone. The white walls were gone. The crinkly bed, gone. Jenna had more freedom, more than she had since last Christmas. She could make decisions now, not just whether she would get out of bed, but important decisions.

Kay had packed the variety packs of mini Kellogg's cereals to take with them on their trip. Oh, the decisions to make! Jenna and her brothers and sister had to get up early if they wanted the good ones, Fruit Loops and Lucky Charms if you asked her.

After inhaling breakfast, it was time to dash off to the beach to spend the day. Like other beachgoers on their getaway, they were there to relax, but relaxing in their family meant competition. Body surfing the waves, challenging each other to sandcastle competitions, and building moats of protection in hopes their castle would be the one to withstand the crashing waves, were only a few of the friendly competitions between the siblings. There was never any downtime to think about what was to come in the weeks ahead; there wasn't a moment to waste.

Long shadows casted over beachgoers packing up their folding chairs, umbrellas, and snack-filled coolers. Daytime activities were over, and the family was off to the next big adventure of the night.

Cruising down the palm tree-lined strip of Ocean Boulevard, Jenna's eyes lit up from the back seat when she first gazed at the giant, 100' Ferris wheel reaching far above the Family Kingdom Amusement Park amidst the twinkling bright lights of the Myrtle Beach nightlife. They stopped, and for hours, they rambled through the park, enjoying its carnival carousels, teacup rides, bumper cars, and other amusements, welcomed distractions for the price of a booklet of tickets.

The night was coming to an end, but before they left the park, illuminating itself to her like fireworks on the Fourth of July, Jenna spotted it, the climax of the evening. The Swamp Fox, the eighth-fastest, wooden roller coaster in the United States, lit up the night skies. Jenna decided it would be a perfect fit for her first roller coaster ride. She hopped into the seat next to Aunt Vonnie, and they were off with no care in the world. On the ground below them, Kay prayed anxiously the entire time the port in Jenna's chest would stay intact as they jostled about.

Other nights they played miniature golf, went to Broadway at the Beach and Barefoot Landing for some shopping, then finished off the evenings at a local homemade ice cream shop. Each night, Jenna's family coveted those special moments, but there would be a night that would transport Jenna out of the reality she was living in. It occurred the moment she walked through the massive arched wooden doors of the Medieval Times dinner theater show.

Jenna loved the Medieval era. Since starting her bout with cancer, she had been so weak and could barely get out of bed at times. Watching television and movies was often the only escape from her continuous pain-filled days. When people asked what kind of things Jenna would like to keep her busy, Kay never hesitated in answering, "movies."

A family friend took that to heart, telling Jenna to list all the movies she wanted. He had no clue there would be a list of about 100, and Jenna could not contain her excitement when she returned home on break from the hospital one day, and all of them were waiting in boxes for her.

Jenna was captivated by the scene at dinner. She felt like she was on the movie set of *A Knight's Tale* or *First Knight*. Between feasting on roasted chicken, butter-basted potatoes, and sweet corn, Jenna watched as the knights would joust and swordfight one another. Whenever a knight heroically won an event, they would pick a maiden from his cheering section and hand her a rose. After their section's worthy knight defeated his nemesis, sounds of clanging metal armor filled the stands as he marched up the stairs to where Jenna was sitting. She did not know whether or not the bald head gave it away, but it was as if the knight knew she needed some loving, so he gallantly offered her his rose.

At the end of the competition, one knight would be crowned victor and get to pick his princess. Each would present themselves to the king and queen, joining them for the rest of the show.

The joust and sword-wielding knights continued to battle as the rally cries from their doting fans filled the arena. While the boys chowed down on their succulent suppers, the girls secretly hoped the knight they cheered for would win, and they'd be picked as his princess. It was a fairytale Jenna hoped would come true for her.

It was the last jousting match, and their knight stood bravely mounted atop his horse, decked out in royal purple gear. All he had to do was knock his opponent off his horse, and victory would be had. With one kick from the iron stirrups, his horse lunged forward with an arched back and raised neck, and they were off. Galloping towards each other from either side of the arena, the knights pulled back their arms, and upon meeting in the middle, they thrust forward their jousts.

Bash!

The knight in red flipped over the back of his horse and hit the dirt covering the arena floor. Purple won!

The chivalrous knight grabbed his last rose, valiantly leaped over the wall, and began climbing the stairs making his way back towards Jenna, getting down on one knee, he grabbed Jenna's hand and asked her to be his princess.

At that moment, Jenna did not need to know her mom and Aunt Vonnie had spoken with the director of the show earlier in the day and told him Jenna's story, asking if there was anything special they could do for her. All Jenna needed was to live in the fairytale for as long as she could.

She needed those days. She needed to be her 11-year-old self and live in a fantasy world of being a princess, even if only for a night. The reality was in the next couple of weeks, she would begin a different journey, one that would not be full of roses and crowns. She would trade the sincerity of her purple knight for a team of nearly a dozen doctors and nurses.

Only for a Moment:

TAKE A VACATION

Amid the chaos and turmoil of life, take a vacation. Jenna's family will never forget the trip to Myrtle Beach for many different reasons. They will never regret the moments taken; the moments not taken are the ones they would have regretted. It's essential to slow down and take in God's amazing beauty around you. So, go enjoy it!

Take a breath, breathe in the moment, and keep going.

15

5200

That's the thing about castles. They transport you back in time to places children only see in storybooks. To an 11-year-old girl, castles are majestic. But as Jenna was helped out of the family van and reluctantly put her feet onto the hot parking lot in Durham, North Carolina, she was met with the beginning of yet another journey. Before her stood another castle made of dark, gray stone. But inside those walls, there would be no fairytale story.

Through the wooden, black steel-framed front doors, the family was welcomed and led down a long hallway, which seemed more like a dungeon to Jenna. It signified her transition from freedom in the outside world to the beginning of her new life. The narrow, featureless hallway led them to a small, cramped waiting room, where they waited for what seemed like hours.

Hannah's friendly nature found refuge in mingling with other patients in the room, and one little girl specifically captivated her attention. Although very little of her face was visible as it was covered with a yellow mask—something all patients wore at that stage—her radiant eyes gleamed. Her name was Katie, and she was just two years old.

Jenna only watched as Katie marveled at Hannah while she tried to conquer hazards traveling through Mushroom Kingdom on the way to rescuing Princess Toadstool. After a while, they shifted to a small child's table where they played with a plastic dollhouse. Jenna could only observe as she was completely worn out from tests she had been through earlier in the day. However, curiosity eventually got the best of her, and she joined them in playing house.

That interaction, although naive, would mark when Katie and Jenna embarked on an inseparable friendship. The nine-year age difference did not matter at that phase in either of their lives. Both were beginning their radical transplant expedition, totally unaware of what lie ahead. But they unconditionally trusted each other. They would innocently follow their parents to each appointment with doctors and nurses. They would feel each other's pain, even though neither of them would ever mention it to the other. They would be each other's strength, cemented in the confiding gaze of Katie's gleaming eyes into Jenna's.

There was a bond built that no one would ever understand, but it was a bond that would give Katie and Jenna the extra boost they needed to keep fighting, to keep pushing forward. They desired the day they would play, not in the white hallways and waiting rooms with masks covering their faces and IVs protruding from their chests, but running through fields in the fresh summer air and beginning new adventures filled with knights, dragons, and princesses on playgrounds outside their medical captivity.

After a long day of tests and meetings, both of their families headed over to the main hospital building, where resident nurses gave them a tour of the unit, Jenna and Katie's home for the next few months. Feeling like they were treated as some sort of celebrities, they were escorted up the back elevator, away from as many people as possible to avoid germs. This was the same elevator many transplant patients' parents would ride during the entire process in order to prevent unnecessary contact with other people and the germs they carried. Once they arrived on their floor, one of the nurses pressed a button, and they entered through the first set of doors to the Duke Pediatric Blood and Marrow Transplant Unit (PBMT).

There were two separate doors to get onto the unit. Only one set of doors opened at a time to decrease the number of germs and other pathogens that could harm the children undergoing treatment. After going through the first door, they entered a small, 12x24' room lined with storage lockers, a special HEPA filter, and a sink for hand washing before walking through the second set of doors. A sign that read, "Wash your hands for 15 seconds before rinsing," lined the wall behind the sink with a small clock next to it to time the 15 seconds. The nurses would also teach visitors to sing *Happy Birthday* twice as another measure to count out the 15 seconds. While slipping on little blue booties over the top of their shoes, they also noticed another sign on the wall that read, "If you are sick, do not come in." The only thing those children on that unit needed to fight was their diseases, not outside illnesses.

Once cleansed, the second door opened. A loud, wooden thwack struck everyone's ears as the doors latched shut behind them, and nurses led them from one end of the L-shaped hallway to the other. They stopped at individual rooms along the way and let their tour guide explain what amenities were offered to the parents staying on the unit.

Each room had its own HEPA filter system that was cleaned daily. However, it was not like normal hospital room cleanings. Each time cleaning personnel entered the room, a new mop head was placed on the end of the mop, and fresh water was added to the soap-filled buckets; decreasing any chances of cross-contamination was a must.

Games, movies, and other kid-friendly objects filled one small room. This room brought back memories of the playroom in their home hospital. Jenna did not plan on visiting it all too often as she was not about to go for round two in that room. Just off the playroom, there was a small area designated for the parents. They could not use the bathroom inside the patients' rooms, and things like brushing their teeth or hair inside their child's room were strictly forbidden. Thankfully, the room offered a shower, stovetop, and washing machine where the parents could have minimal living quarters while joining their children during their transplant.

Hannah looked up at her parents' faces as they walked onto the unit for the first time. It was not an emotional reaction to some grand tour of a luxurious hotel, or a deluxe resort Jenna would enjoy for the months ahead. This place of hope was also a place of heartache, a place where less than 40 percent of the children who walked in were able to walk out. Parents were forced to watch their children endure what would essentially be the worst days of their lives. To contend with this, nurses wore smiles on their faces and brightly-colored uniforms to lift the heaviness that lurked in the hallways.

5200 was etched into a black, plastic placard on the wall. Unlike other hospital floors, the doors to the patients' rooms were always closed to keep out unwanted germs. This was not an ordinary hospital floor, and the scared looks on Ray and Kay's faces reflected that. Despite all the heaviness of its surroundings, 5200 was a place of hope. It was a place where miracles happened daily, a place which gave so many children their only chance for life. It was a place of heroes, where doctors and nurses spent countless hours fighting on their patients' behaves, doing whatever humanly possible to ensure another day for the children.

Jenna knew her parents tried their best to hide the seriousness of 5200 from her, and it worked, sort of. The severity of the situation never really registered with her. In a way, it was a blessing from God she was a child going through such a horrible ordeal. Jenna did not concentrate on the negative because, as a child, she did not think of the worst-case scenarios. So, for her, it was just one day at a time.

As they continued to walk down the hallway, Jenna looked around at what would be her life for the next month or so, white walls lightly showered with children's artwork and medical memorabilia.

16

HELL WEEK

Many have heard the acclaimed stories the recruits of the United States military go through during basic training, with each branch enduring a specific week or weeks of intense training. The Marines call it Receiving Week; for the Army, it is Red Phase; and for the Navy SEALS and special operations teams, it's called Hell Week. Little did Jenna know, the transplant families had their own week prior to transplant they had nicknamed *Hell Week*. It would not involve swimming miles through a freezing ocean or crawling on her belly through mud so thick it felt like quicksand. But in a much different way, those three weeks of Jenna's Hell Week would test her physical and psychological limits. Those weeks would prepare her for what was to come throughout treatment.

Every child's transplant experience was not the same. They did not all have to go through radiation before a transplant, and for some, only certain sections of their bodies had to be radiated. For Jenna, her Hell Week would start with nothing less than total body irradiation (TBI) two times a day for five straight days, beginning with her brain and going all the way down to her toes.

Leukemia is a cancer of the blood, and since Jenna had cancer flowing throughout her frail, 11-year-old frame, total body irradiation was warranted. Every cell, whether cancer or healthy, would be wiped out, destroying Jenna's immune system in the process. Her body would be unable to fight off even a simple cold. Regardless of the risks, the time had come; there was no turning back. With her mask pulled up over her face, Hell Week began.

The doctors had prescribed anti-nausea medicine to take before each radiation session. Of course, that medicine was in the form of a pill, and naturally, Jenna fought her mom over it every morning. After the whole pill-swallowing fiasco during her collapsed lung days, Jenna developed a phobia, afraid the pills may get stuck in her throat like before. After an hour of avoiding the inevitable, she mustered up enough courage to swallow the medication to get her through the first treatment.

As Jenna and Kay arrived at the treatment center, Kay watched as her daughter slowly walked towards the radiation room doors. Walking through the doors, the first thing that grabbed Jenna's attention was a massive cocoon-like machine hovering over a table in the center of the room. It was something she had not seen before. She was frightened. It looked nothing like what a knight in shining armor could fight; this was a different dragon. But just outside those walls, watching Jenna on a monitor, Kay was praying. Six and a half minutes on one side, the gurney turned, then six and a half minutes on the other; her body was scanned. Kay prayed and pleaded, "God, protect and heal Jenna from any harm this could bring to her."

The nurse explained Jenna could have music playing while they completed the treatment as some sort of distraction. To her astonishment, it helped. The dragon was at least momentarily disabled. Before heading down to Duke, a family friend, a teenage girl who had also battled cancer, had given Jenna her first CD ever. It was Shania Twain's *Come On Over* album. Jenna listened to it every day that week during the radiation. Needless to say, by the end of the week, she knew the order of each song on that CD, along with every word. The technicians told Kay they were singing the songs in their sleep. Listening to the music calmed her. It was something new. It took her to a different world, a world where she did not have a machine floating over her head, scanning her body as the radiation slowly killed the life inside her. There were no beeping machines, no IVs, no pain; it was just her singing away in her head with Shania Twain, "*Yeah, I wanna scream and shout!*"

Jenna's thoughts consisted of the story she would make up in her mind while listening as if the song were the life she was experiencing instead of that dreadful reality she was living. Music helped her express herself. She was not good at explaining her feelings, most of the time suppressing them so deeply as if they never existed in the first place. Jenna felt she had to be tough to get through it, rarely ever speaking about the pain she was enduring. Maybe she was just tough, or perhaps it was just another defense tool, but the music seemed to be a voice for her feelings.

Although music was an outlet for Jenna's spirit, it could not soothe the tsunami of nausea crashing about inside her belly. Nothing could alleviate the constant trips to the bathroom. So, she added a pillow to the floor, a comfortable sitting perch as her head leaned over the toilet, just trying to conserve her energy. The radiation was doing its job. The cancer was being killed. Jenna's body was exhausted and weakening.

Every day that week, Jenna had undergone two sessions of total body irradiation, one in the morning and one in the afternoon. In between those sessions, she would return to the clinic to check vitals and receive IV pain medicines and other essential fluids, all were necessary components in preparing Jenna's body for transplant. During one of those clinic visits, Kay sat down beside Jenna in the waiting room, as she had done so many times before, anticipating Jenna to be called back for more testing. She looked over to see a teenage girl sitting across the way. Just like her own daughter, she was bald and weak, identifying them both as cancer patients. But there was one difference between them. Kay noticed the girl had dark, mauve stretch marks covering her legs and arms. She couldn't help but think, "Wow, I wonder what she has been through." The sight of the girl reminded Kay she could only revert to God, her one constant, the only one who offered any peace in that unknown world.

With no break in the misery, weeks two and three were next. Jenna was about to experience the most intense chemotherapy, even more intense than she had at her home hospital. It was the kind of vicious chemo where a nurse would come out in the hallway and gently touch Ray on the shoulder. With pity in the nurse's eyes, he did not even have to ask. Ray knew they were about to do something to his daughter that would cause her a great deal of pain.

The nurses needed Ray to hold Jenna down as they simultaneously gave her a shot in each leg, shots that would feel like two Louisville Sluggers had been swung at her thighs. As Ray stood at the foot of her bed, holding Jenna's ankles, one nurse stood at the head of the bed, holding her arms. Kay held Jenna's hand while looking in the other direction, unable to stand the sight of the torture. Two other nurses stood on opposite sides of the bed and popped the caps off the needles.

One. Two. Three.

Whap!

It was a grand slam. Jenna screamed in agony as the chemo-filled syringes were stabbed into her legs. "How could there be worse than that?" Jenna thought.

Before she could even begin the transplant phase, doctors had to surgically place a triple lumen Hickman catheter in the center of Jenna's chest. Unlike the port, which remained on the upper right side of her chest, the Hickman did not need to be needle-accessed weekly. It was a secured catheter-like line staying in at all times; three lines, each roughly the diameter of a pencil eraser, all connected to one line protruding from the center of her chest. She needed three lines to avoid cross-contamination between receiving blood products, administering drugs, and putting other medications into her body. Each had a different colored top: red, white, and blue. Jenna wondered if it was somehow symbolic of the battle she was about to embark on, her version of the armed forces.

Once the Hickman was placed, the following week would be filled with more tests, spinal taps, bone marrow aspirations, and the fiercest chemotherapy her body had yet faced. Jenna had undergone so many of those procedures, but unlike previous ones, it was much more severe now that her immune system was vastly compromised. At times, her blood pressure would drop to a dangerously low level of 80/25 and her fevers would raise to over 103 degrees Fahrenheit. And Jenna was still only in the early stages.

Her new normal consisted of debilitating bouts of vomiting, diarrhea, itching from hives covering her body like freshly-layered strawberry jelly on a piece of buttered toast, and other allergic reactions which caused her heart rate to rise so high it left her breathless.

Jenna knew what the Navy SEALs endured during their Hell Week and what she went through were two completely different scenarios, but in some ways, the impact those weeks would have on their bodies would be the same. The total body irradiation, surgeries, tests, and chemotherapy had brought her to her breaking point. Jenna's body had been pushed to the brink, driven to the limit.

While the military tested with CS gas, Jenna's body would be tested with chemicals. She was physically weak and in pain; her body was becoming weaker by the day. Mentally, Jenna was subduing the fact this new life was stripping her of civilian life. She was about to enter a world so bizarre and beyond comparison civilian life would remain only a figment of her imagination. This world would be filled with physical anguish and mental instability. But this was only her training for what was to come. This was her Hell Week.

Jenna's new life was not on her terms. She had proven her physical and mental endurance in the past, fighting off the sleepy medicine during surgery, pushing through sleepless nights with her head glued to the toilet, and holding within her the pain and anguish, not wanting to alarm her friends and family. As Jenna's body became weaker, each one of her blood counts dropped further towards zero. With her immune system zapped, she finally recognized the bizarre reality edging closer and closer was beyond anything she could ever imagine. The wooden door would bolt shut until her treatment was over, whether successful or not.

Cancer did not discriminate. It did not care if you were young or old, boy or girl. Cancer did not consider your faith, whether it be in God or your own strength and defiance. Jenna's parents knew the doctors would do everything to save their daughter. But on that unit, the strongest did not always survive. Such was life on 5200.

The timeline of events leading Jenna to the treatment center at Duke were all amazing miracles. Everything was out of their control, from the helping hands the family received, to the over 4,000 who came to give blood in Chesterfield, and to Joe's charge to Liberty's convocation. The past was out of their control, and so would the future. They knew not what the future held, but they knew the one who held it. They prayed. That was all they had in that moment as they walked with Jenna into her new home away from home, room 5211.

Only for a Moment:

MUSIC FOR THE SOUL

What joy music can bring to someone's life! For Jenna, music lifted her soul. It helped her think about something other than what she was going through. For Hannah, it took on a different meaning as she watched it chip away at Jenna's pain. Or, maybe it was just because Hannah loved to sing at the top of her lungs any chance she got. So, listen to music, whether it's a sad country love ballad that helps you get over your devastating breakup or a strong, pump-it-up type of song. Fight back. Sing the lyrics loud and proud. It is such a release.

Of course, Jenna used Shania Twain's *Come On Over* album to conquer her giants. Perhaps, after scanning the QR code below, this playlist of songs will help you will feel like you can conquer the world!

Take a breath, sing loud and proud, and keep going!

17

A BAG FILLED WITH GOLD

The day Jenna's family anticipated for what seemed like a lifetime had finally arrived on August 3, 1999, just seven months after her leukemia diagnosis. Packed tightly like sardines into her tiny hospital room, 11 people nervously waited for the nurse to begin the transplant. It would be the only time so many people would ever be allowed in her room.

For the months to come, Jenna would not have any close contact with anyone except for the doctors, nurses, and her parents. Due to contamination concerns, only two people besides Jenna would be allowed in her room at the same time until her blood counts began to rise. If family members or friends came to visit, the only show of affection they could give her would be blown kisses through the window of her room. She would not be in a bubble, but the lack of human contact made her feel much like *Bubble Boy*, an outcast because of medical circumstances beyond her control.

She rarely thought of what was to come; she knew her faith in the Lord would bring her through to the end. However, it could not distract her from the emptiness she felt being in that room. She was left without the horsey rides with her dad, playing with her brothers and sister, and the comforting hugs of family and friends.

The nurse held a small bag filled with donor hematopoietic stem cells, very much resembling the same bag used for a blood transfusion. Jenna winced, not because of the pain but because of the smell. It reeked of rancid creamed corn and garlic. It was terrible. The odor came from dimethyl sulfoxide (DMSO), a protective liquid solution in which the cells are suspended in during the freezing process to prevent cellular damage to the cord blood. The cells are washed and thawed, but some of the odor remained. Unfortunately, it would be the perfume that would seep from Jenna's breath and through her pores in the days to follow.

Premedicated with Benadryl, Jenna did her best to stay awake to watch the miracle treatment take place. It was the day, the make-it-or-break-it day. With all her blood counts at 0.0, Jenna was getting completely new cells, totally new blood. Her blood type would change from Type O- to Type A-. Even her DNA would change. She was about to get new DNA, someone else's DNA. A baby girl, not even aware of the significance of her life, was about to give Jenna life. The umbilical cord was the key, the key to unlock the door of 5200.

Jenna's nurse, putting on a brave face, hung the bag full of life-giving cells, totally fooling the entire family on the fact it was the first transplant she had ever administered. She carefully hooked the bag up to Jenna's Hickman, and the donor blood slowly entered her body. She told them any time a nurse handled the cord blood, they cared for it as if it were gold, knowing that small bag full of tiny cells was a child's only chance of life.

There was nothing else Jenna's family could do. As the tension in the room rose, stricken with heavy hearts and tearful eyes, they did what they had become accustomed to doing more and more in the last seven months. They prayed. They prayed for that miracle, and those prayers were to be heard; however painful and debilitating, they would be answered.

18

WEEK ONE

Much like the first week following Jenna's diagnosis, Kay was sick and not allowed on the unit. It was as if the rewind button on the VCR in the den had been hit on one of the movies Jenna had been watching. Ray took the reins again, mounting his white horse of fatherhood, staying with Jenna while she started the grueling uphill climb post-transplant day.

Each day, Jenna would walk to the end of the L-shaped hallway to the metal doors that led to the outside of the isolated unit. Her mom would stand on the other side of the door, peering through a small glass window to see her daughter, only further solidifying the seclusion between them. As Kay placed her hand against the glass, going up to mirror Jenna's, the surrealness of that prison-like experience was beginning to depict the magnitude of what she was going through. Unable to bear the sight of her mom behind the glass window, Jenna began to cry, then turned around and shuffled back to her room. It broke her mom's heart.

If Jenna was going to make it through treatment, she knew she had to learn to take the good with the bad. While no one could replace the companionship between her and her mom, there sure were perks to having her dad around. Jenna could get away with a whole lot more!

Jenna was a bit of a rebel with a stubborn streak. Well, as much as she could be locked away behind two doors and hooked up to a pole with at least three IV pumps attached and multiple bags of liquids hanging from it at all times. Given she was now entirely dependent on other people for simple daily activities such as going to the bathroom or eating, just having the right to say "no" to the nurses gave Jenna a sense of control over a situation in which she had very little.

One day, the nurses tried to encourage her to take her morning regimen of pills. As usual, Jenna was having none of it. After the first couple of hours of refusing them, her dad began taking away her *privileges*. Mistake number one as a transplant parent: do not take something away from your child they don't have in the first place.

There were not a whole lot of things Jenna enjoyed that could be taken away. It was not like she had her go-kart she could get in and drive out the unit doors. Grounding was not an option since she already had to stay in her room all day long anyways. So, her dad had to get creative. First, he took away the TV, but that only made them sit in a silent room with each other. Shortly after, the boredom from the monotonous wall staring consumed him, and round one went to Jenna. The TV was turned back on. Then, he chose to punish Jenna's refusals to the nurses by not playing games with her. Once again, it limited his entertainment as well, and round two also went to Jenna.

She was tired of taking pills. She was tired of listening to other people telling her what to do. So, she just sat there all day, arms crossed, with a you-are-not-going-to-win-this attitude. The problem was, she was playing in the big leagues now, and those clever nurses had devised a plan so diabolical that she could not resist any longer.

They told Ray he needed to leave the room. Knowing Jenna had no way of getting out of the bed by herself, at some point, Jenna would have to make a big decision: either pee on herself or take the pills. Eventually, the final round went to the skilled nurses.

Those types of hardheaded games continued while her dad stayed with her. All Jenna could hear was the broken record of the cancer treatment world—take that pill, lay there while I give you a shot that will inflict indescribable pain on your body, and don't forget to do your mouthwash. Jenna just wanted to be a kid, and the only way to do that was to buck the system.

The doctors and nurses stressed how she needed to take a bath every day. Unsurprisingly, Ray would spend the day asking Jenna, "Do you want to take your bath now?" She responded with a defiant, "No!" And every time 11:59 p.m. would come around, Ray would look at Jenna, and she would look right back at him and declare, "The day isn't over yet!" But she would always end up taking a bath, and those days, rounds two, three, four, five, and so on would go to Ray. It was nothing personal against her dad or even the nurses. She just wanted to have some sense of control in that uncontrollable world, so she did as many things as she could, when she wanted to, and how she wanted to. Not to mention, Jenna's skin was becoming more sensitive to touch, so the simple rubbing of a washcloth caused her great pain as each stroke of the cloth grazed over her speckled, bruised skin.

Ray never envisioned he would have to play those types of games; his normal games was coaching Jenna's brothers on the baseball field. He especially never imagined being the cause of physical pain inflicted upon his daughter as he gently rubbed a warm washcloth across her back. No parent ever wants to see their child in pain. And he not only had to see it but at times, he had to cause it.

Trying to escape the heartache of watching his little girl in pain, he slipped outside in the hallway, only to be brutally reminded there was no evading it as he walked past the rooms of so many hurting children. He walked down to Katie's room and motion for her dad, Larry, to come out and join him for a moment free from watching their daughters suffer. There was no denying the weight of the life-or-death situations those two fathers were facing with their daughters.

Looming over them was the knowledge that the month before they came on the unit with their sick daughters, five children had died during the first week of July, and a total of nine had died in the month of July alone. That was over half the children on the unit. Those numbers were terrifying, but they did slightly resemble the 33 percent chance doctors gave Jenna.

With terror in his eyes, Larry looked at Ray and fearfully said, "You know, that means one of our girls probably won't make it."

The reality of Larry's expression hit him hard like the suddenness and ferocity of a Mack truck slamming into a guard rail on a steep mountain bend. Ray needed a moment to escape. He needed to leave the world he was living in, which still did not feel real in so many ways. At that moment, the piercing sound of the latching wooden doors echoed down the hallway; his moment of relief would walk through the unit doors as his sons arrived to greet him.

Tears began to trickle down his face as Zachary and Gabriel walked into sight. It had been six weeks since Ray had seen them.

Gabriel and Zachary had just returned from their escape. They needed to be teenage boys and had spent the previous weeks with their aunt, uncle, and two cousins in Pennsylvania.

Zachary and Gabriel spent their days riding jet skis on the lake, lounging at the pool by the house, and filled the entire experience with boys will be boys' moments. While tubing across the lake, Gabriel and Zachary would taunt their uncle, telling him they could not be thrown off into the water. Upon hearing this, their uncle jerked the boat back and forth at high speeds trying to flip them off the tubes.

On one particular ride, Gabriel and his cousin were in side-by-side tubes, knocking back and forth, soaring over the bumpy boat wakes. With a flick of the steering wheel, their uncle flipped Gabriel straight up into the air in the boat's wake. He grasped the side handles as he came crashing down on top of his cousin's back, narrowly avoiding hitting the water at about 30 miles per hour. With the tube still in his white-knuckled grip, upside down on his cousin's back, Gabriel proudly shouted towards his uncle at the helm of the boat, "You still didn't knock me off!"

Those shenanigans continued throughout their stay as the boys would antagonize the chipmunks roaming feverishly around the yard by trying to catch them with their bare hands, though their aunt would ultimately give the chipmunks the last laugh. While preparing lunch one afternoon, their aunt had placed some sandwiches out on the picnic table while she ran inside to grab the mayonnaise they liked to layer on top of their bread. When she stepped back outside, she was greeted by the sight of one of the chipmunks the boys had chased earlier in the day casually gnawing on the crusts of the bread. With a naughty chuckle, she let the chipmunk take a few more bites. As the boys sat down minutes later to eat their sandwiches, their aunt questioned, "How do you like the sandwich?"

"They're great, thanks," they replied.

She laughed, "That's good because you know that chipmunk you've been chasing all day? He just had part of it!"

But chipmunk-nibbled sandwiches were a small price to pay for a moment of escape from the unpredictable world surrounding them. Smacking your face on an inner tube stung a bit, but spending a month free from watching their sister suffer made those days worthwhile, even if it was only temporary. Because it was always temporary. Zachary and Gabriel were reminded of that as they walked into 5211 and saw Jenna in the frail condition she lay in.

Jenna was supposed to be experiencing the beginning of her seventh-grade year. Instead, she was being taught life science and biology through real-life experiences lying in a hospital bed rather than sitting in a classroom. She now knew the meanings of terms like white blood cell count (WBC), bone marrow aspiration, graft-versus-host disease (GvHD), absolute neutrophil count (ANC), and an assortment of about a thousand other medical phrases. Those words were something no 11-year-old should know the meaning of, but Jenna did. She knew a low WBC meant there was no way to fight off infections, making death an all too real factor in her life. WBC is made of numerous types of cells, lymphocytes, neutrophils, and many more, each having a different job. For example, lymphocytes fight off viral infections, neutrophils fight off bacterial infections, and the mix of those two cell types fight off fungal infections.

Jenna's neutrophils were around 80 percent, and they were supposed to be at 40–50 percent. Her lymphocytes were 5.5 percent, and those were supposed to be at 50 percent. Her neutrophils were so high because of the cellular growth-promoting granulocyte colony-stimulating factor (G-CSF) she was taking. Still, none of her counts were accurate because Jenna was getting an extra boost from medication. Even though her counts looked normal to the untrained eye, the G-CSF she was taking worked like jumper cables to a car battery, shocking the process which promotes the growth of the types of cells that would make up the WBC in her new blood. Even with this drug working its magic, Jenna's system was highly vulnerable to infection.

The ANC was a whole different ball game, as Jenna knew if her levels were below 500, the new cells had not yet engrafted. However, once she reached 500, she ran the risk of developing GvHD, something she would become much too familiar with later in her journey.

After the boys had left, Kay needed to break up the blinding heaviness of her daughter's monochromatic world. She brought Jenna's grandma's handsewn silk pillowcase and draped a colorful quilt over her bed's sterile sheets. She began filling the emotionless walls of Jenna's room with pictures of family and friends, including many of her dog Maggie, beautiful artwork, sports memorabilia, and other colorful touches, anything to do her best to cover the four white walls that seemed to be slowly caving in on them as the days progressed. But that hermetically sealed box was her home for now.

Only for a Moment

ALL FUN AND GAMES

There will be times in your life when the domino effect begins to take over. One after another, the pieces of your life start to crumble around you. It's heavy. It's physically, emotionally, and mentally painful. There was nothing to prepare Jenna for the upcoming days of this battle she and the rest of her family would have to face. Everything cannot possibly be explained because, quite frankly, all the medical jargon would become overwhelming. But that's exactly what it was: overwhelming. It was pain no one would want to inflict on their worst enemies. It was heartbreaking, and there were no pause buttons.

So, take a break when you need it. Take a breath, get out on the lake, and keep enjoying life. Relax and go feed the chipmunks.

19

DAVID JAMES ELLIOTT

A little over a month had gone by, and an exhausted Jenna's 12th birthday was approaching. Unlike previous birthdays, she did not wish for the days leading up to September 11 to fly by. There was not much to look forward to, apart from late-night episodes of *I Love Lucy* or starting a little trouble by climbing out of bed and spraying nurses and other patients' parents with foam hand sanitizer. It was impossible to have a birthday party because groups of people were rarely allowed on 5200. Somehow though, Jenna had an inkling something big was going to happen.

Another game Jenna had become an expert in during her extended stays in the hospital was playing possum. With her eyes closed, appearing to others as if she were asleep, she was able to overhear everything going on around her. The fun part was no one ever really picked up on it. Sneaky, sneaky, right?

Earlier in the week, Kay had been busy on the phone trying to line up something special for her daughter's birthday. Jenna overheard her talking about a mystery person but never could quite make out who the person was. In the back of her head, she thought her mom was trying to get a celebrity to come, but she was not exactly sure how her mom could pull that off. So, for the time being, all Jenna could do was sit and wait.

September 11, 1999 had arrived, and Jenna was officially 12 years old. She woke up nauseated and aching all over her body, not normal for a 12-year-old, but typical for Jenna. Mandy, one of Jenna's favorite nurses, came into the room to administer nausea medicine. She was always so sweet and kind to Jenna, but something about her seemed a little off that day. It seemed like Mandy was avoiding any real interaction with Jenna. When the nurses or doctors were quiet, Jenna's mind tended to wander. Often expecting the worst, Jenna anticipated something was going wrong. "Is Mandy mad at me? Did I do something?" Jenna thought. Little did she know, Mandy was keeping a secret from her, a secret that even a game of possum could not uncover.

About 20 family members and friends were beginning to arrive at the hospital. They were ushered into a conference room just outside the unit doors. This space was open to air filled with germs, so the doctors had to make sure Jenna had the vital signs and blood counts necessary to join them. Still unaware of what her mom had planned for her, nurse Mandy told Jenna to get all gussied up; the best she could, at least.

Suddenly, a handsome, dark-haired, 6'4" silhouette filled the doorframe of her room. Jenna could not believe it! It was David James Elliott, the star of the hit TV series *JAG*. He was at the top of the list of people she wanted to meet when she got sick, and there he was right in front of her. He looked at her, and with that devilish, I-could-mesmerize-any-woman-with-this-smile look, said, "I hear it's somebody's birthday." After that, well, let's just say Jenna had all the ladies jealous of her.

David escorted Jenna down the hallway to the conference room to join the rest of her family and friends like she was the VIP at a Hollywood film release. With her yellow gown wafting behind her, all eyes were on Jenna as the women and girls on the unit thought to themselves, "She's so lucky!"

Jenna celebrated her 12th birthday with nearly two dozen friends, family members, and one TV star. She had to keep her mask on to ward off any germs, which limited her ability to blow out the candles on her cake. Hannah leaned in and blew them out for her, which was something Jenna's younger sister had become accustomed to doing by that point, helping Jenna whenever she needed it. There was no doubt David was tired of smiling and posing for the photos he was bombarded with, but Jenna could not stop looking at his smile, photo shoot perfection standing in front of her. "What a surprise!" she thought. This was the best gift they could have given Jenna, family, friends, and freedom, at least for a little while.

After about an hour, Jenna wanted to take David to Katie's room to see her. Katie's mom, Gina, and her grandma were absolutely in love with him, so Jenna could not wait to give them a much-needed surprise as well. Kay, Jenna, and David walked down to Katie's room, and David, proving himself even more as a gentleman, pushed Jenna's IV pole down the hallway beside her. When his tall silhouette filled Katie's doorframe, boy did their eyes light up too.

On his way back to Jenna's room, David made sure to visit each patient on the unit who was well enough. For the rest of the afternoon, he spent hours with Kay and Jenna in her room. Before David left, he gave Jenna a stuffed, multi-colored bear she named Jag and a stuffed, black and brown cat she named Mac, after the heroine on *JAG*, Lieutenant Colonel Sarah MacKenzie, played by Catherine Bell. These were two stuffed animals she would never want to get rid of.

David was so wonderful to her, talking with Jenna as if he had known her for years. He looked just as handsome in person as he did on TV, better actually. That was probably why all the nurses fought over who would be the one assigned to Jenna's room on that day.

There was no way David could ever truly understand what his visit meant to Jenna and the other families he met. He gave Jenna something to look forward to every week on Tuesday nights as she and her mom watched *JAG*. Even if it was only for an hour, they escaped the world surrounding them with the dramatic legal adventures of two top JAG officers.

While in the hospital conference room, David gave her family and friends a bit of laughter amidst all the negative reports by serenading them with his guitar-playing talents and rock-star singing voice. He even promised Jenna's best friend, Rhonda, a signed autograph picture of him, which was fulfilled a couple of weeks later when she received a special package postmarked from Los Angeles, California. When she pulled out an autographed picture of him as his character from *JAG*, Commander Harmon Rabb Jr., her only thoughts were, "Wow, I can't believe he remembered. He thought of me."

David gave Jenna's cousin a kiss on her cheek she would never forget as he whisked her up in his arms and gave attention to someone other than the sick girl for a moment. For the top-notch nurses who were nonstop caretakers, he gave them an exciting day full of smiles. There was hope in his visit. It could be the recipe for the extra boost of energy needed for one more child to make it off the unit. For Jenna's parents, he gave them comfort in knowing if it were to be

Jenna's last birthday, she had escaped the pain for a little while and replaced the slight grimace on her face with a smile.

Jenna rarely smiled anymore. She hurt all the time. Jenna's parents longed to see her smile, and they would do anything for that, including setting up a television star to visit and spend her birthday with her.

Jenna was so sad when David had to leave. She was not ready for that moment to be over. It was nice to get visitors, but sometimes it just made things all that much more challenging because they always left while she had to stay. There was nothing Jenna could ever say or do to repay David for taking the time out of his busy schedule to come and visit her.

Since the visit was not set up by Make-A-Wish but by special friends of Jenna's family, Ray and Kay would have to pay the hefty tab. However, another moment was about to occur. That time, the moment would be a blessing for Ray and Kay. Upon discovering the experience was not Jenna's Make-A-Wish, David graciously covered all the expenses. One visit from a stranger, stretching 3,000 miles from California to North Carolina, was what it took to give so many blessings to many different people in desperate need of sunshine through those grim, cloudy days. Nothing could ever hold a candle to the relationship they built that day. The friendship between Jenna and David was unexpected, but it remained so special to her that the anticipation of his phone calls kept her striving to get through the next day of treatment and hopefully eventually off the unit.

Give a Moment:

FOOD FOR THE SOUL

Now, this one is an important one. This is for everyone. First, find laughter in the moments. Whether it is binge-watching an *I Love Lucy* marathon or going to a comedy show, find what makes you laugh and do it.

Second, bless someone else. David was a blessing to Jenna's family and so many others during his visit. He brought so much joy to the patients and families up on that unit.

Just like David, there is another man who embodies the spirit of helping others, Tim Tebow. He has blessed so many families with his Tim Tebow Foundation organization. The foundation's mission is simple: To bring faith, hope, and love to those needing a brighter day in their darkest hour of need.

It does not require a lot of money to bless someone. For many days and months, Kay was at the hospital with Jenna away from the rest of the family. The meals that were brought to their family while Jenna was sick were huge blessings and such a relief for an exhausted Ray and Kay. So, here is one of Jenna's easy recipes that would be a great meal to bring to a family in need.

Take a deep breath, give a meal, and keep going.

EASY MANICOTTI WITH CHEESE

Ingredients:

- 32 oz. spaghetti sauce (Jenna preferred Prego)
- 1 c. water
- 8 oz. manicotti, uncooked
- 15 oz. ricotta cheese
- 8 oz. shredded mozzarella cheese
- ¼ c. grated parmesan cheese
- 2 Tbsp. dried parsley
- 2 tsp. garlic powder
- 2 tsp. Italian seasoning
- ½ tsp. salt
- ½ tsp. pepper
- 8 oz. mushrooms (optional)

1. Heat spaghetti sauce, water, and mushrooms in pot.
2. In bowl, mix ricotta, mozzarella, parmesan, spices, salt and pepper.
3. Spoon mixture into uncooked manicotti. Keep any extra cheese mixture to the side.
4. Pour 1 c. of sauce into the bottom of a 9x13. Layer manicotti evenly over the sauce. Do not stack the manicotti.
5. Add any leftover cheese to the top of the manicotti.
6. Add remaining sauce on the top of manicotti and cheese.
7. Cover with aluminum foil. Bake at 400 degrees for 40 minutes or until hot and bubbly. Remove foil and bake 10 more minutes.
8. Add a salad, bread, a carton of sweet tea, a dessert, and you are good to go!

20

THE LITTLE GIRL
WITH PAINTED NAILS

Everything changes. Friends change, time changes, and life changes. It seemed like every day a child on the unit would receive a life-altering change in their progress. Sometimes, rather, many times, their bodies would react negatively to one of the drastic drugs. There was no predicting the future because, at any moment, there may not be a future.

Just down the hall, nurses were prepping Katie for a second transplant because the first one had failed. Both Jenna and Katie walked onto the unit together for that grand tour of 5200's accommodations and had their transplants just days apart from one another. In a month and a half, their bodies had become beaten down from the treatment, but doctors insisted from day one exercise was essential to the engrafting process. Jenna had been walking the L-shaped hallway with Katie since the beginning. Although she was never without a mask, only revealing her eyes, there was always a smile on Katie's face when Jenna would show up at her door to see her. Jenna walked for one sole purpose, to make it to the day they would walk off the unit together, without the struggles of cancer and the veils of facemasks through hospital room windows.

Usually mid-morning, Jenna started her routine preparation for her trek of the day. One arm after the other, Jenna slipped on her yellow-meshed gown overtop her nightgown, slid on her slippers, pulled her yellow mask up over her mouth, and then grabbed her IV pole to make her way down the hall to Katie's room. She had made long strands of beads for Katie to hang from her door, much like the ones she made for her own door. Doctors and nurses would hit them as they entered her room, giving Jenna just enough time to play the possum game so they would not ask her any questions.

Tap, tap, tap.

She quietly knocked on the door. Jenna placed her hand on the metal push handle, and with a bit of help from her mom, she pushed the door just far enough to peek in and see an empty bed.

Tears began streaming down Jenna's face. The worst thoughts started to flood her mind. "Katie is never not in her bed unless she is at my door. No one told me she had to go down for a procedure."

Before Jenna's mind could wander any further, sitting across the room, Gina pointed towards the floor in front of her. Katie was playing on the other side of the bed, away from Jenna's sight. In that split-second moment when Jenna could not see her, there was a lapse in time, like it took away the wind beneath her sails. Jenna's mind immediately sent her to the future of no future at all.

She had seen the worst outcomes. Life was not fair. Jenna was tired of seeing her friends suffer, never really grasping the concept that the survival rate on that unit was less than 40 percent. The reality was the majority of the kids who started that transplant journey with

Jenna, including herself, may not be there to cheer on their comrades as they conquered their diseases.

Jenna had her own conditions even before the cancer was diagnosed, ones which made her survival even more uncertain. The doctors had never treated a cancer patient with fibromyalgia. She was in so much pain all the time, and it soon began to settle in specific areas of her body like her knees, hips, and hands. Side effects from the new medicines she was taking at Duke could very well cause nerve and joint problems, but there were still so many unknowns. The doctors could not accurately decipher if her pain was from fibromyalgia or one of the numerous medicines. But one thing was for sure; the doctors would not let Jenna suffer in pain.

Pain management was a must for them. While they needed to follow specific protocols for a patients' well-being, they never wanted their patients to suffer unnecessary pain. They continuously made sure Jenna was comfortable, giving her as much pain relief as possible, but she rarely complained. In her eyes, she had nothing to complain about. A few of her friends were going through their second and third transplants. Worried for those children, she thought to herself, "Who am I to complain, having undergone just one. I am alive, and my fight is not over. And it is for so many others."

After a while, Jenna's body could not hide the pain. Parents of other children began to notice as she became weaker and weaker. Everyone on the unit became somewhat of a modern family. Those halls were filled with different ethnicities, cultures, religious faiths, and even some were from other countries.

Jenna had become the mother hen to the kids. There were two 16-year-olds, one boy and one girl, who came in a month or so after her, one boy Jenna's age who had been fighting for a while, but other than that, everyone else was five years old or younger. As Jenna walked the halls, she would go to every door to talk to the rest of the patients, placing stickers on the hands of the younger kids. Many of them did not like wearing masks, and if they didn't wear one, they could not walk the halls. So, Jenna bribed them, telling them they could have a sticker if they wore their masks. Those kids didn't need the newest and best video games or the coolest toys. They just needed anything other than something dealing with the treatment. Jenna wanted to help the other kids because she felt the pain they endured. She knew how they wanted to be free of IV lines coming out of their bodies. They wished they were free to run down a warm, windy beach with a kite string in their hands, not an IV pole walking down a sterile hallway. Even if it was only for a minute, she tried to make them happy, which was also the antidote she needed to get through the day. But through it all, there was one little girl's smile she longed for, the one smile she needed to get through her day, Katie's.

Katie did not like wearing a mask either. When she saw Jenna had to wear a mask to walk down the hallway, she decided she wanted to be just like her. Katie put on her mask and walked right alongside Jenna, sometimes riding her IV pole like a carriage with a tiara on her head, truly embracing the little princess inside her. Jenna and Katie were like Bugs Bunny and Daffy Duck, Scooby-Doo and Shaggy, or Batman and Robin, one of them alone just did not make sense without the other.

While lying in bed one day, Jenna heard the faint sounds of little knuckles knocking on her door. As the door slowly opened, Katie's tiny body stood proudly in the doorway with her chest puffed out. Even though a mask covered her mouth, Jenna could see her smiling from ear to ear through the sparkle in her eyes. She mischievously pulled her arms out from behind her back. Her tiny hands were covered by the oversized hospital gown sleeves, resembling Dopey proudly showing Snow White his freshly washed dinner hands as his sleeves draped over the top of them. Gina slowly lifted the gown's sleeves, then gently removed the latex gloves from her daughter's fingertips. Katie fanned her hands to Jenna, revealing her newly-painted fingernails. She and Jenna loved to have their nails painted, if only to give them another reason to see each other. They would walk to each other's rooms to show off their crazy-colored nail polish concoctions.

As their nail polish collection grew, so did their inseparable friendship. They did not have a lot. There was no playground, no carnival rides, no lakes to swim in, or ice cream shops for them to pick out their favorite toppings to put on their sundaes. Regardless, Katie had Jenna, and Jenna had her, and that was the only thing mattered to them.

Many nights, Katie would not be able to fall asleep. There were so many restless nights of pain, side effects from medication, and just being uncomfortable in a hospital bed that left the children stressed and unable to sleep. But Katie's parents figured out a trick, usually solving the problem. They would lean over her bed railing and whisper to her, "Jenna has gone to sleep." Once she realized her playmate was asleep, Katie's eyelids would slowly flutter until she gently shut her eyes to play with her friend in her dreams. Little did she know, however, Jenna rarely went to bed before 3:00 a.m.

As Katie began the process of her second transplant, one morning Jenna set out on another voyage to visit her. Creeping closer to her door, she could hear the faint sounds of Katie moaning and crying. There were many obstacles to overcome during treatment, but by far that was the hardest for Jenna. While she had learned to suppress the pain she was in, watching her friends in agony chipped away at Jenna's heart. She knew they were suffering, and she could literally feel their pain, but she could do nothing to help them. So, she did the only thing she knew to do. She went back to her room and began praying for Katie.

21

A HURDLE RACE

Although Jenna had donor cells floating throughout her body, they were technically not hers yet as they had not engrafted. Her ANC had to be at 500 or higher for three consecutive days before doctors would confirm the procedure as a success. The longest time they had ever seen it take someone to engraft was 59 days, and Jenna was on day 49. The doctors, trying to ease Kay's nerves, assured her Jenna would be within the far end of the engrafting time frame. But, as if her low ANC levels weren't enough to deal with, the doctors also explained Jenna's white blood count needed to read between 10,000-12,000 to fight off infection; Jenna's stood at 1,000.

It was as if she were running a hurdle race. After clearing the first one, momentum would gain, only to see an even higher hurdle in her near future. Once she jumped the hurdle of engrafting, Jenna would then face the grave possibility of graft-versus-host disease (GvHD).

GvHD was complicated. The new donor cells would fight against the host's body. If those cells recognized Jenna's body was foreign, they would begin to attack her cells. Any major organ, including the skin, could be attacked, causing extreme pain and even death.

Those donor cells had to be suppressed by steroids so they wouldn't keep attacking an organ. However, the donor cells were what fought off viral and bacterial infections. Jenna's body was at an even greater risk because her immune system was so greatly compromised. There were children re-admitted a year after their transplant for issues as simple as a spider bite because their immune system just wasn't strong enough.

While everything about the disease seemed horrible, the GvHD also could attack any remaining leukemia cells living in Jenna's body. It was one of those harsh—take the good with the bad—scenarios.

Jenna was becoming restless with her slow progression. She was now much more swollen from the steroids. Her hands, face, and nearly the rest of her body began to look like large splotchy round objects that, in many ways, took away her identity as a young girl. Not only was she big, but she was also shiny. Her face now resembled a polished bowling ball, the type where if you get close enough, you can see your reflection in it. Teamed with her 5'0", 150-pound, Tellytubby-like body, Jenna would not be entering a beauty pageant anytime soon. That would only become more apparent as some unexpected visitors arrived one afternoon.

Jenna's door slowly screeched open. It was family friends from their home church. Their three boys were all close to Jenna in age, so walking on the unit and seeing those children was something they were not prepared for. This became even more evident as their middle son took one look at Jenna in her cramped room, and the room began to spin. He quickly exited the room, but as he stepped into the hallway, completely turned around by the unfamiliar surroundings, he panicked, unable to find the exit. He wanted so desperately to reach the outside of that unit before he became sick, fearing passing along any sickness he may be carrying. But the truth was, he hadn't been sick before he stepped on that unit, nor was he sick the following days after their visit. He had become so overwhelmed with seeing how pitiful Jenna was lying in bed, how completely different she looked, that it had literally made him sick. Jenna's life had changed so drastically, and the mere sight of her in that state was too much to handle.

As the days continued, Jenna's skin continued to stretch to the point of popping like one of the latex gloves Gabriel would blow up and let fly around the room. All the bloating, and none of it was due to Jenna's eating. Doctors became concerned. She was nauseated around the clock but forced herself to try all different kinds of food just to see if it took the edge off.

Eating habits, just like sleeping habits, were very different than from back home. Jenna typically woke up every night between 12:30 and 1:30 in the morning craving a snack. She didn't have refined tastebuds due to the effects of the chemotherapy, so she usually stuck to her standard menu of Campbell's chicken noodle soup, pepperoni pizza Lunchables, mixed fruit cups, Fruit String Things, Fruit Roll-Ups, or Fruit by the Foot that she would wrap around her finger like a roll of paper towels.

Parents on the unit never missed a chance when their child wanted to eat. The children's appetites came and went just as quickly as a Dallas Cowboys' lead in a playoff game—hey, only a fan can knock them.

Between fighting off nausea most of the time, if Jenna woke up hungry at 1:15 a.m. and wanted to eat and watch *I Love Lucy*, her mom jumped at the opportunity. Most children did not even start eating until they were off the unit, but then again, most children were off the unit by now.

One day, when nothing seemed particularly appetizing, Jenna's mom ventured out of the room to see if she could find anything Jenna could stomach. Barely five minutes had passed on her quest for food when Kay eased the door open to walk back into Jenna's room. In shock, she dropped the slice of pepperoni pizza. Kay rushed to the bedside; Jenna was gasping for air. She frantically rushed out to the nurses' station, with the nurse quickly following her back and a stethoscope in hand. Jenna's nurse checked her lungs; they were clear, and the oxygen monitor showed no signs of abnormality. Jenna was panicking. She writhed in the pain of breathlessness, feeling as if she was a circus pedestal and an elephant was acting out its grand finale on top of her chest. Her hands began to tingle. Jenna was now turning blue, so a doctor on the unit was quickly dispatched to her room.

Interestingly enough, he walked in with a brown paper bag in his hand. Handing it to Jenna, he told her to breathe into the bag. Jenna thought, "Great, now I am a part of this circus act." Believing the doctor had lost his mind, Jenna reluctantly decided to become part of the entertainment since she really had no better option. Minutes later, and completely stunned, her tingling began to disappear, and her breathing issues slowly subsided.

An X-ray was ordered immediately. The medical staff fully expected to see fluid in Jenna's lungs as a side effect from all the steroids. Since her kidneys were not functioning normally, the steroids could not exit her system, causing her body to retain fluid like a boat on a lake without its drain plug. The number of drugs Jenna had been on up to that point was affecting her kidneys. She needed those medicines, but the possibility of her kidneys shutting down was high as the doctors knew kidney failure was all too real on 5200.

The X-rays were clear of anything that would worry her doctors, but the situation would remain a complete mystery. They were baffled. The doctors chalked it up as just a Jenna thing, giving them something else unique of hers to learn about. Jenna just laid there wondering where in the talks of percentages that near-death experience was.

22

BIG BIRD

Memories of what it felt like to be normal, celebrating in the dugout with her softball teammates, family gatherings by the backyard barbeque grill, sitting on her couch petting Maggie, seemed to be fading away. It was hard to grasp ever being able to do what she loved again. Even if she lived, how could everything her body was going through not affect the rest of her life? How could it not change her future? With each issue that arose, she could not help but think there would never be a time when she would be entirely out of the woods just beyond the castle walls, no longer surrounded by howling wolves.

It was hard not to think about the constant warnings echoing from the doctors' mouths. Her WBC could plummet to zero at any time, resulting in an engraftment failure, meaning Jenna would need another transplant. Her counts seemed to be on a constant elevator ride, fluctuating by the day, teasing her like a cruel joke. Parents on the unit would come to Jenna's door every day, asking if her counts were up or down, knowing how serious it was. No one could figure out why her body was not fully adjusting to the donor cells. With Jenna's slow progress and the damage done to her organs, Kay's mind couldn't help but be reminded of those dreadful success rate percentages on that unit. One day, she reluctantly asked one of Jenna's doctors, Dr. Martin, what percentage Jenna had of making it through. In all sincerity he said, "Kay, it's 50 percent. She is either going to make it or she's not. There's really no need to worry about the percentages." Even though it was hard to hear, Kay needed to hear those words, because that was the truth. Either Jenna would survive, or she wouldn't.

As new patients arrived on the unit, they would all ask how long Jenna had been there. It took everything in her not to reply, "I pass," and keep walking, knowing if they were to hear the truth, it would just scare them even more than they already were. With a second transplant on the horizon, she felt like William Wallace in the final scene of *Braveheart*. Jenna had battled, she had fought hard, only to reach her ultimate ending.

Jenna just wanted to be her old self. She wanted to be the girl who pitched a no-hitter in that week's softball game against the Alberta Smith Sharks. She would give anything to go to the movies on a first date with her elementary school sweetheart, something his mom was trying to set up just before Jenna heard the word cancer. Kay laughed as if that would never happen—her sixth grader going on a date. But none of that was Jenna. She was now the girl who walked the halls looking into the windows of other patients' rooms to try and bring them joy. When she walked by, those young, innocent faces would light up in smiles. They would weakly wave back, mouthing "hi" as Jenna passed. Her mom jokingly told her, "I think they think you're Big Bird," as the kids waved to their favorite Sesame Street character walking by. Jenna, all decked out in her yellow gown and mask, thought to herself, "Next time, I'll wear a crown of feathers to complete the ensemble."

Like an actor getting into character and leaving behind their normal life, for Jenna, Big Bird was an escape from the harsh realities of that unit. That was until she would get a call from David James Elliott, and conversations about show biz were her moment of relief. David's kindness provided an escape from the pain and realities of transplant life. Even if only for 15 minutes or so, she could hear David talk about life on the set of *JAG*, the sunny days out in California, any small thing that would remove her, if only temporarily, from the emptiness of room 5211. Gina was standing outside Jenna's door for one of those calls. She told Kay she wished she had a camera to capture the look on Jenna's face. She said Jenna's face glowed and gleamed with smiles like she was speaking with royalty. Jenna jokingly said her face naturally glowed because her skin was stretched so tightly.

It was now the beginning of October, and soon the leaves on the trees outside would begin changing color, drying out, and falling to the ground. At 52 days post-transplant, over two months of being inpatient, Jenna was in more agonizing pain than ever. Doctors worried peripheral neuropathy was setting in, damage to nerves possibly from previous chemotherapy. They hoped, in time, it would be reversible. Still, there was no guarantee, especially for someone already suffering from fibromyalgia. Constantly pressing the button on Jenna's morphine pump would no longer allow her to rest without immense pain, so doctors turned to methadone, a drug given to heroin addicts to fight withdrawal. There were times when the pain would become so severe neither her head nor tough skin could block it out anymore, and tears would just stream down her face. Her mom and the nurses knew she was definitely in pain during those moments, even though Jenna rarely said anything.

Jenna's pain level was uncontrollable. Everything in the transplant world seemed to feed off each other like a shoal of piranhas gnawing away at human flesh. Jenna needed a higher dose of a growth factor drug because she was engrafting the donor cells at such a slower rate than most, but the higher the dosage equaled higher pain. Her body became so sensitive to touch even the softest, most plush, feathery pillow that braised her skin made her feel like she was a fish being descaled. The only difference was, Jenna was alive to feel her ashy skin seemingly peel away. The sensitivity of her skin did not help matters when it came time to access her port.

One particular day, a nurse and Sue entered Jenna's room to complete the daunting task. The nurse began the process by pressing and pushing down on the port site, trying to locate it. After a few minutes, the nurse thought she had found it, so she stuck the needle through Jenna's skin. However, she did not hit the site. With the needle still inside her chest, she began to reposition it, trying to make it work. It was painful enough just having something brush against her skin, but being pressed and poked and needles repositioned, Jenna just could not hide the pain anymore. The tears flowed. She screamed and wailed so much she ended up going hoarse. The process of accessing her port was becoming more difficult. The steroids had created so much water weight around the port site that it had been pushed much deeper under her skin, making it nearly impossible to find by just pressing down on it.

David called that night to talk to Jenna, but she felt so poorly she just didn't have the strength to talk to him. He told Kay he would call back later to check on her. Jenna was utterly bewildered as to why someone as busy and famous as he was would take time to worry about her, but he did. However, it didn't matter how bad she was feeling, nothing compared to what Katie was going through.

Katie's health was declining. When Jenna would walk by her room to tell her goodnight, Katie would wave and blow her a kiss. One particular night, Katie's nurse informed Jenna that was the only response she had seen from Katie all day. Those were words Jenna wished she had never heard. They opened up another pit of despair inside her. Jenna needed her beautiful friend with the gleaming eyes and painted nails. She was her inspiration to walk the halls to get better. She had a smile that brightened her day. There was not a whole lot that did that, but Katie did.

23

NEEDING HER

On the morning of day 56 post-transplant, Jenna's ANC levels read 708. These were the levels that needed to be above 500 for three consecutive days in order for the doctors to say she had officially engrafted the new donor cells, and they were now the highest they had ever been. If she could only remain on that mountaintop for two more days, victory would be hers. But on that long and arduous trek, often feeling like the ground beneath her feet would give way, Jenna was anxious to hold steady. She persisted to fight another day, afraid her ANC would drop below 500 and the avalanche of a second transplant would be upon her. But there were too many risks if doctors let the process go on much longer.

There was a knock at Jenna's door later that night. It was Katie's dad wanting to speak with Kay. Larry told Kay he now had two girls he had to keep up with, and Jenna's parents felt the same way too. At that point in both their daughters' journeys, Larry knew Jenna would come to say goodnight to Katie, so he made sure he came to Jenna's room before the trip was made.

Katie's kidneys were not functioning as they should, and fluid began filling her stomach. Doctors were going to take Katie to the pediatric intensive care unit (PICU) promptly to have a drainage tube put down her nose and into her stomach. Larry explained he did not want Jenna visiting and seeing Katie the way she was. But Kay knew what she meant to Jenna, and there was no way she could keep that information to herself. After discussing the situation with her mom, Jenna insisted on seeing Katie before they took her to the PICU.

Nothing could erase the memory of seeing Katie lying there so helpless in the hospital bed. Jenna gave her a teddy bear her cousins had brought, unable to give it to Katie until that point because she had been so sick. Jenna told her she loved her as she laid the teddy bear by her side. There was no wave, no saying goodnight; Katie only moaned.

Leaving her room that night was one of the hardest things Jenna had ever done, knowing many children who entered the PICU never rejoined their friends on 5200. Jenna's room was across the hall from the nurses' station, and at times she would look out her window and see the nurses crying. Those tears only confirmed one of her friends had fallen to their horrible disease. She only hoped now those tears would not fall down their faces because of Katie.

"She cannot go, not her. She's too young," Jenna thought. "I need her."

In the middle of the night, Jenna's mom was able to go down and see Katie in the PICU. She watched her pitiful breaths as her chest moved abruptly up and down. The sounds of her heartbeat were drowned out by the rumble of a room full of beeping machines, all attached to her with either a tube, line, or a sensor. Her internal fluid levels increased, and doctors suggested dialysis would relieve the pressure and get her kidneys working again. But her pancreas was also failing, meaning she could not have any food or liquid. Katie cried and motioned in misery to her parents, wanting a drink of water to quench her thirst. Larry told Kay, "Most parents want their kids to get honor roll or be the star athlete on the team. I just want my little girl to pee."

While Katie was sleeping, Gina came into Jenna's room. She told Jenna the first words out of Katie's mouth when she woke up were, "Go walk, see Jenna." Jenna wanted so badly to be with her. Just like the encouragement Katie was to Jenna so many times before, Jenna wanted to be there for her best friend. The only gift Jenna could give Katie was her mom. So, instead of staying with Jenna that night, Kay stayed with Katie and her parents in PICU.

24

COVETING RAINBOW SPRINKLED PAPER

Every morning, at 4:00 a.m. sharp, Jenna's blood was drawn to analyze her WBC levels. With each reading, Jenna, her family, and the entire medical staff on the unit waited in anticipation for her ANC levels to remain above 500. With those results in, Jenna now had a reading above 500 for the second day in a row. Jenna couldn't breathe a sigh of relief, though. She had already been above 500 two days in a row the week before, only to have it fall on the third day. Although Jenna was showing she had new cells, it didn't mean they had totally engrafted to her body. This too was complicated. The doctors said it rarely happened, but if Jenna did not engraft by the end of that week, they would begin prepping her for a second transplant. The back-and-forth tennis match her ANC counts were playing as they bounced from above 500 to below was just too risky. But Jenna desperately wanted to walk under the coveted rainbow of sprinkled colored paper, when those wooden double doors would open at the far end of the hallway, allowing her to go back to the life she had nearly forgotten.

Every time a patient was discharged, the nurses and other patients gathered together to throw a confetti party. Standing in two rows lining the hallway by the doors leading to freedom, a patient with a successful engraftment would walk through a sparkling cloud of confetti, their own ticker-tape parade for winning such an exhausting battle with their disease. There was no way to tell when it would be someone's turn for the confetti party because every case was different. There was a boy just a few doors down who was on his third transplant. He was suffering from GvHD. Yet, in another room, a 16-year-old comrade of Jenna's was just 25 days post-transplant, and she already had better counts than Jenna.

Jenna knew if there were a discussion of a second transplant, now just days away, it would feel as if a judge had handed her the death sentence. Many children didn't make it through one transplant, and a successful second one seemed like a trip to the moon, only obtainable for a select few. She could only pray tomorrow would be the day those donor cells would finally become hers.

Katie was on her second transplant, but it was not working. Just behind the double latched doors, one hallway separated Jenna from Katie in the PICU. She had been placed on a ventilator to help her breathe. Jenna's mom told her Katie was also struggling with GvHD. The donor cells had recognized her body as foreign.

Her new immune system was attacking all her organs, including her skin, causing extreme pain. There were more tears. Jenna thought it was all wrong. It just didn't seem fair for someone so small and helpless to have to endure so much misery. Katie's WBC was so low, she could not fight off any infection that had taken over her body. Her body was just so weak. Jenna wished there was more she could do for her, thinking if she could just see her, maybe it would give Katie the extra boost she needed to keep fighting.

Knowing that was impossible, Jenna made her a big card so all the nurses could sign it and give it to her. Katie was such a little fighter. No matter how sedated she was, she tried her hardest to do whatever the doctors asked her to do, a lesson Jenna could learn from her.

Jenna began to pray. She prayed God would protect Katie's precious little body, that he would protect her best friend.

In between those prayers, Jenna watched as so many lives around her were changing forever, for the good and the bad. Kay tried sheltering her from the scariness of the unit, much like a mama elephant protecting its young from a pack of roaring lions. But the reality of death could not be hidden as she watched parents, two by two, leave the unit hopeless and totally shattered, forever without their child.

It was now October 1, 1999, just one day shy of tying the 59-day record for the longest engrafting time. That morning's blood work was analyzed and confirmed Jenna's ANC had been over 500 for three consecutive days—she had officially engrafted. And with her good news came more good news. Katie was doing better. Her WBC was rising, and her high lactic acid levels began to fall. The doctors planned for Katie to be released from PICU that weekend.

Since Jenna had reached a major milestone and Katie was on the mend, a relieved Kay headed back home to be with Zachary, Gabriel, and Hannah as Ray took her place at Duke to stay with Jenna. He had taken on that role multiple times leading up to that weekend. Ray knew the drill. He could prepare himself for the bath time standoffs or the 2:00 a.m. snack urges and reruns of *I Love Lucy.* He could even prepare himself to be the designated chuck bucket holder or the hand to hold while a nurse changed Jenna's bandages.

Every week, a nurse had to change the bandage around her Hickman to prevent the possibility of infection, a sterile procedure Ray would end up having to do himself if Jenna made it off the unit. In Jenna's head, she knew that was not nearly as bad as everything else she had experienced so far. Still, it was just another thing to cause her pain and discomfort. Her nurse would slowly peel away the tape around the Hickman site, a delicate yet painful process as the skin underneath was completely raw because of the constant dryness. After the tape was cleared, the nurse would gently clean the area with rubbing alcohol and betadine, an antiseptic solution.

The nurses all knew her skin was extremely sensitive because of the harsh chemotherapy, radiation, steroids, countless spinal taps, needle sticks, port accesses, and an entire team of nurses and doctors poking and pushing on her all the time to check various things. Even the slightest pressure and touch from plush cotton swabs was too much for Jenna.

While she could handle those issues with her dad by her side, Jenna was not prepared for what was to occur the following morning. Even her high pain tolerance would not matter.

25

FALLING TEARS

As the sun rose, Jenna woke up to a scene of chaos on the unit. A day could change everything. In reality, sixty seconds could change everything up there, and it had.

Katie's lactic acid levels suddenly spiked. With levels that high and not decreasing, it usually meant one thing—some organ was failing. Her kidneys were barely working, making her stomach swollen from fluid build-up, which was now pushing against her lungs. Although she had been placed on a ventilator, oxygen was not getting to her extremities. Katie's legs turned from a shade of light blue to dark purple and were cold to the touch. Doctors and nurses worked tirelessly to figure out what had gone wrong so quickly. Katie's pulse became weaker by the minute. Ray ran back and forth from Jenna's room to the PICU, attempting to comfort Larry and Gina.

Jenna asked her dad, "If the doctors can find the source of the problem, they can do surgery to fix it, right?" But once again, there was a Catch-22. The children on that unit had highly compromised immune systems, which made it almost impossible to fight off infection, especially an infection contracted during surgery. Therefore, it was not an option for Katie. Prayer was the only option. So, everyone prayed.

As Ray entered Jenna's room again, his face was unable to hide the inconsolable news his 12-year-old daughter was about to hear. But she didn't need to listen to words. There was no need to explain what happened. The tears streaming down her dad's face told Jenna her best friend was gone. Katie was gone.

In the months she had been on the unit, Jenna had seen many children die. She knew every child there, but Katie was her best friend, her transplant buddy, her joy, and her inspiration. She was the only one who Jenna knew understood her, the one who knew she was not actually Big Bird. Jenna didn't just plan on coordinating fingernail colors; she planned for the two them to exit the unit the same way they entered it—together. Jenna could not even begin to think what she would say to Larry and Gina when she saw them. She could not stand the thought of them, her second parents, leaving the unit. It would just make Katie's death all the more real.

Jenna did not know how to cope with the loss of her friend. There was a hollowness in her heart that would never be filled. She knew Katie was no longer suffering as she was now walking the streets of gold, hand in hand with her Creator. But the aching in Jenna's heart would never be filled until the day she would walk side by side with Katie again.

Only for a Moment:

ART THERAPY

There will be a time in your life when you have to say goodbye to the ones you love. Sometimes life is cut short in an instant, and you never get the chance to say goodbye. There is nothing anyone can say to comfort you. A simple little exercise probably will not help at that moment. But for Jenna, she found comfort and peace in the fact that she would see Katie again in heaven one day, walking the streets of gold instead of the halls of 5200.

So, for Katie, go paint your nails because it is what would have put a smile on her face. Color as a reminder of the pictures Katie colored for Jenna and the unique drawings Jenna would leave on her door. Do what makes you smile. Do what makes you laugh so hard you start crying. Remember the moments you shared with the person you loved, and live in such a way that you change someone else's life.

Just breathe, keep breathing, and keep going.

26

THE WRITINGS ON THE WALL

Everyone's moods were declining. Jenna was missing her family terribly. It had been months since she had seen some of them, and she was ready to go home. The nurses did what they could to try and get her mind off everything going on, asking if any more famous people had visited lately. Meeting another famous person was about what it would take to cheer Jenna up at that point, and that's just about the time Hannah walked in.

Hannah was a little more than two years younger than Jenna, and they had done everything together since Hannah was born, including sharing a bed after the crib stage. She and Jenna would sneak their stuffed animals into bed after their mom had turned out the lights, quietly playing make-believe reenactments of the Lion King until Kay would crack the door open to see if they had fallen asleep, causing Hannah and Jenna to quickly dispose of their stuffed Nola and Simba and pretend to be asleep. These fun antics would only continue to the next morning. Jenna and Hannah would use VCR tape cases to outline their barbie houses, leading to hours of fun coming up with new plots ranging from modern day high school boyfriend-girlfriend fun to wagon trail rides across the western plains. Those were only a couple of the activities that had forged such a strong bond from a young age. Hannah and Jenna were more than sisters, they were best friends, playmates, rarely bickering back and forth. Maybe this wasn't typical for sisters so close in age, but for them it was in their nature to put the other first or let things just roll off their backs. So, when Hannah came to visit it was no wonder that the comfort of her sister—the closest feeling to home—made everything better for Jenna. Hannah's goofy, always smiling personality was often the only antidote to bring a smile to Jenna's face. Even on Jenna's worst days, Hannah, at only nine years old, mustered up the courage to sit there as she watched Jenna moan and wrestle in extreme pain and nausea.

She could play games with her or watch the TV screen as Mulan cleverly devised a plan to beat the Huns, but she would never be able to take away Jenna's pain. She wanted to shield Jenna from any hurt she was experiencing. That was Hannah's nature. She was the caregiver, the servant, and the infectious smile. Her contagious smile only magnified at the mention of the new nurse on the unit, a blond-haired, surfer-like young man from Canada, Andre. Jenna and Hannah both had a huge crush on him, but Hannah had a tougher time hiding it as her face blushed a cherry blossom red as he walked by.

They would tag team and play foam soap fights in the hallway with canisters filled with mousse-like hand sanitizer the doctors and nurses used to rub on their hands before entering the children's rooms. Those moments of child's play—which were rare since Katie became very ill—broke up the repetitive routines Jenna was now accustomed to.

The feelings of joy and community the Big Bird ensemble brought Jenna and her adoring fans on 5200, slowly faded to pain and agitation from the material rubbing against her skin. Those fluffy-mesh feathers had turned into sewing pins poking her with each swish of the gown, now causing her to suffer as she walked the halls, greeting and talking with the other children. Kay tried cutting a slit in the gown to relieve some of the stinging. She could see Jenna was feeling many more of the side effects.

Jenna would get injections of platelets every other day. Leukemia affected the bone marrow, and since platelets are formed there, it put Jenna at a higher risk of bleeding and bruising. Rashes started to appear randomly, and the doctors were baffled as to why. There were tormenting red bruises on her feet, which meant walking was sometimes unbearable. Her body was beginning to turn a bluish-green tint from the bruises collecting all over her, making her resemble one of the speckled trout her dad and brothers would catch on their Chesapeake Bay fishing trips. Despite the tenderness, Jenna knew she could not stop walking. She had to make it to the end of the hall because she now had a mission to complete.

Each day Jenna walked down to the far side of the hallway she passed a blank whiteboard on the wall across from what used to be Katie's room. With only a few smiles and the rare sounds of laughter, Jenna wanted to bring hope through the tears and broken hearts that flooded the unit. After Jenna inched down the hallway, still working through the misery of post-transplant recovery, she sat down in a chair beside the board, staring at the dry erase marker hanging on a string from the wall. Unaware of her inspiration, Jenna began writing an encouraging message for the children to read. It was hard to get out of bed most days, let alone walk the halls, but Jenna knew it was necessary, so she had to find a way to get the kids out of their rooms.

Soon, news spread throughout the unit. The kids had more to walk for than just stickers. They would now walk to see what note of encouragement Jenna had written for the day, what happy picture she had drawn. Those messages, Bible verses, flowers, and smiling sunshine faces were not just for them, but it was also Jenna's therapy. She needed to see smiles. Focusing on making the other children happy and taking care of others gave her less time to focus on the extreme amount of pain she was enduring. It also gave her a little extra push to get out of bed, knowing other kids were waiting for the writings on the wall. She did not know that helping or encouraging other people would be therapeutic for her, but slowly, with each stroke of the multi-colored dry erase markers, she found her serenity.

Jenna's counts improved with each mark of her pen, and the doctors were pleased with her progress, even though she felt horrible most of the time. Her body ached so badly even the water coming from the showerhead felt like sharp thorn bushes being jabbed into her back. Pain medicine helped a little, but she was usually so nauseated she could not swallow the pain pills. Therefore, an okay morning often spiraled downward into an awful afternoon.

Neuropathy had set in, turning her plush, cotton slippers into the backside of a porcupine, the sharp quills lodging into her feet like tiny arrows. The doctors explained it was most likely from a previous chemotherapy drug she took called vincristine and the FK-506 drug used to help prevent GvHD. She had to prepare for two types of GvHD, acute, which goes away in time, and chronic, which lasts a lifetime. The chances were if GvHD was going to occur, it would happen within the first year after the transplant. However, there was a possibility of it occurring later in life. Unfortunately, she had to take FK-506 for nine months after she left the unit, so more than likely, the pain would not be subsiding anytime soon.

Walking, regardless of pain, gave her a slight sense of freedom in that uncontrollable world. Jenna walked from room to room, peeping in through windows and door jambs to play peek-a-boo with all the babies. As Big Bird came by, the baby's faces would light up with smiles as Jenna slipped inside their rooms to quiet the drone of the beeping machines by their bedside. Jenna had been on the unit for so long she had learned some aspects of the IV pumps, quieting them until the nurses could come by and change out the meds. Jenna quickly became known as the *Door Bandit* and the *Writing Fairy*. She would sneak around to every patients' room, leaving individual messages on the whiteboard hanging just beneath the window on their door, and the messages were always topped off with her trademark flower.

Jenna could see how much the parents suffered too, and they needed just as many encouraging words as the children. Parents grieved for their sick children as they watched their young lay in agony, wishing over and over they could take away the pain. But they could not take their child's place.

A father of a patient down the hall knocked on Jenna's door one afternoon asking when the Writing Fairy would be able to come out. He requested a message left for him on his son's whiteboard. He needed a little extra strength of encouragement so he could pass it along to his son. With the stroke of the marker, she wrote on the son's whiteboard, "Take your dad for a walk, because today, he needs the exercise." That family was from Iraq. Jenna and the boy were from two completely different sides of the world; now they were together in one, 5200.

Only for a Moment:

THINKING OF YOU CARD

So many people can use encouragement, and it's something anyone can give. Jenna gave it, and in return, she received it by seeing smiles on the faces of hurting parents and children. You may not have the chance to write on someone's whiteboard, but you can color this card. Write an encouraging message to someone who needs a little pick me up. Put it in an envelope and send someone a little thoughtful happy mail.

Take a breath, keep breathing, and keep going.

Take a deep breath, keep breathing, and **KEEP GOING!**

27

SET FREE

At 75 days post-transplant, Jenna was finally given the green light to go off the unit for a brief walk around the hospital grounds. It had been almost three and a half months since she had felt the sun and warm breeze on her face. She wasn't even sure she remembered what it looked and felt like.

Dr. Kurtzberg required all the kids who came in with leukemia to have a WBC level of 30,000 before leaving the unit. With Jenna inching closer to that number, for the first time since late July, she put on an actual pair of pants and shirt, ditching the Big Bird ensemble. She walked down to her friend Michelle's room to see if she and her dad were ready to step out on an adventure.

Michelle had entered the treatment center as a beautiful, long-haired 16-year-old, and Jenna often wondered if she knew she would lose her lovely locks or even if she was prepared to. But little did Jenna know, Michelle walked on that unit knowing what she would have to endure.

Michelle was diagnosed just two weeks shy of her 16th birthday with chronic myelogenous leukemia (CML), an adult leukemia typically found in males over 40. After given very little hope from the doctor who diagnosed her—telling her she may live to 25 if she responded well to the treatment—Michelle headed to Duke and never looked back.

It was at Duke Michelle learned all about transplants. The same packet Jenna's mom couldn't bring herself to keep reading at the beginning of Jenna's transplant process, had landed in Michelle's hands. At 16-years-old, the doctors wanted her to know everything that could go wrong, and she was petrifyingly reminded of this as she read the last line of every page, "This may lead to death." So, Michelle knew, and because of that, she knew even more how much a trip outside the halls of 5200 was needed.

Both the girls were roughly at the same stage in progression through treatment, even though Jenna had been on the unit many weeks longer than Michelle. With both girls' counts in an acceptable normal range, Jenna thought it would be nice to hang out with a friend and talk about what they would do after leaving the unit, what real life would mean to them.

Jenna borrowed a brown bucket hat from Michelle, put on her mask, then they checked out at the nurses' station, getting their day passes as if they had been on house arrest. The moment the duo walked out the revolving doors, Jenna paused and marveled at the atmosphere around her. It was real air not cleaned through the HEPA filter inside their hospital rooms, freshly-cut grass instead of sanitized linoleum, and rays of sunshine instead of fluorescent lighting. Everything looked different. Everything smelled different. Even the skies seemed to be a different shade of blue than she had remembered.

Jenna slid her mask down and took in a deep breath of fresh air. She felt like a newborn puppy, born with its eyes shut, just now opening them to a whole new world. That new world she stepped into was invigorating, but to be honest, Jenna also thought it was a bit terrifying. She could no longer depend on the safety net of 5200 and now had to face the outside world. She was unsure how she would fit in.

Mosquitoes began biting Michelle's dad, so they decided it was time to go in and avoid any setbacks a bite could cause. There was no way a mosquito would keep Jenna on that unit a day longer than she had to be. So, she took those 15 minutes of freedom and hoped time would bring even more.

Now, when friends and family now came to visit, they could actually have close contact with Jenna. One afternoon, Zachary came. He had not seen Jenna in a couple of weeks, and when he went into the room, their mom told him to put his arm around her for a picture. Usually, there would have been no hesitation as Zachary was the most affectionate of the four kids Ray and Kay had raised. He was the first to hug someone, or rather pick them up and squeeze them as hard as he could, something he inherited from their papa.

Zachary was passionate about everything he did and the people he loved, taking everything to heart. So watching his little sister suffer was torment for him as his all or nothing personality could not save her from this. But there was a pause; there was hesitation in his response. He looked at their mom with a puzzled face. "I can put my arm around her?" he asked with uncertainty. It had been months since Jenna had been able to hug anyone. There were just too many risks of germs.

Apart from relearning physical contact with people, the closer Jenna was to being released, the more she learned just how much life would be different than before.

Nurses began preparing Kay for her role once Jenna finally stepped off that unit. Kay learned how to check her blood sugar and give her insulin shots. Luckily, when Kay had to draw Jenna's blood, she would not have to stick her with a needle but would use her Hickman line. Kay was also instructed on how to operate the different medicine-filled pumps Jenna would still be hooked up to once leaving the hospital. Most nurses spent a whole day in nursing school learning how to put on sterile gloves required for sterile procedures. Kay not only learned that, but a year's worth of nursing, all in just one week. Jenna did not know whether to be really impressed or worried for her life.

But as she watched her mom be trained on the ins and outs of those daily routines, the worry quickly faded into complete awe. Sacrifice didn't seem like a strong enough word to describe the devotion Jenna witnessed. Kay rarely left Jenna's bedside at Duke. Her only freedom from that small room was quick trips to the room across the hall for a shower or meal prep for Jenna on the rare occasions she felt like eating. Occasionally, she would walk down to the cafeteria on Fridays for seafood day, but seldomly able to eat in Jenna's room because the smell would only cause Jenna to become more nauseated. She gave up the comfort of her queen bed to a small cot in the corner of Jenna's room. It was just big enough for her to barely straighten her legs. Jenna never saw her mom complain. Her only sign of faltering was missing her other kids growing up, something Jenna could see written across her mom's face as she hung up the phone with them. But after the phone calls, it was back to her nightly duties of bucket exchanges, to Jenna stating, "Ok, the nausea subsided now, so I'll take a pizza," to the days filled with countless games and hall walks where Jenna and Kay built a bond so deep it became impossible to break. Kay was Jenna's only outlet. Jenna rarely shared her thoughts about what she was enduring, but if she did, it was to her mom. Consequently, turning Kay into Jenna's advocate for pain management and hospital life in general, knowing her daughter would not speak up for herself. Kay's complete devotion to Jenna's well-being was first and foremost and only continued as Jenna's eating regimen would also change.

Burdened with pain in her hands, Jenna could no longer hold a fork for an entire meal as her nerve endings had become so damaged. The stinging penetrated her fingertips while holding utensils and surged through her hands up her arms like a raging firestorm. As if that wasn't torture enough, Jenna's fingernails had begun growing back after her old ones had *fallen off* during transplant. The pain was indescribable. All this, combined with the steroids, nausea, and altered taste buds, made eating just another hurdle for Jenna to scale.

Thankfully, she was blessed with not losing her taste buds like some children due to radiation and chemotherapy. Jenna rarely ever drank anything but water before transplant. However, now there was a bitter, metallic aftertaste when drinking water, and only sweet tea and lemonade still tasted like they had before the transplant. Since her immune system was highly compromised, she could not have any fresh fruits or vegetables because bacteria and fungi could be present on them. Anything she ate had to be freshly prepared in sterile conditions, even ice cubes. Nothing could be re-heated; everything had to be consumed within an hour of being cooked, but there was one massive problem with that.

Jenna would have a mouth-watering craving, and her mom would run across the hallway to grab it out of the parents' kitchen. To no avail, as soon as she opened Jenna's door and handed her the food, Jenna's appetite would disappear, overtaken by nausea. Her appetite tended to be the heartiest sometime after midnight. Jenna saw how frustrating it was for her mom to put on her chef's hat and prepare whatever she had requested at one o'clock in the morning, only then to be told, "No, I can't eat it." It was a vicious cycle.

One day, Jenna had a craving for hush puppies, so Kay rushed to a restaurant, praying on the five-minute ride over Jenna's hankering would not subside. Anytime Jenna wanted something from a restaurant, Kay had to get it specially ordered, explaining her daughter was a transplant patient and needed the food cooked fresh in a clean environment.

One restaurant told her they did not have any gloves for preparation. Even though she probably should have left, Kay knew Jenna's cravings came few and far between, so she asked the cook to wash his hands thoroughly. With a nervous look in his eyes, like what kind of germ-freak mother are you, he kindly obliged. However, if need be, Kay would stand over the cooks' shoulders inspecting their every move if it meant keeping her daughter safe.

Thankfully though, most restaurants located near Duke were familiar with transplant patients, and when an order for one came in, staff yelled back to the kitchen, "transplant patient." They say ordering as a vegan is hard; they have nothing on transplant patients.

28

BUDDHA BABY

There was no more daydreaming about what it would mean to finally be able to step outside those two tightly-latched, wooden doors at the end of the hallway because the day had finally come. After a grueling 84 days post-transplant, Jenna was headed off the unit. It was finally her turn for the confetti party, to walk out and not come back.

An overwhelming feeling of guilt came over her. Out of the 16 beds on 5200, she would be walking out without eight of her friends she started with, and four more of them would later have failed transplants. Jenna was one of four to make it off the unit during her in-patient timeframe, something that was just unfathomable to her. She felt like she was abandoning the rest of her transplant buddies, not finishing what she had started as the writing fairy of 5200. All her friends, still locked on the unit, staying behind to keep fighting. Almost like a soldier sent home from war without their unit, there was a sense of unsettledness, of betrayal. Jenna knew that was not how it worked, but she could not help but feel a sense of fear for the ones she would leave behind. She could not encourage them anymore; she could not make them smile with stickers as they walked the halls.

She got an award from Sue for all her hard work. The certificate read: "This is to certify that Jenna has officially become the Duke PBMT Program's Top Walker!" Having worn out her slippers in the process, Jenna had walked more than any other patient who had come through those doors, earning her a $50 gift certificate to Lady Foot Locker. Michelle wasn't in the least surprised. Her mom and her nurses would tell her, "Jenna already walked ten laps and you haven't gotten out of bed," a nice wake-up call Michelle received every, single, day.

After the confetti had fallen, Jenna stepped through the first door, then through the second, both doors latching behind her for the last time, hopefully.

Five minutes from Duke, Jenna and Kay settled into an apartment. The transplant team liked patients to stay close to the hospital for at least 30 days after leaving the unit. With their immune systems still so compromised, daily, all-day visits to the clinic were required. Jenna would spend time in the clinic receiving platelets. The normal range was between 150,000 and 450,000; her levels only read 8,000. While Jenna had reached a major accomplishment in her journey, to a 12-year-old, going to the clinic daily to be given even more medicines and fluids than what she had already taken during breakfast, didn't seem like too much of a change.

Besides the five-minute drive to the clinic, Jenna stayed out of the public. Her WBC was staying in the normal range, but since the growth factor medication hindered her immune system's production, it was safer for her to remain indoors. The doctors told Jenna her immune system would not go back to what it should be for a typical 12-year-old for at least one to two years after transplant. Hearing that hit her hard. Although she was moving in the right direction, many physical setbacks led to a steady decrease in her emotional and personality traits.

Whenever someone came down to visit, Jenna would sit up for periods of time to play games or talk, rarely doing that if anyone wasn't around. Sitting up for longer than an hour was a huge accomplishment in and of itself. Ray and Kay watched with saddened eyes as their once outgoing, people-oriented daughter withdrew inward like a hermit crab. It was as if she slowly ducked her head into her shell, trying to shield herself from the harshness of the world around her.

No one on the unit really knew who Jenna was because, most of the time, the personality they got to see did not reflect who she was on the inside. Quite frankly, some of her actions would have resulted in getting a switch across her butt had she been a healthy, active child.

That was one of the most challenging parts of the whole ordeal for her parents to navigate. There were times they wanted to crawl under the table and disappear as Jenna responded to the doctors with sarcasm and disdain. Sometimes Jenna wouldn't respond to doctors' questions just because she could, with Dr. K usually getting the worst treatment. In most cases, this would be considered rude, but for some reason Jenna's doctors and nurses didn't seem too shocked by her behavior, with Dr. K always assuring Kay her actions were ok. It was as if Dr. K understood Jenna in a deeper way than most. She somehow knew this wasn't who Jenna truly was. It was the response of a young girl in extreme pain and unable to express how she really felt about that process. The grace Dr. K bestowed upon Jenna was a genuine gift.

But Ray and Kay struggled with the disciplining dilemma, the fiasco of knowing if and when it was worth correcting her. As their child's life hung in the balance, day after day, there were just not as many things that seemed as important as they were before she was diagnosed.

Being off the unit only exaggerated the fact there had been multiple physical changes to Jenna's body. Halloween that year was spent inside the apartment. As costumed-dressed kids knocked on the door, Kay opened it with a candy-filled, pumpkin-faced bucket in hand.

"Trick or Treat," the children exclaimed.

The looks on their innocent faces would turn from smiles to frightened stares as they caught a glimpse of Jenna sitting on the couch out of the corner of their eyes. She knew she didn't look normal. "They probably think I am a real-life, scary Halloween decoration," she thought to herself.

Besides the fact she had no hair, her weight had gone from one extreme to the other during that process. The intense chemotherapy during the first six months after diagnosis caused Jenna to become so nauseated no food was appetizing except her grandma's spaghetti. She had lost so much weight, something the transplant changed drastically. Jenna's skin was stretched so tightly the freckles that lightly covered her face and the dimple on her right cheek had vanished. She was hard as a brick. The massive amounts of steroids made her uncomfortably bloated, and she just wished someone would take a pin and pop her.

Gabriel decided her new appearance needed a nickname. From that point on, Jenna became Buddha Baby, a rather large, bald, Asian-looking man. The nickname didn't bother Jenna so much. Perhaps that was because she barely looked in the mirror, but either way, whatever she looked like before was gone.

Jenna understood that was Gabriel's odd way of showing he loved her. It was his love language. Being a boy of few affectionate words, he joked his way through the discomfort of awkward silences. If he didn't pick on you, you probably weren't his favorite person. Jenna must have been one of his favorites because the picking started early on.

Gabriel loved playing with Jenna as a baby. As a two-year-old, he took his 19-month, age advantage to stuff five-month-old Jenna under the couch. Their mom's only chance of finding her was the minimal view of her tiny legs sticking out from underneath. Getting older and playing tag throughout the house was also a great time for antics, especially when Gabriel let the swinging kitchen door slam into Jenna's face, leading to one of many ER visits for stitches. But Jenna loved on him right back when she *accidentally* pushed him out of the 10-foot-high treehouse in their backyard.

Calling Jenna Buddha Baby was Gabriel's way of coping with the fact that Jenna looked nothing like his sister. It was also some comic relief Jenna needed at the time. It was one of the few constants she could cling to, his sense of humor. For all they knew, she might never look the same again.

To Jenna's dismay, she was looking more like her dad every day. She wore his shirts and pants as she was now too large to fit into any clothes made for a 12-year-old girl. To add to her dad bod, she now had a substantial unibrow, mustache, and a carpet of hair growing down her back. All she needed was a few hairs poking out of her chest, and Ray could have called her Junior. Regardless, Jenna never really cared about how she looked on the outside. Too much effort was put into surviving, and she never stopped to face the mirror. Either way, those physical changes were pieces of the process that had been easier to handle than others.

29

HOME, HOME

As Jenna inched closer to that 30-day mark, Ray was instructed on how to prepare their house for her arrival. Medically-approved air filters needed to be put in their house to prevent post-transplant complications. They had to hire professionals to deep clean the entire house from top to bottom. The duct system had to be cleaned and sanitized. The carpets, the curtains, and the furniture all needed shampooing. Anywhere mold could grow had to be painted. No living flowers and plants could be in the house due to bacteria. Jenna also could not come into contact with babies who just had their live vaccinations. Flu shots were a must for the whole family and anyone who planned on being near Jenna for long periods of time.

After a day filled with testing her immune system, Cobalt studies to check her metabolism, thyroid inspection, reticulocyte counting, chest X-rays, echocardiograms, and a three-hour infusion including FK-506, IVIG, and other confusing medical acronyms, Jenna sat on the examining table like she had so many times before, waiting in anticipation as news of her departure had been lurking in the conversations she was hearing.

She could hear Dr. K just around the corner outside her room, and the sound of her voice did not have the same cool, calm, and collected demeanor she generally had. As Dr. K walked in, her eyes told a different story than usual. In Jenna's mind, they usually mirrored the image of bad news, and typically, Dr. K would just smile because Jenna would not talk to her. That day was different. She walked in with a smile and, after only a few questions, told Kay and Jenna they could go "home, home." The parents and children knew it wasn't until the word *home* was repeated twice, they could actually return home to their families.

A feeling of happiness and fear overcame Jenna all at once. Much like the hand-sewn, silk blanket her grandma gave her which never left her side throughout her four-month journey, Duke had become a security blanket for Jenna. Her nerves were beginning to set in as she realized she would no longer have her safety net. Three hours seemed like an awfully long way away, especially for those rare medical emergencies she had grown accustomed to.

For the last 30 days, Jenna had only been five minutes from a place she now saw as her safe place. During the weeks of horrible preparation before the transplant, Jenna's family was able to stay at a house in Raleigh called Christian Life Home. It was built as a house for unwed mothers to take refuge during their pregnancies, but they had not yet opened their doors for that purpose. Therefore, friends and family who visited Jenna could stay there. Many days and nights were spent at that house, and tearful goodbyes became a part of the routine. The worst for Jenna was watching Hannah looking out the back window of a friend's car as they veered left heading back to

Chesterfield, and Jenna and her mom went right back to the house in Raleigh.

Hannah had so much to deal with as a nine-year-old child. She was the only girl left with three boys. Ray had to learn to fix her hair but never quite mastered how to pull up her long-curly-red locks into a ponytail. But no more, as the day had arrived for Jenna, November 19, 1999, when she and Kay could make the 130-mile drive back home, relieving Hannah from being the only girl in the house.

A new set of emotions came flooding in as Jenna was not ready to see everyone. There was a weird feeling about going home and seeing friends and family she had not seen for the better part of a year. She would no longer be around people without dancing bears on their uniforms and stethoscopes drooped around their necks. "Would they understand what I have been through? Do I even understand?" Jenna thought. She knew she would get emotional, and tears to Jenna just meant she could not handle what was being thrown at her. Just a mile from home, so many thoughts began to run through her head. "What would I do now? Does this mean I do not have cancer anymore? Does life just go back to normal?"

When Kay pulled into their long gravel driveway, Jenna saw yellow ribbons lining the trees down to the house. "What was this?" Jenna thought. "I am not a soldier coming back from war. I have not given my life for my country. Who am I to get this type of treatment?" Jenna questioned. She did not feel like a hero. She felt beaten down and lifeless. But as the view of their front yard peeked through the trees, that was exactly how she felt as she saw a large crowd of people standing and cheering. Truthfully, Jenna was returning home from a battle. She had seen her comrades suffer, not making it home to families that crowded their front yards. Jenna nearly died from the enemy she was fighting and was mentally and physically torn apart.

A huge banner reached from column to column across their front porch that read "Welcome Home Jenna" in bright purple letters—Jenna's favorite color. Overcome by the cheering noise as her mom pulled into the garage, tears came flowing from Jenna's eyes like a rushing waterfall, with no dam to barricade them in. It was as if that applause was some sort of curtain call, finally recognized by the audience for her courageous performance, the heroine of an epic play, the girl who had finally made her way back home.

Wiping away tears of joy, Jenna gathered her composure and walked out onto the front porch to join the crowd amidst the November frost. They had witnessed a miracle. Their prayers had been answered. Jenna did not know if she had really experienced the feeling of being humbled before, but that day she was. God spared her life.

30

FEET ON HOT COALS

As Thanksgiving rolled around, Jenna's typical thoughts would have consisted of her grandma's turkey, mashed potatoes, stuffing, freshly baked rolls, and the other sweet and savory treats family members would bring to Grandma's house. But in the few short days following her return to normal life, she had not eaten anything besides one pretzel, a bite of a saltine cracker, and a few ice chips. A terrible, feverish headache quickly turned into bouts of intense stomach pain.

As Jenna awoke on Thanksgiving morning, she swung her legs over the side of the bed, placed her feet on the ground, and the most excruciating pain shot throughout her body as if she had just placed her feet on hot coals. Normally she would be thanking God for saving her life, but the three pain medications she had taken stopped working. Jenna tried to use reverse psychology on herself, pretending the pain was all in her head. However, the pounding in her head from the debilitating headaches had now overtaken those mind tricks she had used for so many months. Her joyful reminiscence was overshadowed by the agony, and she could not suppress it any longer. Tears rushed from her eyes.

Kay hurried into Jenna's room after hearing the all-too-familiar sound of her daughter in pain. Bent over in anguish, it took all of Jenna's strength to whisper to her mom, "I'm afraid." Kay rarely heard her talk like that or express herself in that way, so it scared her too. They had no choice but to head back to Duke.

Upon arriving, Jenna was pumped full of morphine but received only a few hours of relief before it stopped working. There were no words to describe it. Her pain was getting much worse. Giving herself a rating of eight on a pain scale of ten being the most immense pain was more like a 20 for the average person. Her nurses had come to know her well and knew she was suffering. Natalie and Jen, two more of Jenna's favorite nurses, brought her gifts and games in an attempt to give her some sort of relief. If only for a moment, those gifts gave Jenna a mental break.

The nurses on 5200 were a different kind of species. They rarely sat down. If they weren't caring medically for the patient, they were their playmate. Their patients were not just children they cared for, but family. Patients were their daughters and sons, sisters and brothers, and nieces and nephews, or at least that was how they made Jenna feel. She could see it in their faces. Although they tried hiding it with a crooked smile, they were hurting too. Watching their patients lay in constant, extreme agony and not being able to do anything to help them had to be mentally and emotionally taxing on them. But they carried on, trying to make their patients as happy as possible. They were true heroes, and extremely special people.

A gastroenterologist came in to examine Jenna, and when he pressed down on her stomach, she screamed. Jenna wanted to punch him in the face. She was in so much pain. Jenna knew he was only doing what he had to do, but pressing on her made the pain worse. The doctor told them she needed a surgical procedure but was nervous because her platelets were very low, which could lead to bleeding out as clotting was unlikely.

Nurses began prepping Jenna for surgery, meaning an increased dose of steroids, a platelet drip, insulin shots, and a total parenteral nutrition (TPN) supplement since she had not been able to eat for days because of the pain. Jenna was also back on blood pressure medicine because the stress from the intense pain was giving her hypertension. Adding even more to the stress, the anesthesiologist said he must postpone the surgery because there were no open beds in the PICU.

For transplant patients, they were overly cautious. If something unexpected happened in surgery, they wanted the PICU opened as a possibility. Sue and Dr. K, who both had daughters Jenna's age, showed their motherly protection over her as they were upset Jenna was put through the pain of pre-testing. They informed the surgeon they would not put her through that again, and he would have to do the surgery without it being done. Jenna was so tired of fighting. Having Sue and Dr. K protect her was as if she had her own Adrian standing in the corner of her boxing ring, giving her weak and beaten Rocky spirit time to restore.

A few days later, Jenna scooted from her bed onto the operating room table, prepped and ready for surgery. Beforehand, nurses injected more platelets into Jenna and started her on a 30-minute breathing treatment, something Jenna had to do every month to try and prevent lung disease in the future. The operating room staff tried talking to her to get her mind off her surroundings. "We're going to give you a little medicine now to help you go to sleep," one said.

As the first dose of sleepy medicine was given, it was no surprise Jenna's eyes remained wide awake. Even though she was still coherent, the side effects of the anesthesia caused her to lie there on the table, limp and unable to physically stop anyone from beginning the procedure. It was not the most comforting feeling hearing the surgery was about to start while she was still waiting for the medicine to completely kick in. Still able to mumble to the operating room nurses through the oxygen mask covering her mouth, they gave her the heavier stuff. Jenna took one last look over the nurse's shoulder, checking to make sure her dad was still in the room. She knew he was her only ally to ensure they did not start the procedure before she was completely asleep. Jenna did not want another bet over a six-pack of Coke to occur that day.

Sue took full advantage of that procedure and accessed Jenna's port while she was asleep and changed the bandage over her Hickman. She knew what an ordeal it was for Jenna, and Jenna was never so thankful to have someone put her first over protocol. But that was Sue.

Sue would bend the rules, something Jenna so desperately needed many times. Sue's quiet, sweet demeanor was an excellent cover because when it came to her patients, she did what was best for them. If that meant taking up the first five minutes of surgery to access Jenna's port, then that was what she would do. Sometimes it meant mustering up her stern, Army-colonel attitude to protect Jenna from being subjected to more pain.

The surgery was a success, but as Jenna woke up, all she could do was moan. She felt so badly as she lay there, repeatedly crying out, "Maaaa-ma, Maa-ma!" It may have had something to do with the seven biopsies he took, two of the esophagus, three of the stomach, and two of the colon. To everyone's surprise, however, Jenna's appetite was in full force.

Jenna could not remember the last time she had eaten real food. Steroids had given her particular cravings, and that day it was a McDonald's Filet-O-Fish sandwich. Although it was not the healthiest option, it was food, which was all that mattered. So, her dad left and got one on special order for her.

Only 24 hours after surgery, the results showed Jenna was suffering from mild GvHD in her stomach, the new donor cells were destroying her stomach tissue. Tests run before the surgery showed her immune system was barely working. What was left was trying to fight off the GvHD, which left other areas of her body at a high risk of infection. So, more steroids were given to suppress the donor cells.

Laying as still as possible in bed, Jenna tried to avoid any movement, fearing more pain would flood in. Then, her emotions started getting the best of her. It was hard being back on the unit. She saw more of her friends dying around her, some of whom had come back for a second transplant. Those kids would randomly walk up to her in the hallways and give her big hugs. One boy, in particular, would walk up to her, arms opened wide to give a big bear hug, wearing his winter jacket. He had a high fever due to his drug protocol, which left him cold, but burning to the touch. Thoughts overwhelmed Jenna.

"Will this be me?" she constantly asked herself. "Is all this pain because something is failing? Am I relapsing? Is this about to be my permanent home until I meet Jesus, face to face?"

Peering out the window of her room, Jenna noticed a friend's stepmom in the hallway. She knew he was in the PICU, so Jenna asked her mom why his mom was on the unit, knowing she should be with him. Trying to spare her feelings, Kay gave Jenna some phony reason. Naturally, Jenna probed a little more and asked how he was. Not able to come up with a different reason, she took a deep breath and told Jenna the sorrowful news. Her friend had just passed away. That day was his sixth birthday.

Only for a Moment:

PUT YOUR GAME FACE ON

Weep with those who weep and rejoice with those who rejoice. Don't run from the pain. Be present with those who are hurting—share in it. The nurses of 5200 did just that with Jenna and all their other patients. Whether it was putting a Lego dinosaur together, playing with Barbie dolls, or doing word search puzzles[2] with the older kids, the nurses tried easing those children's pains in any way they could.

Some of Jenna's Favorite Things

```
R M H O R S E S L S U R V I V O R P W K
M B B J U T C X E A Q M W M O V I E S Y
S N E I F C I F P U Z Z L E S M G V C Z
P B S A B F T L C F M H S P A V C A W N
W R J D C L R W O O H L L S N B E G L R
I E S P D H E I Y V F I Q C O O K I N G
R W S Z U J A E E W E Z W D Y C V E P A
O I Q T N T S X U N Q L V V F W Z H Y M
O C P F E C T D W A D V U J N A I A P S
K H S C L R V P N S V S D C O A T L Q C
Z R Y X Z O N G U F H S I C Y H R V Z T
E I O O C M W S Q T D A S I E O J T S R
Y S D A J M U E C D T V N N N V A P O A
U T E U S R A F R E X O E I U U G V Y V
Q M M M P X S G C S C K Y N A Q D A I E
Z A G J A L C P G M S U R P R I S E S L
U S H G D C I R O I Y F A S H I O N X G
U Y X E E O D I W R E A F A M I L Y D H
M Y A F S Z H T S Q T V A O I G S G U C
I J V F R M X H B Y U S O M U S I C Q Y
```

I Love Lucy	Surprises	Christmas	Bible
Survivor	Westerns	Putt-Putt	Art
Cooking	Flowers	Puzzles	JAG
Friends	Movies	Fashion	
Spades	Sports	Travel	
Horses	Disney	Shania	
Maggie	Family	Music	
Beach	Rook		

31

BREATHLESS

Quite frankly, Jenna was tired of sickness and death. The pain she was in had spread all over her body, now in both ankles and legs. But it was not just the physical pain tormenting her but the heartache it caused her family. It was 17 days shy of Christmas, and the doctors were telling Jenna if she was released within the next week, she would still have to stay in Durham for at least another week so they could keep a close eye on her.

They could not have a live Christmas tree that year, and they also could not use their wood stove in their basement because of the dust that circulated in the air. Talk about hacking away at the Christmas spirit. The doctors did allow for a fire in the fireplace, mercifully allowing Jenna to keep at least one of her favorite things ablaze at Christmas, even though part of her felt like she would not be there.

Jenna already knew she was the cause of breaking the family tradition of going to the tree lot and picking out a Christmas tree. Now she had the burden of knowing her mom had to be away, and her brothers and sister would have to take a backseat to her . . . again.

While Jenna didn't like talking on the phone with Zachary, Gabriel, and Hannah because it only made her miss them more, she would sometimes hear her mom talking with them. She was missing her kids grow up, something that not only brought her much guilt, but also caused her to worry as she was not there to parent during her boys most critical teen years. All she could do was give her kids completely over to God as she knew He loved her children more than she did. That was her only solace.

"Hey, Mom! I made the basketball team!" Gabriel exclaimed while on the phone with her one day. He had just made the middle school's basketball team. "I tried getting the number 22 as my uniform number, but the jersey fit another player better," Gabriel said with a bummed spirit echoing from his mouth. Kay thought he chose that number because one of his best friend's favorite numbers was 22, but no. Gabriel told her he wanted that number because it was Jenna's softball number. In that moment, Jenna knew her troublesome treatment was affecting him somehow, as his once rolled-up sleeves were slowly unfolding, revealing his emotional heart.

Hannah and the boys were missing their mom. How could they not? A person could only take so much of their dad's specialties: Italian sausages, egg sandwiches, and bean soufflé. So, Kay headed home to be with them and get the house all decorated for Christmas. Jenna knew it was good for her mom to go home and reenergize herself by being in the normal world with the rest of the family.

While Kay was gone that weekend, two more of Jenna's friends died, one boy just seven months old and another who was 20. The saying, age is just a number, was all too real up there. Even the so-called healthiest of kids could be taken at any moment. The 20-year-old boy was a cyclist in excellent shape before taking the elevator ride up to 5200. Jenna only wanted to show her mom his newly-shaved head when she returned from her weekend away, but after an acute reaction to one of the chemo drugs given before transplant, his body shut down. He did not even make it to his transplant day. It was those sudden bursts of cruel reality that put life into perspective for Jenna. It made it so hard to catch her breath every time it happened, afraid the next breath she took could be her last. There was no sheltering Jenna from that life.

Jenna was at one of her lowest points. The pain in her knees, ankles, and wrists had intensified. One of her knees was bright red and hot like a schoolgirl's cheeks who had just seen her crush walk by and acknowledge her existence for the first time. An X-ray showed nothing. The doctors were once again bewildered. But even through it all, nothing would stop Jenna from fighting her dad during the dreaded bath time.

Jenna did not think the doctors realized just how hard it was to push that ten-pound IV pole. It held three pumps resembling a snow cone machine, with bags of different colored liquids waiting to be poured on top of the shaved ice cones she missed so badly. Jenna would shuffle her feet to a bathroom that was too small to fit two people inside. Afterward, she contemplated how to lift one leg over the side of the tub, knowing lifting that leg meant putting all her 150 pounds onto the other. Once one leg was in, she had to swing her second leg over the side while aiming for a hard wooden bench inside the tub. Then her dad, with all of Jenna's privacy gone, would pour the water over her ever-so-sensitive skin. It pounded on her head like pellets of hail falling from the sky.

Within seconds of bathing, Jenna could not catch her breath. The pain in her stomach was unbearable. Her dad rushed her into bed and pushed the nurse call button, or at least that was what he thought.

He had accidentally pressed the emergency button, comparable to a code blue.

Just a few panicked seconds passed by, and Jenna's room was filled with nurses and doctors. They rushed around her, putting an oxygen mask over her mouth, and hooked her up to all sorts of machines to monitor her condition. All her functions were normal, and once again, there was no explanation from the doctors. Their only guess was the severe pain in her stomach had literally taken her breath away.

Jenna could not take anymore; she had hit her breaking point. There was not a day that went by she was not in pain. It had been so long since she had a normal life; she could not even remember what it felt like. Jenna laid in bed quiet and beaten down. She looked over to her dad and softly whispered, "Daddy . . . I'm tired." She was tired of the bad news, tired of death. She told him she was tired of fighting, done with the pain.

With tear-filled eyes and determination in his voice, he looked at Jenna and declared, "No! You are not going to give up. You are going to keep fighting. And you're going to keep fighting because one day, I am going to walk you down the aisle."

In a way, Jenna's dad needed to hear those words more than she did. That position of caregiver was not the most ordinary or comfortable job for a man. Men were not typically designed to be encouraging and nurturing creatures, so Jenna knew her dad had been thrown into an alien world. He was the provider, the hard worker, and the protector of their family.

Ray was accustomed to working overtime so all the kids could participate in whatever sport or extracurricular activity they wanted. More past times included going out in the woods and sitting in a tree stand all day until he saw an elusive wall-hanger in shooting distance. There was nowhere in that scenario where he cared for the deer and nurtured it back to health. Instead, he would take the deer back to the house, gut it, and then send it to the butcher, where it would provide food for some good home-cooked meals for the remainder of the year. Jenna knew all of it was hard on him, and she thanked him for trying, for having compassion, and for fighting for her when she could not. But Jenna was sure he was never so happy for Kay to take back the reins at the end of that weekend.

32

A MOUTH FULL OF COPPER PENNIES

With Kay back at Duke just ten days before Christmas, Jenna had the same punishing experience during bath time the next day, so doctors ordered a CAT scan of her stomach. Reluctantly, Jenna lifted her oxygen mask just long enough to gulp down the thick chalk-like liquid contrast before the scan.

Jenna's chest and arms were so heavy, forcing her to lie limp in the bed as if her muscles had disintegrated entirely. The nurses knew she was exhausted when Jenna did not even react to the six tubes of iodine and medication pushed quickly through her Hickman lines. Typically, Jenna wanted them to push it slowly because it made her nauseous. She could not only feel the liquid being pushed through her lines, she could taste the chemicals that were flushed through her veins, leaving her with a metallic taste of a mouth full of copper pennies.

The results of the slew of tests came up empty, so it was back to the drawing board. Although she wanted to, Jenna could not even scream in frustration because she did not have the strength to do so.

Her potassium levels rose way too high, and so did her glucose, so doctors placed Jenna on a continuous insulin drip as her pancreas was not making the right amount of insulin. As if she was not having a hard enough time sleeping through the pain, now she was awakened to take blood every two hours to check her glucose levels, which turned to every 30 minutes when the insulin was increased. Then within minutes, her heart started beating way too fast, so yet another monitor was added to the wall behind her hospital bed.

Jenna's triglycerides, fats in the blood, were exceedingly high, causing her blood sugar to be way above the normal range. Doctors said the root of the issue was probably due to the high amounts of steroids, but she needed them to fight off infection. A normal person has a triglyceride level of 200 or less; Jenna's was 21 times that at 4,220.

The nurses could not even get the tubes of blood back to the nurses' station right across from her door before the blood coagulated from such a high fat content. The rest of the day, they had a relay system in place. One nurse would draw the blood and immediately hand the tubes off to another nurse, who would then run it back to the nurses' station to be put in different tubes before the blood turned to a thick yellowish-red paste. At one point, Jenna's nurse could not get anything to come out of her lines and could not push anything in, not even heparin, a blood thinner. Now the blood baton passing was not even an option.

That thick, jelly-like blood was attempting to flow through Jenna's veins, and it was extremely dangerous. Jenna's pancreas would become completely compromised if the doctors did not figure out how to get the blood flowing inside her. Pancreatitis could happen if triglyceride levels reached over 2,000, and Jenna's was more than double that. She was in trouble.

The doctors were now placing Jenna on a diet. The high dose of steroids gave her an uncontrollable appetite, and now they wanted to limit what she could eat? Talk about cruelty. It was like telling a child they could not eat any of their own birthday cake. They had taken away the only foods that were appetizing to her in between her bouts of nausea: McDonald's fish sandwiches, barbeque platters, hush puppies, cream cheese on blueberry bagels, spaghetti, and pizza. What was a girl to eat? Eating those foods was the only thing she looked forward to every day. Now she was in excruciating pain and being starved, it was torture.

After more tests, the doctors had no clue what was happening inside Jenna's body. They thought it could be an allergic reaction to CD-25, an immune modulator Jenna was on. Since that drug was relatively new to the process, as it had only been in use for nine months, many unknowns came with it. They had never seen a reaction from the drug, but Jenna liked to keep the doctors on their toes by taking the roads less traveled. One night, an on-call doctor came into her room to observe Jenna. He had heard about her legs and arms becoming inflamed, red like Santa's rosy cheeks, but he had never witnessed the phenomenon until his shift that night. Jenna's knees were in the most excruciating pain. Redness and warmth had started in her left knee, then moved to her right, eventually spreading up and down both legs. Morphine was barely taking the edge off the pain. Once again, there was no explanation, just something for the doctors to write in a medical journal. That's what Jenna felt like she was, just some article in a medical journal.

33

A DANGEROUS GAME OF TETRIS

Kay tried to rub lotion on Jenna's dry skin to alleviate the pain from the forming cracks that were beginning to appear. With each stroke of her hand, it felt as though a piece of sandpaper was peeling away at her rough, desiccated skin. Kay would do anything to rid Jenna of the pain she was living in, especially knowing Hannah was showing up later that afternoon.

Hannah did not get to visit much, and when she did, she could not stand seeing Jenna in so much pain. Hannah wanted to be able to do something with her just like they had the previous year, playing dress-up, pretend Miss America pageants with Rhonda and her sister, and then scoring and crowning the winner. Instead, Hannah walked out of the room to draw on the whiteboard outside Jenna's door, trying to escape from watching her sister in misery.

Doctors continuously returned to the room with negative test results showing Jenna's blood counts were slipping lower and lower. Kay was in panic mode as her first thoughts were, the leukemia was back. Sue placed her hand on Kay's leg and tried to calm her tearful worries, explaining she did not believe that was the culprit. The GvHD in Jenna's stomach was still suppressing her immune system, which dropped her counts. Of course, that did not happen to all GvHD patients, but doctors had seen it in some cases before.

The next doctor walked into Jenna's room with more test results in hand. It was as if Jenna was playing a real-life version of the game Tetris. Slowly, each complication was falling on her, echoing from the doctors' mouths standing over her bed. The more specialists that entered her room, the faster those complications would fall. If they didn't stop falling, surely her game would soon be over.

That doctor standing at the foot of her bed stated Jenna's triglyceride levels needed to be less than 1,000 before taking her off the insulin drip. That alone would keep her up on the unit past Christmas. After she was off the drip, she had to begin insulin shots twice a day, but Jenna would have to prick her finger four times a day. "Why not add more needles to the mix?" Jenna thought, as if she was not in enough pain already, now having to voluntarily inflict it on herself. She refused, but her mom worked to convince her otherwise. Nurses wanted Kay to begin practicing giving Jenna insulin shots, knowing it was the only means of getting her closer to going home. But it just meant more of what was probably her least favorite thing . . . needles.

The specialist first gave Kay a shot filled with saline. She wanted to show her how it would feel to Jenna. What the specialist was not prepared for was Kay's reaction. As the needle penetrated her skin, her eyes quickly bulged, and her mouth quivered as she could not hide the fact being stuck by a needle was uncomfortable, no matter who administered it. Kay then practiced on two of Jenna's nurses. Although they did not seem to mind, that would not change Jenna's opinion on the matter. She was so over needles, so over being the pin cushion. She hated them, and now she had to get stuck by them six times a day, two insulin shots and four finger pricks.

Between the finger pricks, insulin shots, oral medications, doctors pressing on her, new doctors talking to her about diets to avoid high triglycerides and diabetes, and the constant pain no one seemed to have an explanation for, Jenna was worn out. The transplant doctors got together to discuss the patients' conditions every week, and they were all at a complete loss about her symptoms. But that only fueled their fire even more. They had no clue what could be causing her pain, swelling, and migratory inflammation. So, they studied and compiled research to ensure they did everything humanly possible to rid Jenna of this pain. They reached out to other doctors around the world in hopes someone would know a different way to treat her.

An endocrinologist said she had never seen a child with triglycerides that high. Being such a mystery case, Jenna knew she would not make it home in time to run down the stairs with Zachary, Gabriel, and Hannah on Christmas morning; well, maybe not run down the stairs, but at least watch them do it.

As her struggles increased, there were simply not enough days between Thanksgiving and Christmas that year. Jenna's eyes slowly opened much earlier than usual that morning laying in the hospital bed. Still, with a hazy, half-opened view, she caught a glimpse of a rather large man in a red suit standing beside her bed. Santa had come to visit. Although Jenna was happy he had come to visit her, the picture taken of Santa smiling while leaning over her bed as she lay there with her eyes nearly shut, proved Jenna was anything but thrilled to have Santa there so early in the morning. Santa obviously did not get the memo things didn't start happening up there until around midday, as most of the kids were sleeping in their pictures with Jolly Ol' Saint Nick.

Jenna couldn't help but begin to feel guilt creeping over her. It was day 145 post-transplant, Christmas morning. Jenna was glad her mom was there watching over her, but the family was split apart. Being apart was difficult. So, she was thankful for the breaks when family and friends came to visit. That usually involved a rousing game of Racko, Rook, or Spades, but she never turned down anything. And everyone who came to visit had better have their game face on.

Jenna had such a competitive spirit. Growing up with two older brothers who were athletic instilled that in her. Whether she was running with the boys just to show she could keep up or slapping a spade on top of an ace of diamonds, Jenna was no quitter. She wanted to win, just like every time she stepped up on the pitcher's mound. But for now, playing cards would have to do.

Only for a Moment:

ALL FUN AND GAMES

Jenna needed distractions as she was struggling with pain. Those distractions were card games, board games, and mind games.

If you're at an all-time low, grab a couple of friends and play a game of Rook. If you can't muster up the strength to be with people, grab a pen and drown your woes by adding a little pixie dust to your life with this Disney crossword puzzle.

Disney Crossword Clues:

Down:

1. Fearsome tiger
3. Dumbo's ears help him _____
5. Sophisticated felines
6. Missing fish
7. Unlikely Princess
8. Orphaned kitten
9. She saves China
12. Ho, Ho, Ho movie
13. Tod's best friend
16. Mice guardian angels (Bernard and Miss Bianca)
17. Two dogs and a cat adventure
18. Fawn
25. Lightening McQueen
27. Jenna's favorite non-animated Disney movie
28. Prankster twins' movie
30. Lover of spotted fur
31. Underestimated football team
32. Heavenly baseball players
38. Swiss Family Robinson dwelling
39. Signed paper of unlimited funds
41. Plays "The Glad Game"
43. Mush, mush
45. Newspaper deliverers
48. Colors of the _____

Across:

2. Steals from the rich
3. Green, rubber-like substance
4. Five dozen egg eater
10. Man cub
11. Means "no worries"
14. Tale as old as _____
15. The Jamaican bobsled team
19. Beats his chest
20. Preys on poor unfortunate souls
21. god of strength
22. He's gonna be a mighty king
23. Most athletic dog
24. Chunky rodent
26. Jenna's favorite animated Disney movie
29. Wooden boy
33. Chimney sweeper
34. Doggy dinner for two
35. Jungle 2 _____
36. Flying nanny
37. Mighty _____ Young
38. Misfit soccer players
40. Genie's home
42. Singer of "Let It Go"
44. Tarzan's mate
46. Locked in a tower
47. Captain Hook's left hand
49. Awoken by a kiss
50. Lost her glass slipper

34

KISS ME

Jenna began to regain some of her strength, and the pain subsided enough for her to walk that familiar L-shaped hallway. That meant more encouraging messages and flowers on patients' whiteboards with Pollyanna moments that revealed parts of her sunny personality often remaining covered by dark days. It just so happened one of her male doctors would catch a ray of Jenna's sun as he walked into her room one morning.

Dr. Martin, a quiet, gentle-mannered, ponytail-wearing man, placed his stethoscope on the lower extremities of Jenna's back, checking her breathing, then switching locations to check her heart. As usual, Jenna lay there acting completely bothered by the examination. Midway through, Jenna looked up at him and asked if he wanted a kiss from her. He paused, in complete amazement that she actually talked, stuttered a little, and then started blushing. Knowing she caught him off guard, Jenna opened her hand and showed him a Hershey kiss. Later that night, the same doctor walked by her room and blew her a kiss through the window, and for a brief moment, there was a smile on her face.

With Christmas in the rearview mirror and New Year's Eve having arrived, Jenna was still in that crinkly hospital bed. While the nurses on the floor were busy making the unit as festive as possible, one knocked on Jenna's door, came in, and told her she would have to get her port accessed. Jenna just sat there in silence, thinking to herself, "What better way to start off the new year?"

Jenna probably had her port accessed over 100 times by that point. Back at her home hospital in Richmond, during the first six months of treatment, her port had to be accessed multiple times every week. With the port placed so deeply, each week proved to be a tormenting experience. After pressing and pressing and pressing, trying to find the port, something that normally didn't need to be done with a correctly placed one, the needle then penetrated the skin. This often resulted in blood running down her chest from the constant sticking and maneuvering of the inch-and-half-long needle. Knowing the trauma Jenna had been through with each access, trying to ease the blow the nurses gave Jenna a choice of three people who could do it for her. To no surprise, Jenna picked Sue.

Jenna had built trust in Sue. Although she never shared that with her, it was something Sue probably needed to hear at times. There was comfort in knowing she was taking care of her. Even though Jenna felt she was often the bearer of bad news, somehow, it did not seem as scary when the news came out of Sue's mouth. It was almost as if she was her protector. Jenna had seen her time and time again step in to shield her from unnecessary pain. However, when Jenna's life depended on the harsh treatment, Sue remained tough, knowing it was vital, though inside, she was hurting for Jenna.

Sue also made Kay feel at ease. For Jenna, anyone who could do that during those times must have been exceptional. There was no way to describe it; Jenna just knew Sue would do everything in her power to make sure that dreadful ordeal was a little less daunting. However, all of Jenna's bad port access experiences combined would not hold a candle to what was about to come.

Sue came in with another nurse practitioner, and when they walked through the door, Jenna could tell she was not going to enjoy what was about to happen. Despite handpicking Sue to inflict that torture on her, she fought with them just like every time before.

Jenna pleaded with them, "Please, can I have sleepy medicine?" She wanted so desperately not to feel the upcoming brutality. They fought back, telling her they could not give her any. "As if this experience is not as bad as a surgery!" Jenna thought. Being the determined person she was, Jenna continued to argue with them to give her something for the pain. There was not much fighting or fleeing she could do lying there in the bed. Still, after multiple minutes of arguing back and forth, wiggling around so they could not pin her down, they halfway complied and said they would give her something to calm her down, but not anesthesia. That was a feat in and of itself as nothing was normally given when accessed. Jenna knew that was all she would get. So, she took it, and the torment began.

The first needle pierced through her skin, and the screaming began. Apparently, the needle was not long enough, so needle number two was prepared. There was 45 minutes of sticking, turning, and repositioning the needle as the two nurse practitioners took turns holding Jenna down while the other tried finding the port. Although it was placed just beneath her skin, the fluid buildup from the steroids had created a cushion around the port. The pressure from the fluid had pushed the port even deeper than it already was. They could not get the needle to reach it.

Sue decided to roll Jenna down to the X-ray room, with the needle sticking out of her chest, to see where it was in reference to her port. After a cruel three hours, the nurse practitioners came to the conclusion the entire port needed to be taken out as there was no needle long enough to reach it. They later told Jenna they were glad she pushed so hard to get some type of pain suppressant. They never thought it would be that hard to access. Jenna was traumatized, but as the old song says, "the sun will come up tomorrow," and it did. Jenna received good enough test results and was cleared to go home, home again.

Jenna had been in the hospital all but 30 days since July. Most of those were spent just minutes away from the hospital in the apartment where she lay her head at night after spending all day in the clinic to receive medicines and such. She was home in Chesterfield for only 5 of those 30 days. But now, in the middle of January, she was going home to celebrate Christmas.

35

BLASTS

Christmas Day for Jenna's family did not arrive on December 25 but rather January 18, 2000. However, out of all the abnormalities over the past year, their Christmas morning started just like any other. After waking up before sunrise, Zachary, Hannah, and Jenna had to drag Gabriel out of bed. They sat at the top of the staircase, anticipating their mom's red camcorder light to flash on, preparing themselves to rush downstairs into the den and pounce on Santa's gifts.

Jenna did not run down the stairs. She barely had enough coordination to walk in a straight line, let alone run. But the four of them still turned that same corner from the hallway to the den and saw the Christmas tree lights blazing bright. To their delight, there were mounds of presents at the base of the tree, many more gifts than they ever had before.

Many of Ray's coworkers got together to make that happen. Those things may have just been Christmas presents to other children and teenagers, the latest toys and clothes, but Jenna so desperately needed it. It allowed her to be a child for a little while, not worrying about medical terms, medicines, and needles. She could just enjoy opening presents with her brothers and sister.

Jenna sat in awe of the compassion shown by people who did not even know her. Her parents smiled as they watched Jenna sitting on the floor, putting together the last puzzle piece of Belle's beautiful yellow ball gown. They hoped it was the finale of God's miracle they had prayed for.

Puzzles, painting supplies, hunting gear, and tons more were not the only gifts Ray's coworkers had given his family that year. Many of them also gave up their vacation time so Ray could have more time to spend with Jenna and the rest of the family as they all coped with the tragedies that swallowed their lives whole. They had given up so much time his place of employment ended up putting a cap on the amount of vacation allowed to be given.

Students at Bailey Bridge Middle School had sent Jenna hand-written Christmas cards, 1,200 in all. Weeks before, when the rest of the world celebrated Christmas, every sixth, seventh, and eighth grade class at Bailey Bridge made a beautiful bell garland with individual students contributing a bell. They were put into huge sacks Jenna's mom, dad, and siblings brought while she was in the hospital. The school even had an entire display case dedicated to her recovery journey.

Jenna honestly could not believe she was even remembered at school since she had only attended for such a short while. Jenna had been gone for more than a year. She had barely completed the beginning three months of her sixth-grade year, and now half of her seventh-grade year had come and gone. Not one textbook had been opened, not one class was attended.

Days were busy with nurses checking on Jenna, but instead of those gathered across from her hospital door at the nurses' station, they came from a home health company. Kay took the reins as a full-time nurse with no trained nurse around, which made it a bit weird for Jenna.

Kay started Jenna's daily routine by pulling out eight different syringes for filling five tubes of blood, a two-hour infusion of cyclosporine was needed to accept the donor cells, a five-minute infusion of steroids, and then an insulin shot. Believe it or not, all of that had to be done before eight o'clock in the morning while Kay, who wore her Supermom cape proudly, also got Zachary, Gabriel, and Hannah ready for school.

To both of their surprise, Jenna was tolerating the insulin shots and finger pricks, but her glucose level was still too high. Jenna's blood pressure, platelets, and a list full of other things she could not pronounce were not where doctors said they should be. That far outside transplant, going on five months, Jenna's immune system should have been more robust. The medical team had to suppress it due to the GvHD in her stomach, therefore throwing a wrench in her recovery. It didn't help either that most of Jenna's medicines were in pill form. The anxiety brought on by swallowing pills coupled with the fact that her only water intake was in the form of ice chips only made recovery slower.

The side effects of the drugs were becoming even more evident. Doctors had conducted various muscle tests on Jenna and identified the carnitine in Jenna's muscles was extremely low. The steroids were killing her muscles, wasting away like the dried leaves dropping from autumn trees.

It made sense to Jenna for her muscles to be weak after all those months of being in bed. Still, no one told her that her medications might permanently damage anything. There were already so many unknowns that it was just another added blow. The only option she had was to wait it out, sit around the house, and wait until her next clinic visit.

Jenna was still going to Duke for weekly check-ups every Tuesday on clinic day, which was no easy task. Kay and Jenna never knew what kind of news those visits would bring, so they had to be prepared for the worst, another in-patient stay in the hospital. So Kay prepped, throwing videos, clothes, pictures, and games into an overnight bag.

The constant reminder Jenna's world had changed continued on their three-hour car ride down to Duke. Since the radiation, certain aspects of her body had changed, like how the sun affected her skin. She could not go anywhere without sunscreen, which included being in the car. It needed to be layered on constantly so her delicate skin wouldn't burn as it would do so in minutes. Lotion needed to be applied quite often as well, as her skin resembled the cracked earth of the Sahara Desert.

As the middle of February rolled around, the family prepared for Hannah's birthday party. January 19 was her actual birthday, the day after they celebrated Christmas that year. Hannah wanted the party at their house because she did not want to celebrate unless Jenna could be there. With Jenna's immune system compromised, they had to make sure all the girls invited or anyone in their family had not been sick.

They were able to have four girls come over. It was nice to play games, even if Jenna never did get up from the recliner. Hannah saw Jenna laugh and smile for the first time in over a year during the fun. It was also the first time Jenna saw Hannah as happy. Jenna could see it on her parents' faces, almost a sigh of relief, a light at the end of a long, dark tunnel. Jenna watched her brothers' faces, and even they looked shocked she was sitting there laughing and playing games with friends.

As the party died down and all the balloons were deflated by Zachary and Gabriel popping them, Kay prepared Jenna's second dose of insulin. Her eyes bulged like Bugs Bunny after seeing Lola Bunny in the distance. She realized she had just doubled Jenna's insulin dose, having given her the morning dose instead of the night dosage. After a frantic phone call to Duke, doctors prescribed a buffet platter of sweets as a remedy. That was music to Jenna's ears, as there was nothing a girl on steroids with no nausea liked more than to be told she had to eat more. For the rest of the night, Kay woke Jenna up every two hours to draw her blood to ensure her sugar level did not drop too low.

Although at home, Jenna never really relaxed because all her levels, organs, and bones were not regulating as quickly as they should have. Her WBC and platelets were only slowly creeping up to a normal level, like the turtle's pace in the popular children's story *The Tortoise and the Hare.* Her hemoglobin level was on some type of seesaw at a children's playground, and her blood pressure spiked to resemble that of an older man and then dropped to that of a small child. Jenna had so many headaches now and a deep, raspy cough. The doctors started her on some preventative treatments for pneumonia. To top it all off, Jenna's hearing was randomly declining, which meant the television volume increased immensely despite who was in the room. She felt as if she was bobbing up and down in an ocean full of problems, waving her hands around to grab someone's attention.

The next day, blood results drawn a week earlier from Jenna's home hospital were in. Kay received a call from a nurse who proceeded to give the latest update on Jenna's tests. The nurse explained that her platelets had dropped. Kay looked as if the life had been blasted out of her, and fear began to surge over her.

Dr. K had been concerned that Jenna's counts were not growing as fast as they should. Previously, she informed Kay if there was a decrease in platelets, it may mean the cancer was back. Nearing the end of the phone conversation, the nurse told Kay two words that jumped out on the pages of results: *blasts seen.* Abnormal immature white blood cells associated with leukemia had been seen.

The confetti-sprinkled safety net that held Jenna was ripped from under her. Quickly, Kay hung up the phone and called Duke. She frantically alerted Dr. K and Sue of the news. Trying to calm her down, Dr. K informed her they would run more tests before confirming anything. There was nothing to do now but wait for the new test results.

After a long ride back to Duke, Kay, Ray, and Natalie sat waiting in the clinic trying to keep Jenna busy while they waited for the test results to come in. Much like that day over a year ago, they waited to see if they would hear the dreaded word *cancer* again, that time knowing full well what it meant. As they rolled the Yahtzee dice over and over, hours of fear passed by as they waited. Typically, results from blood tests only took about an hour to come back, so the extra time only left room for their minds to wander, mainly about the worst possible news.

Then they had it, the news they had anticipated. Multiple doctors had confirmed it; no *blasts* were found. They explained the only things they saw in the results were newly-forming red blood cells, platelets, and white blood cells. Jenna's body was finally making new cells on its own!

Kay started crying. Mothers of other children in the waiting room started coming over one by one, hugging her and crying with her.

There was nothing more radiant than seeing transplant parents cry over good news. It was the crescendo of a conductor's masterpiece, the grand slam in the bottom of the ninth inning, the Apollo 11 mission splashdown.

Only for a Moment:

LET'S DANCE

Jenna's friends and family had watched her suffer so much. The thought she would have to do it all over again or maybe not even get that option was an indescribable pain. But instead, that day Jenna received the best news; the transplant was working! When moments of joy happen, celebrate them.

Take a moment, scan the QR code below, get up, and dance it off. Blast your music right there in your room, and dance like you don't have an audience because if you did, we all know you wouldn't be dancing quite the same!

Take a breath, dance it off, and keep going.

36

MORE QUESTIONS, FEWER ANSWERS

In her delicate condition, one of Jenna's new hobbies was counting the number of bruises dotting her arms and legs, very much resembling a white-furred Dalmatian puppy receiving its black polka dots for the first time. She watched closely throughout the day to make sure the blemishes did not grow larger, stay around too long, or turn colors that did not resemble traditional shades of blues and purples. A bruise was not just a bruise for her. It could become infected or bleed excessively, meaning another setback. Sometimes she thought it was harder being home, confined to the recliner in the den. There was no L-shaped hallway to travel. She could not cheer up her adoring Big Bird fans or color cheerful artwork on their whiteboards. Staring at the walls inside their home was different but, at the same time, similar.

She should have been getting off the bus with Hannah. Instead, Jenna limped halfway up the driveway to greet her after returning from school in the afternoon. Jenna should have been cheering at the top of her lungs from the dugout for her teammates, but she was so weak she was limited to writing down what she wanted to eat on a sticky note to her mom because it just took too much energy to talk. And, she should have been playing outside with Zachary, Gabriel, and Hannah, riding go-karts and playing wiffle ball in the field. But Jenna was bound to counting bruises.

It was hard to see her brothers and Hannah come home from school and hear about their days in the outside world. They would try and talk quietly in the kitchen, one room away from where Jenna was. She was an expert at playing possum by now and would hear everything about their different activities and outings with friends. Jenna would not say much. When she did, she tried to act interested, but it hurt to be interested. There were so many more bruises, invisible to the naked eye. Jenna was missing out on normalcy.

Everything in her life had changed. Jenna did not necessarily look older like the other girls she use to go to school with. She just looked balder and a lot rounder.

Life did not stop for Jenna, but her life had stopped. It was like she had been placed in another universe, one where she was happy to be alive, and the other girls were happy putting on make-up. Jenna fought to stay alive; they fought over which boy to take to the seventh-grade dance.

Jenna thought there was supposed to be a time when all of it just went away, a time when she could actually play or go to school. But that day just seemed further and further away as she continued to struggle with the side effects of the transplant process, the side effects no one could seem to figure out.

Luckily, the testing was less frequent now. Jenna only had to go back to Duke every three months. Still, it was crazy how she was told the transplant could be failing one week and the next told she only needed to be seen every few months.

Shades of bright green returning to the trees in the front yard came just in time for Jenna's first real public outing, eight months after the transplant process began. On a Sunday night in March 2000, Jenna's family packed their minivan, leaving Jenna in complete disbelief she was allowed to go somewhere other than a hospital or clinic. Their family had not been to church together since June of the previous year.

Jenna sat on the front row of the service in a rocking chair set aside for her to be more comfortable. Although weak, she was excited she could at least watch kids her age performing dramatic skits, singing, and preaching.

Midway through the service, the preacher announced to the congregation how blessed they were to have Jenna, not just in the church, but alive. Hundreds stood to their feet, and an exploding applause filled the air around them. Jenna did not know if it was from pure exhaustion from the night's activities or out of complete humility, but tears started filling her eyes. In one way, she did not like the attention, but for everyone else, they were looking at a miracle.

Many of those people had spent hours praying for Jenna, sometimes all night. Twenty-four-hour prayer chains were warranted on many occasions. But it wasn't just those people inside her church walls who prayed. Since the beginning of her journey, Joe had insisted Jenna's story get out to the masses. He not only knew money needed to be raised to cover the bone marrow drives, living expenses, and the mounds of hospital bills to come, but he also knew if Jenna was going to make it, people would have to pray. Joe equipped Kay with a laptop and told her she had to start writing, a very difficult task for her to complete.

Unfamiliar with computers, and feeling totally ill-equipped to write, Kay's only driving force was her daughter's life, and what a force that would be as the roadblocks began. Almost every night while at Duke Kay would wait until Jenna would fall asleep, typically way past midnight, before she would begin her CaringBridge updates, a blog-like health journal site. After spending an hour writing a draft, Jenna would wake up needing something to eat or assistance to the bathroom. Once Jenna would fall back asleep, Kay would return to the journal only to discover the draft had been deleted, often resulting in another hour or two of writing. As frustrating as it was, Kay knew those messages were reaching people all over the world. Thousands upon thousands of people from around the globe were giving money and praying daily for Jenna, and Jenna's home church was now seeing firsthand how God had answered those prayers as Jenna leaned back in the chair and watched the service. Jenna was glad they had that moment because, by that time, many of them needed to see an answered prayer. After the night's end, Jenna was encouraged leaving her first outing. However, she was quickly brought back to her stark reality.

Once again, the next day, Jenna was sitting on an examining table, and another doctor, probably the 100th or so, came in to examine her. A geneticist had checked her carnitine levels, a compound involved in metabolism. To no avail, there wasn't even enough to test because Jenna was so deficient. Dr. Kurtzberg said she had never seen such low levels of carnitine in a patient.

At that time, Duke had the most specialized geneticist in the world on staff. Just ten years prior, not too much was known about carnitine, but at that point, newborns were being tested for it so specialists could prevent any significant issues if they were deficient.

This deficiency wouldn't have been as massive an ordeal to some transplant patients, but since Jenna had fibromyalgia, it was a big deal.

There were still so many unknowns with fibromyalgia, but hopefully, now that she was seeing a muscle specialist, the world's best at that, she would get some answers. It was crazy to think that out of all the tests she took to find out that she had fibromyalgia, that specific carnitine test was never given.

After meeting with a metabolist and a pediatric rheumatologist, to no surprise, they had no idea what was causing her pain. The lack of carnitine only accounted for the weakness of the muscles but not the pain in them. They had no explanation for the redness and hotness of the skin on her arms and legs. The only thought was it could be an allergic reaction.

The pain throughout her body had become so intense that for many days, Jenna sat doubled over in her dad's recliner, yearning for relief. The doctor's solution was to triple the dosage of steroids.

The steroids didn't always cause transplant kids problems, but Jenna seemed to react strangely to them. Her counts had dropped even lower than they already were. Her insulin level increased, as did her blood pressure, triglycerides, and not to mention weight gain, all of which could cause organ damage.

Jenna was more than worn out after meeting with the multiple doctors, but the day's tests weren't over. Jenna's blood counts taken earlier that morning were in. They were so out of balance that she was given two units of blood. The cyclosporine, an anti-rejection and anti-GvHD drug, was too hard on her red blood cells. Even though her marrow was making the cells, they were not surviving long enough. Jenna was prescribed vitamin E and folic acid to try and strengthen the red blood cells. But after inconclusive blood work, she showed no deficiency in either, and her doctors were again at a loss for why her red blood cells were not surviving long enough.

As Kay and Jenna began the three-hour trek back home, pain and weakness flooded Jenna's body. Kay pulled over and took her blood pressure. It read 164/115, which was way, way too high. In a panic, Kay called Sue, and she explained to Kay Jenna needed to take an oral nifedipine to bring it down.

After finally making it home, Kay put a blanket on top of Jenna, and the weight of the blanket sent sharp pains throughout her body. She took Jenna's temperature, and it was 101 degrees Fahrenheit. After multiple phone calls back and forth to Duke, Dr. K said to stay near the local hospital because the trip back to Duke would be too risky.

Not long after, Jenna's temperature hit 102.6. Kay knew she couldn't wait. They dashed back down to Duke. After dealing with so many unknowns, Kay had learned most of the time it was just better to be closer to the experts.

With her blood pressure still elevated, doctors gave Jenna extra medicines to get the bottom number below 100. It must have helped with the blood pressure and her kidneys as she had continually been playing musical chairs, hopping from the bed to the toilet seat as the fluids rushed through. But like so many times before, only minutes passed by, and the tables would turn.

Eventually, her blood pressure spiked back up to 180/98. Even though her blood pressure was too high, the doctors concluded from further tests she did not have GvHD. The last time she had it, back in November, she had to stay in the hospital for two months.

Although it was good news, it meant they still had no clue what was causing her pain and inflammation. A CAT scan was ordered for her stomach, brain, sinus cavity, and chest to ensure everything was as normal as it could be. Unfortunately, the CAT scan came with contrast, so she had to drink that thick, nasty, curdled milk-type liquid, then six big tubes of solution pushed quickly through her lines. Not long after, the results were in. There was still no answer. So Jenna was sent home, high blood pressure and all.

37

BEAR ATTACK

After the school administration allowed Jenna to skip the rest of her sixth-grade year without taking anymore classes, she had attempted to start seventh-grade several times since coming home in January. With all the interruptions caused by chronic pain, she did not complete any schoolwork until April, just a month and a half shy of the academic year's end. Jenna was in a homebound program and talked back and forth to different teachers through a headset. They had to be highly flexible with work because her energy level could drop suddenly, causing any desire or ability to do schoolwork to cease.

At times, Jenna was too sick to show up at her scheduled hour, so they would reschedule, only for her to cancel the rescheduled meeting because of bouts of hypertension-induced headaches, fatigue, and horrible nausea. For the remaining of her seventh-grade year, Jenna did very minimal schoolwork, receiving her only education through episodes of *Bonanza* for history and *Wheel of Fortune* for language arts.

Jenna was now allowed to be outside in the fresh air, so putt-putt became her new favorite outing. The medications she was taking caused her to be very hot and sweaty, much like an overweight, middle-aged man after a ten-mile run. But that was also what Jenna looked like, apart from being painted white like Casper the Friendly Ghost from all the sunscreen she had to wear to prevent further damage to her skin.

Shaded by the fake palm trees, Jenna was just glad to be doing something resembling the life she had forgotten. Rhonda, her mom, and her sister joined Kay, Hannah, and Jenna on one outing just as they had many times before. Jenna was knocking brightly-colored golf balls down the green felt carpet, even bending down to pick the balls out of the holes. That in and of itself was a huge feat as just a couple of months previous, she would have toppled over like a wobbling bowling pin. It was a feeling of freedom, a freedom Jenna fought very hard for. She was making huge strides, even better than her newfound short game, but it did not come without some drawbacks and reminders that her life was now different.

The children playing putt-putt near her would stare, almost in amazement, as she did not even look normal for a guy, which was who she resembled the most. She knew children were curious, and who could blame them for marveling at that wonder of a creature. Some of them, even the children's parents, could not take their eyes off her, like they were afraid of her. Jenna would laugh it off and say she was fine with it, but it was just a defense mechanism. She knew she would look normal one day; at least, that was what she hoped.

Jenna's body had been through a war, and she would forever have the scars to prove it. There were so many emotional scars she had not come to terms with, but she could mask those. However, there were physical scars, ones that could not be hidden. As the excess weight brought on by the steroids slowly shed away, it left behind remnants of the battle wounds she had endured during her war. Deep, bright, mauve stretch marks now covered the front of her body, the same ones Kay had seen those many months prior during Hell Week. As they started to appear, they didn't really bother her. She was still dealing with pain on a daily basis and rarely looked at herself in a mirror, so in a way, they were just a mere afterthought. Jenna still avoided the public most days, but on those rare occasions she did get out, she would quickly be reminded those new marks on her body were not just a figment of her imagination.

One time while on their way back home from a check-up at Duke, Kay and Jenna stopped at Cracker Barrel like they had done every time on their rides home since she had been given the green light to eat in public. As they were waiting in the gift shop for a table, admiring the knickknacks in the store, a grown woman stared at Jenna in astonishment. She looked down at Jenna, and with curiosity and concern, blurted out, "What in the world happened to you?" Caught off guard, Jenna paused for a moment, confused about what the lady was talking about. Then it hit her—the stretch marks.

Jenna proceeded to tell her the short version of what they were and why they were there, watching as the lady's eyes grew as big as the plates of biscuits on the tables around the corner in the dining room. It was as if she wasn't listening to what was coming out of Jenna's mouth, only considering the following words out of her own. Jenna quickly wrapped up her story, clearly seeing the lady had lost interest from the moment she opened her mouth to explain. Not even a second passed, and with the lady's mouth wide open in all seriousness, she said, "Well, my goodness, I thought you got attacked by a bear!"

"What do you even say back to that?" Jenna thought. "Well, Mom told me if I don't have anything nice to say, don't say anything at all." So, Jenna just looked at her, smiled, and walked away.

Unsurprisingly, that would not be the only bizarre experience for Jenna as she was also asked if a stingray attacked her, if she had survived a fire, or her personal favorite, being referred to by her younger cousin as a tiger or zebra. Although those statements seemed harsh, in a weird way, Jenna understood them and learned to use them to make people smile instead of feeling sorry for herself. When Jenna was around children or other kids her age, it was only normal for them to ask what had happened. So, she would casually say, "I got attacked by a bear." It was definitely a more exciting explanation than to tell them, "I take steroids."

Although those questions seemed insensitive, and maybe they were, or maybe they were out of genuine concern, they taught Jenna a valuable lesson, one most have yet to learn. Never ask a woman how far along she is. Chances are, she is probably not pregnant.

Only for a Moment:

CHECK YOURSELF IN THE MIRROR

Jenna seemingly shrugged off the random comments because of the way she looked, but that certainly wasn't always the case. Sometimes she needed reminders she was beautiful despite her outward appearance.

It's important to remember and focus on what makes you appealing. When you look in the mirror every morning, tell yourself you are beautiful. Tell yourself you are handsome. Tell yourself you are worthy because you most certainly are!

Use this mirror or your mirror at home and write positive words on it to remind yourself, you are deserving. The world just wouldn't be the same without you!

Take a breath, keep breathing, and keep going.

38

SALAD BAR OR BUST

Apart from trips to Cracker Barrel off Interstate 85, Jenna's family did not eat out a whole lot. When they did, it was usually kids eat free night at Shoney's. Jenna could count on one hand how many times she had been to a restaurant in a year. She did not need a five-star accommodation, she just needed her favorite choice of food, and that was a salad bar. Therefore, as Jenna was sporadically given green lights from doctors, she knew Ruby Tuesday was in her sights. But it didn't take long for her mom to throw a huge wrench in the plan. She had called Jenna's transplant doctor to get her okay on the choice of venue. Jenna was not too upset when her mom said they had to go to the restaurant when the least amount of people would be there, fewer people, fewer germs. It was then her mom crushed all Jenna's hopes and dreams after telling her Dr. K had put the gavel down and said she could absolutely not eat off the salad bar.

"What?" Jenna exclaimed. "That's why I wanted to go to Ruby Tuesday in the first place." Jenna begged and pleaded, using all the tactics she knew. But this was no fight over bath time, the salad bar was serious business, and the answer was still a solid no. There were just too many bacteria and germs on the fresh vegetables, shredded cheese, and miniature ham cubes.

Dr. K's concerns surrounded Jenna's absolute lymphocyte count, which fought off bacteria and viruses. The standard count was in the thousands, and Jenna's was a mere 280, meaning she was just too susceptible to germs.

Jenna was not going to let that burst her bubble, so they headed to Ruby Tuesday anyway. As they turned into the restaurant parking lot and put the car in park, all Jenna could think about was that salad bar. She was ordinarily nauseated, so food was rarely appetizing, but that day, her mouth was watering, and she was fixated on the salad bar.

As Jenna walked through the doors, she only wanted to look at it in all its glory. Not caring about anything else around her, Jenna focused on peeking over the chest-high wooden wall separating the waiting area and the salad bar. With her eyes still locked on her favorite foodstuffs, the host began walking them to their seats. Jenna walked as fast as her little sloth legs would take her, still fixated on the salad bar and being able to taste the goodies, if only by sight. Her mouth now watering, she reached up to look over the wall. Blinded by her desire for the taste of ranch dressing over a fresh bed of lettuce, she completely neglected to see the bench sitting there in front of the wall.

Bam!

Jenna bashed her right shin against the front of the hard, wooden bench.

In the middle of the restaurant, tears started to flow as extreme pain began shooting up her leg. Within seconds, a large multi-colored bruise formed on her shin, with a knot bulging in the middle. Jenna didn't even hit the bench hard. She could not move quickly anyways. After all, she was the tortoise in this story, not the hare. Not wanting to ruin that special outing, they ordered food as Jenna sat there with her leg throbbing.

Later that night, the bruising became more severe. Kay was on the phone with Aunt Vonnie, who said they had some medical magnets used for arthritis, pains, and bruising. Dr. K had heard of this technique before, but other doctors were unfamiliar. Naively, they put Jenna in the van and ventured down to Aunt Vonnie's house to see if the magnets would positively affect Jenna's swollen lower leg. After two hours of sitting on the couch with the magnet on her leg, the swelling began to subside. Kay thought it would be good to leave it on for a few more hours since no issues arose. Usually, she would have called Dr. K or spoken with the medical team at Duke before she did anything, but that time, she did not. Bad decision.

After about five hours of the magnet lying atop the bruise, Kay lifted it, and the knot on top had turned into a massive white blister. It had burned Jenna's skin. It was the latest reminder Jenna's body did not react like everyone else's, fragile and sensitive because of the chemotherapy and radiation.

The doctors were so observant of any bruises that would come up. Jenna had bad ones before, but none had blistered, not to mention her foot was now swollen and turning shades of blues and purples, with a touch of murky green on the sides. They had to keep an extra close eye on it because if the bruising continued, it meant bleeding could still be occurring.

A few days had passed, and the bruising and blistering were looking worse. All the bleeding from her shin was now falling to her foot, turning her lower leg into a multi-colored, abstract watercolor collage. Jenna was sent to Duke over the concern the blister could break, leading to a bacterial infection that could cause her to go septic. Dr. K categorized the blister as a second-degree burn, but the rest of her team agreed nothing serious had occurred.

That visit, although there for a minor setback, brought positive feedback neither she nor Kay was expecting. Jenna's doctors had not seen her in a few weeks. In that short amount of time, apart from the brief setback from the magnet, they saw improvements.

The swelling in Jenna's face was coming down. They could no longer see their reflection in her mirror-like cheeks. Jenna almost had a full head of peach fuzz, which was still accompanied by a mustache, sideburns, and a unibrow. The most significant change doctors commented on was that Jenna was actually talking with them. They only knew her as quiet Jenna, rarely speaking a word unless she was forced to. The nurses on the unit knew she had spunk to her, but that was because she did not associate them with bad news, pain, yes, but bad news, no. Jenna's body was healing; she was recovering.

Only for a Moment:

THE GLAD GAME

It's often hard to find joy through the pain. Jenna was reminded daily as she sat in painful agony most days. But Jenna tried putting her Pollyanna attitude on and found the good in the bad situations. She chose to play the *Glad Game*. Instead of wallowing in the disappointment of no salad bar option, she was just glad for the chance to eat at a restaurant. Whatever the situation, look for the good in it, because when you do, a little piece of gladness will be added to any sorrowful time.

39

HIS FAMOUS BACK FLIP

Jenna's hemoglobin, platelets, and WBC remained somewhat normal without frequent trips to Duke, as she was weaning off the steroids, blood pressure medication, and methadone.

Anytime she was given the green light, Jenna would take a trip to the grocery store with her mom because they definitely came few and far between. Jenna had to use the store wheelchair, which was risky because of all the germs on it, but if she wanted to make it through the store, it was what she had to do, of course, after Kay sanitized it. The bruise on her foot had spread, causing her leg and ankle to look like Van Gogh's *Starry Night*, and each of her toes resembled Vienna sausages dipped in ketchup and mustard. Regardless, that did not stop her from doing pretty much anything outside, which was where she would have rather been anyway.

Jenna had to avoid mosquitoes because of the diseases they could carry, and she needed to be very careful with her sun exposure. Unlike a normal sunburn, it could cause an infection, leading to GvHD. So, layered in DEET-free bug repellant and sunscreen spread like cream cheese on that morning's blueberry bagel, she would go to Gabriel's baseball game and return to keeping score. Jenna sat in the announcer's box behind home plate. High above the diamond, she counted balls and strikes.

Jenna could not help but notice two friends from school, the school she had not attended in person in a year and a half, walking down the stairs towards her. She did not want them to see her. Although she was not the size of a barn anymore, more like a large shed, she was not concerned with her appearance and her wardrobe reflected that. As they walked up into the booth with Jenna, they began conversating with her, a natural social skill she had forgotten how to do. They talked about everyday life as a seventh grader, something that seemed irretrievable to her. It was hard seeing them. She was reminded of everything she had missed out on. Those were friends she had in elementary school and started middle school with. Jenna had grown up with them, played with them, and had been to their houses for birthday parties, but yet now, they both just seemed like memories from another lifetime.

Like those social skills she would have to learn, homelife was also a new balancing act. Jenna shared a room with Hannah and felt terrible her little sister had to deal with her being sick all the time. Even though Hannah was so young, at times, she would take care of Jenna like a nurse's aide, but that was her spirit.

Hannah had experienced some of her own moments while Jenna was in the hospital. For her, the simple acts of planning out whose house she would stay at during the week fulfilled any need for more moments, because the truth was, Hannah never focused on herself. She would do anything to help make her sister's life easier, and Jenna wanted the same for Hannah, so she made sure any special moments she was given, Hannah got to enjoy as well.

They went to see *Stars on Ice* because a friend of theirs pulled some rather large strings so the experience would be something special for Jenna. Like royalty, they were placed in a separate section, keeping them away from the paparazzi, rather, the people's germs of course. Jenna was given her own private wheelchair chauffeur and covered her face with a mask. She could only sit up for about half of the show as her muscles could not keep her perched for very long. Jenna had been watching those skaters over the last year while lying in a hospital bed and sitting in a recliner. Now, she was there, alive and in person, watching Scott Hamilton gracefully glide across the ice, plant his blades firmly before he bent down, pushed up, and landed his famous backflip.

At the end of the show, Jenna got an autographed picture of Scott Hamilton, Kristi Yamaguchi, Steven Cousins, Tara Lipinski, and many more famous skaters to commemorate the night. It was such a night of relief for Jenna. For Hannah, too.

Jenna did not get too many of those nights. Although her battle was mainly being fought at home now, Jenna often thought of those fighting back at Duke. There was a 17-year-old boy Jenna would ask about quite often. Just like many others, she frequently wrote on his door. He had broken a record, being released from the hospital just 26 days after his cord blood transplant. Yet, that same month, only two children out of the 16 children on 5200 would ever walk under the falling confetti.

Months after leaving Duke, Jenna's nightly schedule hadn't changed much. On multiple nights, she still wouldn't go to bed until midnight. Once, around 1:00 a.m., Hannah woke their mom up because she could hear her sister moaning in the bed across the room. Jenna's chest was so heavy it had taken her breath away. With nothing Kay could do but resituate her, Jenna fell back asleep. Not even a couple of hours later, Hannah woke their mom up again. Kay walked into the girls' room to find Jenna covered in vomit. Her body was still so weak she did not have enough time to sit up before getting sick. So, at 3:00 a.m., Jenna was given a bath, and Hannah went downstairs to sleep on the couch so their mom could stay with Jenna in case of another episode.

Walking was becoming more of a challenge. Jenna could barely walk up the stairs most days as a new pain began gnawing away at her left upper leg and hip. Her mom emphasized being extra careful if she got up in the middle of the night. Making light of the ordeal, Jenna shrugged it off and said, "If you hear a loud thump in the night, it's just me."

40

THE CULPRIT

On August 3, 2000, Jenna celebrated her one-year, post-transplant milestone with a complete and comprehensive bodily study at Duke. Sitting in the waiting room at the hospital preparing for a long day of testing, Jenna marveled at the wonder of the new DNA inside her. From then on, she had two birthdays to celebrate, her birthdate on September 11 and August 3, when she received new cells. She had been given life two times.

The day started with the usual height, weight, blood pressure, and temperature check. Jenna stood stretched out as high as she could go. The scale read 5' tall. It was the same height she was at 11 years old, a year and a half ago when she began her transplant journey. After being told the radiation and chemotherapy could stunt her growth, the news did not come as too much of a shock. It was just one of the many possible side effects of the life-altering measures taken to keep her alive. Patients who survived transplants around Jenna's age, 11, 12, 13, or 14, could also have growth plates altered, leading to hormone replacement therapy to counteract treatment side effects. Physically, those kids were all at the developmental stage in their growth into adolescence, which made their results much more complicated.

Besides drawing 22 tubes of blood to analyze lists full of levels and counts, doctors also ordered a pulmonary test to check Jenna's lungs, an electrocardiogram to check her heart, and X-rays on every square inch of her body. It was a long day, but she would take one long day at the hospital, knowing she would go home later that night, remaining cancer free.

Gabriel and Zachary had gone with Ray to a Bass Pro Shop in Charlotte while Kay and Rhonda stayed with Jenna to keep her company. The boys finished up a little too early, so they ended up stuck with the girls for the majority of the day. That was definitely not their cup of tea. The only type of waiting they liked to do was while sitting in a tree stand waiting for a wall-mounter to walk beneath them; the whole hospital thing, not so much.

The doctors did an X-ray to check Jenna's hip. More than half of young transplant patients who received high doses of radiation could develop joint problems, especially in the hips. The radiation deteriorated the bones. Some kids even needed hip replacements following treatment. Jenna hoped it would not be the case for her. To try and get to the bottom of Jenna's hip pain, Dr. K sent her to the imaging room to have an MRI. She was without her typical Shania Twain CD and had to endure the loud clinking and buzzing sounds from the MRI machine as they echoed throughout the room. Jenna was so worn out from all the appointments during the day she took full advantage of the 45-minute MRI to take a nap.

When the results of the blood tests came in that afternoon, her cortisol and cyclosporin were low; the only two Jenna did not want to be low. This only meant she would continue on with the two-hour morning infusions her mom gave her as Zachary, Gabriel, and Hannah got ready for school.

More importantly, the results of the MRI were in. For weeks, nurses at the clinic back home could not find anything wrong with Jenna's hip. But most days, she needed extra help from her mom to support her. Sometimes Jenna walked by herself, but she would walk with a limp almost daily. After lying around the house, the combination of the pain in her joints, lower legs, right big toe, and left hip, Dr. K grew more and more concerned. Now, the culprit was identified: avascular necrosis (AVN) in her left hip.

Avascular stood for no blood, and necrosis meant death. Essentially the bone was dead, and there was no blood flowing through it. Jenna's bones in her left hip were deteriorating. The high doses of steroids she had taken for a year were killing her bones. They were weak and brittle from blood not flowing to them. It was even possibly the reason Dr. K thought she had fractured her right big toe weeks ago. Jenna's bones were breaking and giving away as she took the few steps to make it from her bed and into the recliner.

As Sue explained more about the condition in Jenna's hip, Kay asked what preventative measures could be taken to stop the progress or reverse it. Sue simply responded, "The damage has been done."

Jenna had the disease, and there was no getting rid of it. A piece of Jenna's lower leg bone would be taken out and engrafted into her hip, with a lengthy rehabilitation to follow. Kay asked Sue what percentage of transplant kids got that disease. "About 11 percent," she said. Normally AVN issues started five to eight years after the steroids stopped. Jenna was only ten months post-transplant and had not even stopped taking the steroids yet.

Jenna was not in the room when the doctors told her parents about the disease. Kay told her later that night. Jenna just sat there, not saying a word, but the tears welling up in her eyes told the story. The words out of her mother's mouth covered Jenna in a heavy, emotional fog as she had heard what the doctors had said about that disease. It was painful and required surgery. There she was making progress, and it was happening again; more pain, more surgery, and more time in the hospital. Unfortunately, if God didn't decide to make a Lazarus story out of her bones, then surgery would be Jenna's only option. After the heaviness of that report, the family decided to take a quick weekend trip to Pennsylvania so Jenna could enjoy some fun times with her cousins. And what a quick trip it was.

41

BELOW 20

Sounds of a whirring jet engine filled the humid air as an ambulance with sirens blaring, lights flashing red and white, sped onto a small local airstrip. As the ambulance screeched to an abrupt stop, three medevac personnel dashed down the stairs of the clamshell door of the plane to meet the paramedics hastily pulling Jenna out of the back on a stretcher. As they swarmed his fragile daughter, Ray watched, speechless from what was happening.

The medevac personnel placed a blood pressure cuff on her arm, sticky adhesive covers of medical leads on her chest, then hurriedly attached bags of vital fluids to her Hickman. Blankets were placed over Jenna's shivering body to keep her warm and keep her from going into shock from the unknown infection coursing through her body. Her temperature was over 105 degrees Fahrenheit. Her oxygen level fluctuated between 20 and 25 percent. The normal range being 95-100 percent. As the clamshell was shut, Jenna's blood pressure dropped to 60s/30s. Medical personnel onboard explained to Ray if the bottom number fell below 20, there was no coming back for her.

As the plane hit takeoff speed and the landing gear retracted, miles away, Kay was back at the house. She quickly grabbed an extra pair of clothes for herself and Jenna, then raced out of the driveway on her way to Duke. If there was ever a real-life *Chitty Chitty Bang Bang* story, it happened on that long stretch of Interstate 85 as Kay flew to Duke.

With each increase in cruising altitude, Jenna's diastolic pressure decreased—23, 22, 23, 21. Her dad, scared to death, prayed that number stayed above 20. It did not.

The airplane touched down in Durham after less than an hour of flight time, and another ambulance raced Jenna towards Duke. Kay arrived not too long after Jenna was frantically wheeled to 5200 suffering from septic shock.

The emergency room doctors in Chesterfield were right; had Ray and Kay driven Jenna, she would not have made it in time. Even the flight paramedics were shocked they had made it, just in the nick of time.

Three different antibiotics were started as Jenna's medical team had received the blood culture results run at her local hospital in Chesterfield just before she was whisked away to the airfield. Jenna's white blood count read 2.1, far less than the 4.5-11.0 it should have been. She was low on platelets too. Her level was barely over 100,000, far below the minimum of 150,000. Doctors determined a gram-negative bacteria was in her bloodstream: klebsiella. Although it was resistant to many antibiotics, thankfully, Jenna had already been placed on the correct one.

She curled up in bed like an unborn baby in their mother's womb, clenching her stomach as horrible pains shot throughout. Jenna only lifted her head every couple of minutes to rekindle her relationship with Chuck, a relationship she thought she had left in the past. In between bouts of projectile vomiting, her parents tried to help her shuffle towards the bathroom as nausea ravaged her body, only to lose that battle every single time.

Doctors put Jenna on dopamine to get her blood pressure to rise, measuring it every 30 minutes. The Phenergan she was taking could no longer ease the nausea overtaking her body, so Ativan was added to her medication regimen to help relieve the overwhelming sickness. Luckily, it made her sleepy, which gave her some relief from the constant puking. Jenna only woke up a few times that night to use the bathroom, many times also holding the bucket with her eyes closed as the acidy liquid poured out of her mouth.

She was drained. In tears and barely able to whisper, Jenna mumbled to her mom, "I just feel so bad."

Her face, neck, and chest had been turning red all night and became hot to the touch. Maybe it was due to the fever, or it was just another mysterious thing with her sensitive skin. Regardless, her body had just survived something medevac personnel thought was impossible. The next days would prove to be even more critical.

42

BOBBY COX

With her fever managed and blood pressure inching towards an acceptable level, Jenna was told her port needed to be removed. This was already planned for when she would have her hip surgery, but the infection could have taken refuge inside, so it needed to come out. It could not be treated without a needle long enough to access it, and there was no way doctors would clear Jenna for hip surgery with the possibility of a deadly bacteria still lurking in her body. That same issue presented itself as the doctors also began talking about removing her Hickman due to infection being in the lines.

Jenna's body continued to be pumped with steroids to fight the infection, and the extreme pain she had in her left hip was now in her right knee. An MRI was needed to determine if the AVN had settled there too. If it had, there was no way both the knee and hip could be operated on at the same time. The extensive rehab could not be completed together as the disease was in opposite legs.

Jenna was confined to her bed, which was now her personal boxing ring as her cancer-life opponent continued to knock her to the ground. In her eyes, Jenna's opponent had just jumped on top of her to administer the final blows. First a right hook to the jaw, Jenna would have to undergo surgery to have her port and Hickman removed. Then with a left punch to the gut, hip surgery would be the second blow. With a knockout body slam coming down on her in slow motion, a third and final knee surgery would surely take her out.

Jenna threw her hands up in defeat and exclaimed, "Aren't I supposed to be cured?" But she was not even given a minute to comprehend the curveball that was just thrown at her as she motioned to Kay. Vomit spewed out of her mouth, mixing at the bottom of the bucket with the salty tears that streamed from her eyes.

A wave of sleeplessness came over her as she restlessly tossed and turned in the bed. All Jenna could do was moan from the pain. Her usually stiff and somewhat lifeless body flapped around in the bed like a small-mouth bass on the floor of her dad's jon boat. More tests showed the port and Hickman cultures were still positive with klebsiella. The infection was not going to back off easily. The doctors told Jenna they would conduct one more test. If positive, there was no choice but to remove the lines. A temporary line would be put in place, and possibly a new Hickman after that. Jenna needed that Hickman; it meant she did not have to be stuck with needles all the time.

Suddenly, every machine Jenna was hooked to filled the room with a barrage of beeps and sirens. Her blood pressure dipped to 85/19, then rose to 196/149, erratically fluctuating from exceedingly high to exceedingly low. Her temperature climbed past 105. Jenna was in septic shock . . . again.

Nurses smothered Jenna with blankets, trying to control her vibrating chills. The highest allowable amount of dopamine was injected into her to increase her blood pressure and avoid cardiac arrest, but even it had to be counteracted as her blood pressure shot back up again, well into stroke territory. Then, the unremitted vomiting began.

The nurses were in and out of Jenna's room for hours, doing everything to keep her from crashing. Jenna had seen it before. She knew when a child had more than one nurse assigned to them, and doctors were continuously outside their room, something was very wrong.

Kay was in the corner, wondering if she had horribly failed as a mother. She had let Jenna sit on the steps of her aunt and uncle's pool just a day before infection had taken over her body, fearing the chlorine had splashed into Jenna's lines.

As one nurse after another came speed walking into her room, Jenna looked over at her mom with fear in her eyes. She reluctantly questioned through labored whispers, "Am I in the worst shape of anyone on the unit?" Jenna knew once a patient hit that point, parents usually left the unit without their child.

A few days later, just one year and nine days post-transplant, the doctors huddled in a conference room across the hallway from her room. They contemplated whether or not to do emergency surgery to remove the port and Hickman. Surgery was very risky because she was extremely unstable. The doctors doubted she would make it through the procedures. At that time, the nurses explained to Kay she needed to call Ray and tell him to make his way back down to Duke.

With Jenna's numbers continuing to plunge and tensions at an all-time high, Ray stormed through the unit doors after beating Kay's record drive-time to Duke that had been set earlier in the week. He took one look at Jenna lying lifeless in the bed and could not stand the sight as flashbacks pierced through his head of Katie. Ray knew those nurses, the same ones who stood outside Katie's door during her final hours. Being the protective father he was, Incredible Hulk mode kicked in. He marched with a fury in his eyes across the hallway and beat his white-knuckled fists on the conference room doors. With tear-filled eyes and a cracked but fiery voice, Ray declared, "Y'all better figure out what to do because if something happens to my daughter, I am going to own this hospital!" Like legendary Atlanta Braves head coach Bobby Cox, he stormed off the bench, standing in a face-to-face ejection battle with the umpire after a horrible call, using whatever tactics necessary to overturn it. Ray had hit his breaking point. His patience was gone. He highly respected those doctors, and they were doing everything they could to keep Jenna alive, but they were not moving fast enough for him. And although Ray had said those words out of complete desperation for his daughter, security officers were perched at Jenna's door for the rest of the night.

Around 2:00 a.m., the decision had been made. The doctors wanted to take Jenna to the PICU. She would have her port accessed, which had not been done in eight months, have her Hickman taken out, and doctors would put in a temporary line. To Jenna and her parents' unbelief, all of this had to be completed without anesthesia. The doctors had no choice. Anesthesia was too risky with her levels fluctuating the way they were. Time was out, and they had to cure the infection immediately because there was a big possibility if they did not, Jenna would not see the sunrise.

Ray knew Jenna was barely making it, and he would not let them subject any more stress on her body. With his adrenaline still pumping, he fought the doctors, demanding, "Either a surgical team and anesthesia will be there, or my daughter will not!"

Jenna's blood pressure had now skyrocketed to a dangerously high level, and the potential of a stroke was massive. If they did those procedures without anesthesia, there was no way Jenna could have physically or mentally handled the pain and anxiety, making a stroke inevitable.

While the doctors collaborated, Jenna's blood pressure began to decrease. As suddenly as the infection started wreaking havoc on her body, her blood began to circulate at a more stable rate. The doctors hit the pause button and decided to wait until morning to remove the catheters. But if her blood pressure took a dive again and her fever rose, all negotiations were off the table, period. They would have to work fast to get everything taken out with no anesthesia.

The monitors beeped softly throughout the night. One nurse was always in her room, while others watched the monitors from outside. Ray and Kay prayed. At times Jenna would whisper to them to pray out loud. She needed to know that people at home were praying too. They were. Those same thousands of people who had prayed many days and nights for Jenna throughout her journey were back on their knees. Dozens from their church at home and thousands all over the world gathered in their sanctuaries throughout the night to pray for Jenna. There was even a large local church in Raleigh with a prayer room above their sanctuary and many people were in and out the entire night praying for Jenna. Those prayers were answered. Her blood pressure remained stable all night, in the low 30s, but stable.

The next afternoon Jenna was finally taken down for surgery, unable to make her scheduled time at 7:30 a.m. due to complications. Both catheters were removed, and a temporary line was placed. Both her port and her Hickman were tested for bacteria. Since Jenna abruptly went into a septic state a second time, it meant the antibiotics were not killing the bacteria, and the lines were most likely the source.

As the results came in from the catheters and lines, it was concluded she had four different bacterial infections, and there could be more. One of her doctors had never even heard of one of them, and the fourth bacteria had not even been identified yet. He said that was uncommon. They determined the bacteria started in her intestines but found a constant breeding ground in both her port and Hickman, sticking to the lines and making it impossible for the antibiotics to kill them. The bacteria could have also retired in another area of her body, her organs, bones, skin, anywhere. It was not probable, but with Jenna, doctors were always prepared for the unexpected.

After being back on 5200 for just a few days after surgery, Jenna was ready to be freed, but there was no option of going home now. Her spirit was broken; her body was broken. Jenna was trying to be strong, but the tears poured out. She had asked her mom many times that week if she was going to die. Jenna had never asked that question so often before. She was scared. So were her parents, the nurses and doctors, too.

Infectious disease experts came in and out to examine Jenna. They said three types of bacteria had been identified and there were three more that could not be. One of the three identified bacteria was exceptionally rare. It was also rare to have that many growing at once.

With breaks in the pain, doctors would jump at the chance to complete more tests. Jenna was sent to the radiologist to X-ray her big toe and have an MRI done on her right knee. It had been scheduled twice before, but she was too sick to do it. Even though Jenna was still weak and recovering from surgery, she was injected with pain medication and pushed through it.

The X-ray revealed her big toe was fractured but healing. It had been hurting for over two months by that point. Jenna did not remember stubbing it. She definitely didn't injure it while running. The only other explanation was the steroids weakened the bone enough to where climbing in and out of the recliner in the den had probably caused it.

Each day brought new medical mysteries. Kay had stepped out of the room to retrieve ice for a few minutes at one point, and when she got back to the room, Jenna was stiff and still, nearly paralyzed from pain in her back. She was having a reaction to one of the many drugs she was on. Shortly before that, the nurse had given her morphine and the G-CSF, a growth factor to boost her WBC. Jenna was then given a strong dose of morphine, but the pain kept increasing. The pain was at the base of her spinal column and went all the way up to her neck.

For over an hour, Jenna screamed in agony. Two milligrams of morphine were not enough, so two more were added, then two more, and then two more. By the end of that ordeal, Jenna had been given eight milligrams of morphine, none of which ever helped her sleep or completely knock out the pain. Now hooked up to even more monitors because of the high dose of morphine Jenna had just been given, the doctors agreed they would never give her G-CSF again.

43

STILL BEATING...BARELY

Zofran and Ativan could not stop Jenna's nausea. Doctors added more Phenergan and some Benadryl to hopefully put Jenna to sleep. What a mistake that turned out to be. Jenna's arms began flailing around in the air, jerking as if there was a punching bag she was aiming for. Her legs stiffened and shot straight out like someone who had been electrocuted. She had uncontrollable spasms, and her incoherent yelling echoed from the room and into the hallway. Jenna knew everything going on, but she just could not control it. Weirdly, she was not in any pain, but the freakish movements and outbursts were irrepressible. So, she and her mom continued to play Racko until the doctors were called in.

Doctors explained they had seen reactions to Phenergan before, but nothing that major. It was an extrapyramidal reaction, drug-induced involuntary movements, yet on a severe level. Jenna had taken Phenergan many times before but never had any negative responses. After a few other medications were tried, the jerks and outbursts subsided. Jenna would never be put on Phenergan again.

Although Jenna's body temperature and blood pressure were hovering around the normal range, she was still unable to eat or drink because of the constant puking. An assembly line of those infamous hospital buckets rotated in and out of Jenna's hands as her mom could not empty one quickly enough. None of the medicines offered any relief. If she did not start eating soon, she would be put back on TPN, receiving her nourishment from a bag of viscous yellow liquid.

It was imperative to find the source of her nausea, so a Contrast CT was ordered. The new lines in her chest were sensitive, so the thought of them pushing a large quantity of contrast liquid through them terrified Jenna. Instead, a nurse walked into her room with a large Styrofoam cup. Jenna knew what it was; the same chalky substance she had to gulp down, time and time again.

Jenna looked at the nurses, and her face told them exactly what she was thinking. "You have to be kidding me. You want me to drink this when every liquid you are putting through my IV is projecting out of my mouth like I'm some kind of water fountain?"

Nonetheless, for their entertainment, Jenna drank half the cup. To no avail, she could not keep it down. After waiting a few minutes to drink the rest, attempt number two occurred. Once again, Jenna could not keep it down. Needless to say, no CT was completed, and another one was ordered for later in the week. Jenna's only other option was nasogastric intubation if she could not keep the liquid down.

While she had her head in the bucket, Jenna saw a large white silhouette enter her room out of the corner of her eye. Yet another doctor in front of her, Jenna could tell by the look on his face whatever news he was bringing was not good. "You have AVN in your right knee," he said. Jenna was not shocked. She saw that coming. The pain in her knee felt much like the pain in her hip, but that did not make the punch to her morale hurt any less. There was much more ahead of her. Jenna did not even have time to process the news before forcing her head back into the bucket. Yet, another white lab coat entered her room when she stopped heaving. An orthopedic surgeon discussed the AVN in her hip and knee. After examining Jenna, he was concerned about how her ankle felt. He did not spare Jenna any heartache as the details of that disease swept away nearly all of her hope.

The disease was rough and progressive. There would be a lot of cutting, drilling to the hip, and joint replacements in the years to come. Jenna laid her head back down on the bed as the explanation continued. Tears filled her eyes as she realized, according to those doctors, her life would never be the same as it was before. As if she was not already suffering enough, now they were telling her to brace herself because there was a lot more to come over the course of her life. That was if she ever got out of the hospital. But Jenna clung to the only ounce of hope she had left. The doctors had been wrong before. Jenna had beaten the percentages in the past. Yes, it was usually in the wrong direction, but it could be different that time. Jenna could be a first but in a positive way.

A week or so later, nurses wheeled Jenna down to the radiology room. Desperately needing to find the source of the pain that consumed her body, the doctors ordered an ultrasound to check her abdomen, appendix, liver, and other organs. Jenna fought her stomach the entire way, trying not to throw up all that hard work she had just sipped down. As she was transferred onto the table that would slide underneath the massive humming metal donut, which all the kids on 5200 knew as the CT machine, Jenna overheard the nurses whispering to each other. "We are not supposed to move her even if she throws up," one murmured. With tears rolling down her face, Jenna gagged violently as if everything she swallowed was soon going to be all over the nurse's clean white uniform. She sat up quickly, reaching for the bucket next to her, but nothing came up. Jenna heaved, fighting so hard to push through, knowing the next option was a tube down her nose.

The ultrasound would soon reveal the culprit behind all the vomiting. Doctors told Jenna she had gallstones and sludge. "Sludge? Did they mean fat?" she thought. "Are they trying to tell me that underneath my watermelon belly, there is fat?" Jenna's gallbladder was distended and swollen from fat and bile accumulation. She thought back to when the nurses created a relay team to draw and then analyze her blood in the moments before it coagulated into a yellowish mixture from too much fat. Jenna's gallbladder was failing to regulate the fat content in her body, which could soon lead to fatal damage to her liver. It meant yet another surgery. She could not believe her ears.

Jenna sat there, barely shaking her head from side to side with a slight roll of her eyes. Frustrated, she wanted to look at the doctors and say, "I'm not some cadaver you're working on here! My heart is still beating . . . barely." At that point, Jenna did not care, as long as she made it out of that place by her birthday. She didn't care who was coming to visit her; she did not want to spend back-to-back birthdays on that unit.

Thinking the pain would not be so bad since her gallbladder was removed laparoscopically, Ray, Gabriel, and Hannah came down after surgery for a visit. That was precisely the wrong move. They all had to leave the room as Jenna squirmed, screaming in agony, clenching her arms around her stomach. Unable to take the sight, Ray thought it best to take Gabriel and Hannah back home. Before they walked out the door, Jenna grabbed Gabriel and Hannah's hands and told them she loved them and wanted them to stay. With a smirk on his face, Gabriel turned to their dad and said, "It's just the meds talking." He was wrong.

Jenna's pain level was so high it was literally taking her breath away. She did not want them to leave. She was afraid it would be the last time she would see them. The morphine was no longer working, and the nurses were doing what they could to keep her comfortable with her 100-plus-degree fever.

While throwing up old and new blood, Jenna could not believe she had only been in the hospital for three weeks. It felt like a lifetime, and she still had one more surgery to go. Jenna had only mustered up the strength to walk the hallway twice. Therefore, the writing fairy hadn't spread her encouraging messages and flowers over other patients' doors or on the whiteboard like before.

In between infrequent breaks from nausea or pain, Jenna would walk door to door, telling the kids she was praying for them and God loved them. As she passed one little boy's room, Jenna stopped and paused for a moment. That friend had been up on the unit a lot with her, fighting the same in-and-out-of-the-hospital battle. The one difference between them: he was on his third transplant. With small strokes of a dry erase marker, she wrote, "Praying for your third transplant to be the one!" Her hand shook as she wrote each word, knowing the young boy's time was precious.

44

THE WHITE COATS ARE COMING

Knowing Jenna needed encouragement, Hannah, Natalie, and a friend came to visit. Unlike many visits before, Jenna now feeling a little better, was riding bikes in the hall with Hannah and another little girl on the unit. They were not real bikes; they were kids' tricycles. But for the excitement it gave the normally bed-ridden Jenna, her tricycle might as well have been a crotch rocket.

All three girls thought they would play Charlie's Angels as they rode around on their bikes, squirting the nurses and doctors with foam soap canisters as they rode by. One boy joined in on the fun, sticking out his blue tongue—a side effect from his treatment medication—and spraying the ladies in dancing bear uniforms with a you-can't-catch-me spirit inside him. But the nurses were not going to go down without a fight. They pulled out syringes filled with water and started shooting them at Jenna, Hannah, and other parents on the unit. Foam and water covered everyone's uniforms, including Jenna's Big Bird gown. As she ducked around corners trying to avoid more foam to the face, there was something very different about the sights and sounds she was witnessing. It was not the beeping machines or cries of children in pain; it was laughter and smiles.

The doctors and nurses were usually the ones who, by no fault of their own, caused the pain. Those syringes usually carried medicines that made the children nauseated for hours, or blood they had just drawn from their red-capped Hickman lines. They did their best to provide them the pain relief they needed, but that day, they brought a different type of relief, laughter.

Jenna never really thought about the nurses' days, but they were also filled with pain and heartache. It may not be physical pain, but it was emotional. The nurses cared for the children, becoming a part of their lives for weeks and months, only to have them pass away while in their loving care. The doctors and nurses needed those foam-filled syringes of relief just as much as the children and parents did.

As Jenna turned to shoot the last of her ammo out of the soap canister, she could see her anesthesiologist walking towards her. Playtime had ended as the *White Coats* were coming, a nickname her mom had given to all the doctors that had been camped outside Jenna's door for the past three weeks. He was there to discuss Jenna's final surgery, replacing the Hickman, insisting she would not be in as much pain as she was after the gallbladder surgery. She did not put much faith into words those days, so instead of focusing on the negatives of surgery, Jenna continued to enjoy the small outlets of positivity around her.

Jenna met up with some of her *cellmates*, a nickname they all called each other. The nickname had nothing to do with the lack of freedom in the atmosphere on that unit, rather their desire in wanting their bodies to make new cells, making the chant "Grow cells, grow!" 5200's motto.

As the sun came up the following day, Jenna's body was prepped for surgery. Three surgeries, three times being put to sleep, all done in a mere two weeks. The surgeons even looked at her as if they thought, "Um . . . this is a little much."

Her Hickman was replaced with no complications. Afterward, with no room in the recovery area, Jenna lay on the surgery table. Her eyes were still bound tightly shut as she waited for the effects of the sleepy medicine to wear off. Her parents usually stood over her when Jenna awoke from surgeries, but they were not allowed back with her at that time.

All Jenna could hear was the minute hand on the clock ticking as her eyes were shut. Five minutes passed, then 10, then 20, then 30. Recovery was taking much longer than expected. Something was wrong.

Her eyes slowly blinked once, then again as she woke up from the anesthesia. Suddenly, the pain poured in. It was not some gentle mist falling from a pale gray sky. No, it was a monsoon. Ray and Kay were rushed back to the operating room to try and calm Jenna down. The pain was so intense she could not control her movements as she wailed in agony. Jenna begged and begged for more pain medicine. She wanted so desperately to go back asleep and escape the torment. The doctors stressed there was no way she could be given more medicine. She had been given so much already any more could cause her to stop breathing.

Jenna had been on so many narcotics for the last few weeks they were no longer effective for her. She had been given the cocktail of all cocktails, but she still lay there in indescribable pain. The transplant team was called in. It was their decision on what else she could be given. Their answer was enough Benadryl to knock her out. Jenna could sleep for now, but that could not erase the reality of what she would face when she woke up.

The doctors knew it was not good for Jenna's body to go under anesthesia constantly. The pain her body was enduring had now become too much for the medicines to handle. They were saying she could not take another surgery like the last one. However, the reality was she would have another in just over a month, and that one was supposed to be the mother of all previous ones. Until then, she was given the green light to go home. Jenna could not walk off the unit without stopping at each door, writing something encouraging like many times before. She had lost count at that point. There was no place like home, but 5200 had been her home for the majority of the past year. So, she hugged her nurses as they threw the confetti in the air and walked out the wooden double doors, yet again, hearing them latch shut.

Only for a Moment:

ACTS OF KINDNESS

It's hard for friends and family members to know what to do when someone is going through a trial like cancer. What can you do?

Jenna's Mema and Papa drove Kay and her down to Duke for many of their appointments, spending many hours waiting with them in the clinic. A young girl who barely knew Jenna spent her weekends raising money for Jenna's fund.

It doesn't matter your age, you've been given the time, so make the most of it. Visit a bone marrow unit, nursing home, pediatric floor, or a homeless shelter. Find any place where people are suffering and spend time with them.

Jenna had many visitors when she was hospitalized. Some carolers came and sang Christmas songs in the hall. Too sick to get up and see them, her mom would hold open her door so she could hear them. A group of people came by dressed as the cast of Star Wars, and the NHL Carolina Hurricanes hockey team came by to offer a little joy to the children.

Anything you can do for someone going through tough times means so much, even if it's just a simple act of kindness.

Take a breath, keep breathing, and keep going.

45

DRILL BITS AND WHAT?

Jenna celebrated her 13th birthday at home, but it was different. Last year, a famous TV star came to see Jenna, walked the hospital halls with her to meet some of her friends and their families, gave her royal treatment, and still called her on a near-weekly basis to check in with her.

That year, although out of the hospital, Jenna could no longer get up from playing games on the floor without the assistance of someone or something else. She was learning to be a pretty good butt-scooter, using what little arm strength she had for pushing down and pulling up on objects. Her left hip and right knee were getting worse by the day. With scar tissue already building inside, the seriousness of AVN was escalating. If the disease progressed to a higher stage, the percentage of the procedure being a success was much smaller. The issue was not that Jenna was dealing with pain in two different joints, but rather those two joints were on opposite legs, leaving her no good side to put the majority of her weight on. Walking wasn't an option any longer. Preserving the joints as long as possible meant she would be confined to a wheelchair everywhere she went. What little independence she had was now gone.

Jenna had tasted a piece of freedom just a few months before. She was starting to go back to church and be a part of the youth group, hanging out with kids her age. Jenna tried her best to keep up with them, playing games with them just to end up falling to the ground, unable to get up on her own. No matter how much spirit she had in her, her body could not physically do it.

It had been a year since Jenna lost Katie, and it still felt like it had just happened the day before. Katie's parents, Larry and Gina, wanted to be with Jenna's family that weekend. Even though they were not blood-related, they had become family, and Katie had become like a sister to Jenna.

The families went to church together that morning. Jenna desperately wanted to show them just how much Katie meant to her. Though her voice and legs were weak, she slowly stood to her feet among a silent congregation and sang a song describing the life Katie and Jenna had been destined to live. She read a poem that honored the children who never walked through the hallway lined with everyone under a cloud of confetti.

Jenna had lost a piece of herself the day Katie went to be with Jesus. She thought of all the other children, some close friends, and others just faces she passed in the hallway. Just like it had been every time before, saying goodbye to the people who visited Jenna was emotionally taxing on her. That same emotion stirred up inside when it was time for Larry and Gina to go, and life got back to her normal routine.

Hip surgery lurked over Jenna's head. The house was prepped for her recovery. Ray built a ramp from the front porch, down the stairs to the sidewalk, and halfway down the sidewalk to the driveway. Woodworking, just another skill in his repertoire. Usually, people going through that specific surgery would use crutches for six months post-surgery, but Jenna's only option was a wheelchair. Her right knee could not take the weight of her body, so for the next six months, Jenna would be stuck in a wheelchair. Her bed was moved downstairs to their family living area, knowing transferring her to and from her wheelchair daily would be challenging enough without adding stairs into the mix.

There were many obstacles to come from that surgery. Most patients only had a four-day, post-surgery hospital stay. With Jenna's track record, the doctors said at least a week. The disease had progressed further in the few weeks she was home. Ray and Kay were told even if the surgery worked, Jenna would need a hip replacement in 10-15 years.

Nevertheless, on October 3, 2000, just over a year post-transplant, her dad walked beside Jenna as her bed was once again rolled into the operating room. He had taken that walk with Jenna many times before, calming her down until she went to sleep, but that time he was not quite prepared for what he was about to see when they stepped through the swinging doors. The operating room looked like the construction site at their house just a week earlier as Ray built the ramp. Lying on metal trays next to the operating table were gadgets labeled drill bits with handheld drills lying next to them. Prongs, knives, screws, cable cutters, and wiring lined the table. And then he saw it, the one last tool.

As Ray glanced around one of the nurses, a shiny silver saw caught his eye like the ruby diamond Aladdin's Abu could not keep his little paws from grabbing in the Cave of Wonders. He looked at the nurse, and with apprehension in his voice, he asked, "You're going to use that?" She simply smiled and nodded.

A saw used for sawing through wood would now be used for cutting through about five inches of his daughter's fibula. A screw would be placed in her ankle to help support her lower leg where the bone would be removed to use in her hip. The drill would be used for multiple stages of that surgery, one being the hole they would bore into her hip. Then they would cut through the veins and arteries to supply the blood from her hip to the grafted bone in the hope the newly-engrafted bone would live. It would all take four hours. Ray had walked into many procedures and surgeries, waiting until Jenna had fallen asleep to slip out before the surgeons began cutting. That time, slipping out of Jenna's view, he left early, unable to bear the sight.

Within three days of surgery, the orthopedist was ready to take off the bandages that covered her lower leg and hip, remove all four drainage tubes, and then re-bandage it. There was no time to waste. Jenna needed to start physical therapy. She pushed herself, something not uncommon for her. If they said it could not be done, Jenna wanted to prove them wrong. So she put as much effort as she could into therapy, counting down the days when she would get the green light to go home. The physical therapist wanted to get her walking comfortably on crutches around her house, but that was it.

As the therapy intensified, so did the pain. Jenna was finally given Dilaudid, a drug five times stronger than morphine, and that didn't even take off the edge. Just hanging her leg over the side of the bed felt as if she had been upside down for days, all the blood leaving her legs and rushing to her head. With her leg tingling and hip throbbing, she knew the only obstacle in her way from going home was the pain itself.

Jenna had a tough time learning to walk on crutches. As all her weight was put on her right knee, shooting pains would cause her to want to put her left foot down, something that could cause the hip engraftment to fail. With the muscles in Jenna's arms more like jelly, she could only do very few short walks. She had barely used her arms for over a year, and coupled with the steroids, there was no wonder she could hardly hold herself up. Despite that, she needed to get use to the crutches because her only other option was a walker. Jenna was already looking like her 40-year-old dad, and she was not about ready to let her 75-year-old, golf-playing Papa look better walking than she did.

Apart from two weeks of grueling physical therapy, for the first time ever, Jenna left the hospital on time. There were no setbacks, and no complications. She was finally heading home.

Jenna was not mentally prepared for what was to come. The whole ordeal had taken away all her independence, not just the cancer treatment but everything that followed. She had to depend on so many other people throughout the last two years that it would seem to be a natural ordeal for her, but it was not. Yes, she was used to someone accompanying her to the bathroom, wiping her with a sponge in bed, and helping her to other patients' rooms to be an uplifting spirit. Still, something about what was occurring now seemed a little more intense to her. Jenna couldn't walk on her own. It was dangerous. Since she could not put any weight on her left leg, it all had to go on the right one. Her right knee was just not strong enough for all the pivoting and bending that was now solely required of it. Jenna did not anticipate a wheelchair during all of this, but unfortunately, it had become her new best friend. It was now a necessity.

46

HERE COMES SANTA CLAUS

Jenna wasn't a typical teenage girl. She did not possess some incredible athletic ability. She wasn't freakishly smart or blessed with a unique artistic ability. Nonetheless, she still stood out from her peers, as Jenna started her eighth-grade year after doing very little schoolwork for most of the previous two years, going straight from fifth-grade math to eighth-grade Pre-Algebra. She couldn't fathom the days ahead when she would finally walk down the school hallways to her next class, filled with 25 other students, healthy kids who walked, talked, and acted just like her. That was not her life. And from the look of the incision on her leg, it would not be her life for quite some time.

A local orthopedic doctor began to carefully unpeel the adhesive tape lining the gauze bandages protecting the two incisions on the outside of Jenna's left leg. One incision reached from her ankle to the bottom of her knee, and the other a horseshoe-shape, her good luck charm, at her hip. Just as the doctor lifted back the bandages, everyone in the room paused and a look of oh my goodness, overwhelmed their faces as the gaping incision allowed everyone to see the inside of her leg.

Jenna looked at her mom and, in turn, she looked over at the doctor. The steroids Jenna had been on were not allowing her to heal properly. It was almost 20 days post-surgery, and the incision should have been closed by that point. The three layers of stitches underneath her skin seemed to be holding everything into place. So the incision was cleaned, new Steri-Strips were placed back over it, and Jenna was back on the road to recovery.

With Halloween just around the corner, Jenna would step slowly into life as a regular child. For the first time, Jenna was going to get to buy a store-bought costume.

Usually, Kay made their costumes. Zachary and Gabriel were always hunters, borrowing much of their design from Ray. Jenna and Hannah would alternate between princesses and puppy dogs. Knowing Jenna looked and felt more like a Pekinese-Bulldog mix breed than a princess, Kay thought it would be nice for her to get a store-bought costume for once, but Jenna didn't want that. All she wanted was a little piece of home.

Kay wet Jenna's hair to make her curls more definitive rather than her new look of the soft side of a Velcro pad. Jenna placed two little barrettes on both sides of her head, put on a short-sleeve shirt, gently pulled her jean overalls up, carefully avoiding the two fresh scars on her leg and the Hickman protruding from her chest, placed a mask and eyeglasses over her face, and tucked saline syringes into her pockets. Although she decided to rock out socks and slippers instead of neon yellow tennis shoes, Jenna was ready to go as her heroine, Dr. K.

Dr. K was much more than just a doctor. She was kind but firm. Much like a guard dog at a junkyard, she fought so hard to protect her patients. To say she cared for them would be a vast understatement. With only a few hours of sleep a night, she researched and studied to find cures for those children. Her sole mission: to keep kids alive.

Ray and Kay took turns wheeling Jenna down the streets of Aunt Cindy's neighborhood. Hannah would walk up to the houses, knock on the front door, and say, "Trick or Treat!" with two bags in hand. With puzzled looks on the homeowner's faces, Hannah would point back to the rest of her family standing in the driveway and explain, "This bag is for my sister." As Jenna watched her little sister go from house to house, she could see it was just as unusual for Hannah as it was for herself. Everything in Hannah's life was always centered on Jenna. "What does Jenna want? What can we do to make Jenna feel better?" was a constant thought on Hannah's mind.

Many days, Jenna would sit with a bag or bucket close to her side, unable to reach the bathroom quick enough when she would belch chemical-laden liquid from her mouth that would forever leave stains on the bedroom carpets. Her body ached all over. Kay asked if she had ever had a day without pain. With no hesitation, Jenna responded, "No."

Jenna asked her mom if her gallbladder could grow back, thinking to herself that was for sure the reason she felt poorly all the time. But the reality was, it was just all a part of the healing process. Weirdly, it was hope more than anything. And more hope was just around the corner as the most wonderful time of the year was ringing in.

For Christmas, Jenna would be going back to 5200, not as a cellmate but as an inspiration. Knowing how hard it was to be up on that floor during Christmas, Jenna and her mom wanted to do something special for the kids and their families. With the help of many stores like Toys R Us, Zany Brainy, Family Christian Bookstore, Cracker Barrel, Hallmark, Ben Franklin, their family's church, and many more, they were able to purchase all sorts of fun gifts for the children and bake fresh cookies for the parents. The family stuffed the gifts into two vans because one could not hold the presents, Jenna's wheelchair, and all of them.

Jenna rolled onto the unit, sporting a Santa hat covering a somewhat impressive amount of hair. She may not have been the perfect uplifting picture of life on the outside for a transplant patient, but she was living, and that was hope enough. Jenna was also able to spend Christmas with her whole family, something most, if not all, of those children wouldn't be able to do.

One by one, Jenna would roll up to their doors. She had been on the other side of the door so many times before. Being the girl looking in from the glass window was new to her. Jenna knocked on the door of one boy's room who had been up on the unit for two years straight, fighting right alongside her since the beginning of her whole ordeal. Jenna could not even begin to complain about her multiple long-term stays when her complications were nothing compared to his.

Smiles and tears came from both patients and parents, seeing Jenna return as a survivor. One year ago, Jenna was in that same battle, spending Christmas away from her family, only wanting the pain to disappear. Most kids, too sick to talk, just laid and played with their new toys on their beds. But the parents wanted details.

One mom asked how long Jenna was on the unit, a common question asked to a transplant survivor. Kay paused, trying to think of an answer that would not scare her. A nurse walking by smiled at the mom and said, "Which time?" Needless to say, that was true for them, but for that mom, whose son had just begun the transplant process, a state of more confusion flooded her mind.

Jenna and Kay dodged the bombardment of intimate questions as much as possible because those patients and parents needed encouragement. Jenna was the one on the other side of the window, now looking in when before she could only see out, but they did not need to know there was probably more to come. That life was scary enough as it was. There was no need to tell of all the bumps and forks in the road.

It was hard to fathom being able to leave the hospital that day. The previous year, Jenna woke up on Christmas morning to Santa standing over her hospital bed and her looking at her mom, completely annoyed. Now she could revel in her dad's fresh seafood meal he fixed only once a year at Christmas time. Actually, Jenna had already started eating some steamed spiced shrimp when her mom, in a panicked slow-motion fashion, smacked it out of her hand. She was left to only enjoy the savory smell of the shrimp and buttery fried oysters because of her weakened immune system. A few tears fell, but that was progress.

Those kids on 5200 were still at stage one, and she was leaving that day, going home to spend Christmas in her own bed, thinking of her grandpa's Christmas trains chugging under the tree as she drifted off into her dream world, a momentary dream that would abruptly transform into a nightmare.

47

ADAPTING

Chugggaa, chuga, chugga, choo . . . putt, putt, putt, putttt.
The propellers slowly started spinning faster and faster, with Jenna only wishing they were the same propellers she had seen a few weeks prior at the Red Baron Air show her family had been invited to. They had eaten more Red Baron pizzas than anyone that year. Well, Jenna had at least. It was her number one steroid-induced craving for breakfast, lunch, dinner, and meals in the small hours of the morning.

Yet, the thumping and buzzing sounds of the aircraft were not a part of a grand show. It was the cruel reenactment of a helicopter filled with medical personnel. Only one day after Christmas in 2000, the whirring med-flight helicopter flew Jenna to Duke. Her fever spiked, her blood pressure plummeted, and chills covered her body. She was in septic shock . . . again.

Steroids were given. Jenna's body was still not making natural steroids to fight off viral infections, and she would be at risk of going septic until she started making them. The diastolic number had once again dropped to below 20, a level most people did not wake up from. Much like a cat with nine lives, Jenna was running out. After a short stay at Duke, Jenna was sent home, only to be reminded a new year didn't necessarily mean a new life.

Only a few days after coming home from Duke, Jenna was admitted to their local hospital after contracting two viruses. Instead of playing in the snow that covered the frozen field beside their house, the only snowflakes she touched were the beautifully-colored, hand-cut paper ones Jenna and Aunt Cindy hung from the four white walls of her room to get her mind off the constant vomiting and diarrhea.

Through it all, Jenna kept climbing. In reality, she could see the mountaintop more clearly now, but occasionally, the wheelchair she was sitting in made the roll up the slippery snow-covered ridge a bit more treacherous. The physical pain was something she would just have to deal with. Jenna was looking forward to the new adventures fitting in as a teenager would bring, starting high school, making friends, keeping score at Gabriel's baseball games, but it carried new emotions and struggles.

Jenna had not been out in public much other than church and Shoney's on kids-eat-free night. She had interacted with ten or so teenagers in her church youth group, but those were kids Jenna had grown up with her entire life. They had prayed for her and were familiar with her progress over the past three years. But as Jenna got out of her mom's car in front of the school on eighth-grade graduation day in June, Jenna had to face a different unknown, the classmates she had left behind three long years ago.

Jenna hobbled down the halls and through the door to the back of the auditorium, one crutch at a time. She sat there in a near-empty room where, in just a minute, 500 of her classmates would turn the corner, walk right past her, and fill the seats. Technically, they were her classmates, but Jenna didn't have much of a connection to anyone anymore. Just weeks before the ceremony, Rhonda had reluctantly informed Jenna her elementary school sweetheart now had a new girlfriend. "How could he? Just because he has not seen me in two years does not mean he should move on without me." Jenna naively thought.

The bustle of a crowd of hundreds of middle school graduates walking down the corridors became louder. The last time any of them would have seen Jenna was when a local news station produced a TV special on her bumpy recovery, and many teachers showed it in class to students, just one of many supportive gestures Bailey Bridge Middle School did for Jenna during her cancer journey. She was no longer that five-foot, 150-pound, mustachioed bald creature. She had lost most of the weight put on by the steroids, and her hair was thick, black, and curly, just long enough to wear clips and headbands. It was not much but the most Jenna had since she was 11 years old.

But seeing everyone in person would be different. Jenna would not have a TV screen protecting her from the odd stares or confused looks that would be beaming back at her. She thought to herself, "If it goes really badly, I could just pull up my mask over my eyes to hide the embarrassment."

One by one, Jenna's entire eighth-grade graduating class poured into the auditorium. A few of them waved, and many of them stared. Jenna could not blame them. Many people had stared before, but this time it was her friends staring.

Jenna thought they stared because they had just seen a girl who had survived a bear attack and did not know what to say, but that was okay. After living in a bubble for almost three years, it was as if a pin had just poked it, causing it to deflate in a crumpled heap around her. She struggled with the fact life had continued without her. She had missed so much, and everyone had moved on and grown older.

Looking around the packed auditorium, Jenna saw nothing but kids her age eagerly waiting for the summer to begin, launching them into new adventures, filled with social and scholastic challenges, high school. It was as if she had been transported to a foreign land where she did not speak the native language or know the local customs.

Jenna had not been able to wear the cutest, trendiest clothes like everyone else; dresses did not come in an adult men's, extra-large. The popular trends she knew before were not in anymore. Her fellow graduates listened to different music, watched TV shows she was unfamiliar with, and played new games foreign to her. Jenna knew if there had been a most-changed-since-sixth-grade superlative, she would have won it, and not for any glorious reasons either.

In only three months, Jenna would have to learn how to be a teenager before walking through a new set of wooden double doors, with much larger hallways and way more than 16, single-patient rooms. She would be walking the halls without IV lines coming out of her nightgown or an insulin pump draped over her shoulders. The only things she would carry would be colorful purses filled with pens and pencils. Girls' faces would be covered with make-up to hide their adolescent blemished faces. Jenna's face would be covered by a mask to protect her from germs and the five o'clock shadow on her upper lip. If that pesky mustache was not tamed soon, she would look like Tom Selleck, a slight exaggeration.

That summer was filled with a surgery to remove the last six-inch Hickman line protruding from Jenna's chest; a piece of her was gone forever. Her legs wobbled as she learned how to use them again after eight months of relying on a wheelchair and crutches. Looking much like a newborn fawn, she learned to balance herself on weak, brittle legs. Jenna pushed herself to be involved in whatever activities Zachary, Gabriel, and Hannah took part in.

She would sit behind home plate during Hannah's softball practices, not squatting like a normal catcher, but rather, she sat Indian-style with her butt flat on the ground. If the ball was pitched in her vicinity, she would catch it and throw it back to the pitcher. A 15-year-old boy stood behind her, protecting her from any stray balls.

Jenna would keep the score at Gabriel's baseball games and was the announcer at Zachary's American Legion baseball games anytime she could stand the heat of the press box with a big box fan sitting by the door. "The shortstop hits a line drive down the first-base line. It's Israaaelll Gonnnnzagaaaa for the double!" she would shout into the microphone. The crowd clapped and filled the stands with feel-good laughter from Jenna's announcer's voice. Well, everyone except for Gabriel, who was slouching down in his seat as if he had no clue who she was.

It was hard for Jenna to keep up as she did not have the same stamina most 13-year-olds had. She went to those games and practices, church activities for the teenagers, and family events with broken toes that just happened while she lay in bed asleep because her bones were so brittle, they broke on command. Her knees would take turns giving out as she climbed in and out of their family minivan to ride to the next endeavor.

At times, Jenna's knees would lock up. A piece of dead bone would lodge itself in the joint, causing her knee to bend at a 90-degree angle up at her chest. Ray would eventually massage it back into normal position. Jenna did not want to be the weak one who could not keep up. She was not in the hospital anymore, so she had to do what everyone else was doing to be the normal one.

Only her family knew Jenna's constant pain because they were there at night to see her in tearful agony. Gabriel would tell her, "You just need a whole new body." He was pretty much right. Her brothers and Hannah would watch Jenna struggle to get up off the floor or out of the minivan. It took strength in her hips, knees, and ankles to do those things, something she did not realize until she was stripped of that strength. But Jenna had to build back the strength because ninth grade was just about to begin. After three years of not being in school, both Bailey Bridge Middle School and Manchester High School administrations allowed Jenna to graduate despite only completing half of her sixth-grade year and a minimal hours of classes since then. They may not have known this at the time, but the kindness given by those two administrations to allow Jenna to *skip* middle school only meant that despite all Jenna's setbacks from the cancer, being held back in school would not be one of them. With this accommodation given, Jenna knew the stamina she would need to go back to school, would take more grit and determination than simply going to ball games and swimming in the pool all summer long.

48

THE NAKED COWBOY

Just before 10:00 a.m. the day after Labor Day, Jenna stepped through the front doors of Manchester High School. The halls were empty, and students were waiting in their classrooms for the bell to ring for the next period to begin. Jenna was about to enter an English classroom for the first time in three years. Although she would only take two one-and-a-half-hour classes, instead of the standard four a day, it would be tough for her in more ways than one.

Known colloquially as a city within a city, Manchester had nearly 3,000 students in it, 550 of which were in Jenna's ninth-grade class alone. Jenna felt as if she stood out like the Naked Cowboy on the streets of New York City. All eyes focused on her as she left classes early to avoid super-crowded hallways because she was more apt to fall if someone bumped into her. Her muscles and bones were too weak for her to carry books, so they were placed in each classroom she attended. She even had a second set waiting for her at home. Jenna couldn't do P.E. She could barely walk, let alone run the mile alongside her classmates.

Teachers were prepped about Jenna's needs, but the students were not. That made her feel different. Students were typically scolded for putting their feet on the seat at their desks. Jenna would look around, making sure no one was watching, and slowly lift her knees to her chest. Sometimes she could tell her classmates were looking at her, thinking, "That isn't fair. Why can she do that, but no one else can?" Yet, if she kept them bent at a 90-degree angle for too long, they would lock up, and then she would have to sit in even more embarrassment trying to massage the bone back in place.

The second bell of the school day had rung. If she had not felt out of place yet, there was no denying it as Jenna entered art class and sat down at the rectangular, wooden six-person table.

One by one, students filled the empty chairs around her. Jenna sat quietly as they all shared their life stories and fun summer adventures. After each had taken their turn, one boy looked over at her and said, "Well, we've told our life stories. What's yours?" Thinking to herself, "I hope the teacher starts talking soon because I don't think we have enough time," Jenna just said, "Uh, there's not much to tell." She did not want to scare everyone off the first day of school or be known as the class storyteller, so she had to fib just a little.

Socially, Jenna didn't belong. She did not know how to communicate with teenagers. She looked at them talking about their boyfriends and girlfriends and their weekend plans, and she would think to herself, "Wow, it would be nice to fit in." Jenna could not hold a conversation in that new world she was in. For years, she had barely spoken, and now she was expected to have a conversation about topics unfamiliar to her. So for the rest of the year, Jenna just went to class, waited in the distance as her brothers hung with the cool crowd in the lunchroom at the end of the day, and dodged the, "What's your story?" questions as best she could.

In so many ways, Jenna was more grown-up than all of those kids because she already had to face the harsh realities of life, but in other ways, she was years behind. Jenna didn't know the social norms. She did not understand it was out of the ordinary to ask someone to turn down the music in their car because there was cussing in the rap song playing on the radio—yeah, sorry about that, Wes.

Jenna would watch her brothers holding conversations with their friends while she sat by herself across the lunchroom, thinking, "How do they do that so effortlessly?" Occasionally peaking over their shoulders, with a concerned look on their faces, her brothers wanted to protect Jenna. But this was something she would have to learn on her own. She couldn't hide the fact her life had changed tremendously as her elementary sweetheart walked by her one of those afternoons. After seeing her, in all sincerity, he went home and told his mom, "She looks like she has been through a lot." Jenna couldn't hide it. She looked and acted differently than she used to. That was apparent, as she didn't realize it was unusual to walk in front of a camp full of kids and adults and announce she had been bald longer than any other guy had in that room, such an embarrassing story to admit.

Throughout the first couple of years of high school, Jenna still lived in an alternate world, missing school because of random colds or viruses. Most people with a working immune system would be able to fight them off, but she could not, and it would knock her out of school for a week or two. But in that new world of hers, Jenna quickly realized it did not revolve around her. Life did not stop if she was sick with the flu, and she was not the only one who had to deal with tragedy.

Jenna understood that very well after turning on the TV, when she woke up on September 11, 2001, fully expecting to celebrate her 14th birthday. She watched the tragedy unfolding on the East Coast, knowing thousands of kids would now be without one or both of their parents, and hundreds of men and women without their spouses, brothers, sisters, aunts, uncles, and grandparents. Lives were forever changed.

Five short days later, Gabriel was involved in a four-wheeler accident leaving him pinned underneath a 1,000-pound recreational vehicle. Just 15 years old, he had broken two ribs and three vertebrae in his back. After a serious surgery, it would be months of pain and therapy before he would walk normally again.

Later that semester, during Zachary's senior year of baseball, he contracted a bad case of mono. His shot for Division 1 universities to scout him was no longer an option. For three weeks, he joined Gabriel and Jenna at the kitchen table for homebound schooling.

There was more to life than just what lingered throughout the halls of 5200. As Jenna watched and heard the smiles, laughter, tears, and fears of the people around her, she knew the world was bigger than she ever remembered. Although standing on the mound as starting pitcher for the softball team was out of the question, Jenna joined clubs and got involved with theater outside of school. But just because she was doing those activities did not mean her life wasn't still haunted by her past experiences and the side effects that came along with them.

Jenna had many days when she would wake up in the morning puffy-faced from throwing up constantly during the night, which developed into a deep raspy chest cough. But as soon as she caught a breather, she would slip on her baggy jeans and hobble to the minivan to be taken to school.

Jenna had lost a lot of weight from only eating one meal a day. She only weighed 79 pounds, and quite frankly, she looked pitiful.

The good thing was, she still lacked the realization of social norms, so she did not know those baggy jeans were not really *in* for girls in the early 2000s. Jenna did not want to miss anything, so she did it all, anything and everything she was permitted by the doctors to do.

Jenna completed her ninth-grade year, then attended her first full day of school in five years as she started her sophomore year. She leaped for joy later in the year when she received a C+ in history on her report card. She had not taken any history classes since the beginning of sixth grade and had no clue what the teacher was talking about for the majority of the year. She would look around the room at the other students intently taking notes, thinking to herself, "Columbus who? We did what in the Civil War? Wait, there are still 50 states, right?"

Lip reading was something she became an expert in doing. Midway through tenth grade, Jenna fought severe ear infections that had limited her hearing. Tubes were put in to eliminate the problem.

The post-transplant years were filled with doctor visits to try and figure out why Jenna's immune system was not back to normal. She would cry herself to sleep at the end of the day because her body was so worn out, but three years after her transplant, she defied the odds. Doctors said she probably would not grow any taller, but she did. She now stood at a firm 5'2", was getting her learner's permit, making money by babysitting two children, and feeling like she was accomplishing something. She was living her life like there was no tomorrow. She knew the real possibility of there being no tomorrow, so with the time and freedom she was given, she would live, and she would keep living like tomorrow was never promised.

49

WISHES DO COME TRUE

On a hot and humid Virginia summer day, two ladies dressed in fun, vibrant colors walked up the front steps of Jenna's house and knocked on the door. Kay walked from the kitchen down the hallway and answered. Greeted with big smiles, she quickly called Jenna to the front door. With stuffed animals and balloons filling their arms, Jenna smiled at what was printed on their purple-colored T-shirts in big, white letters: Make-A-Wish. It was a scene she did not think would replay, but there she was reminiscing on a day that occurred years ago.

Four years ago, when just beginning her long, cancer journey, a hematologist referred Jenna to the foundation. Jenna knew only children with life-threatening diseases got those wishes. Even though Make-A-Wish no longer defined its recipients as children with fatal diseases, it did not shake the stigma that came with it. For months, Kay could never bring herself to return their phone calls because she knew she would be facing yet another harsh reality of death and pain. Regardless, Make-A-Wish wanted to make Jenna's dreams come true.

They wanted her to think big. She could sail across the oceans on a pirate ship, be sprinkled with pixie dust, and fly away to Neverland or join the Seven Dwarfs as they searched the caves for buried treasure while singing, "Hi, Ho, Hi, Ho!" Well, no, it wasn't really like that. They were not her fairy godmothers, but there to grant a wish just the same.

As Jenna sat in the rocking chair on the front porch, beaten and weak from the effects of the chemo, there was nothing she wanted more than to have them to wave a magic wand and transport her away to the grand duke's ball at the king's castle. Although they could not grant her glass slippers, they could give her something that would excite her just as much.

They told Jenna she could choose an item or a trip somewhere in the United States for her family to enjoy. She did not have to think long; she knew what she wanted. Jenna wanted what she played with on the floor while Natalie and her sat in the room with the steeple-high ceilings just a couple months previous, a horse; not a plush stuffed animal, a real one.

Jenna had grown up watching shows like *Bonanza*, *The Big Valley*, and other cowboy shows and movies starring John Wayne and Clint Eastwood. She watched them with her dad and Grandpa and fell in love with Little Joe Cartwright's white and black spotted paint horse, Cochise. Knowing the comforts her dog Maggie had brought her every time she was able to make those short visits home, Jenna knew a pet horse would greatly add to the certain joy that only animals could bring her.

Unfortunately, it did not take long for Make-A-Wish to deny that request. Liability would prevent her from getting her own paint horse. Kay sighed in relief as she knew just how much upkeep a horse was. But Ray would have promised Jenna the moon if it meant she would feel better as he watched his little girl slouched over as she walked, stopping at times just to catch her breath. So, Ray promised his daughter her very own Cochise. Kay nudged him as to say, "What in the world are you doing?" Jenna's grandpa didn't help matters when he promised the saddle and everything else needed to help his granddaughter become her very own Victoria Barkley.

Both Kay and Ray got their own wishes fulfilled a couple of years later when their neighbors across the field added horses to their land. Ray was off the hook, and Kay was excited she would no longer be on horse duty. But it was back to the drawing board for Jenna to choose something that would be possible for Make-A-Wish to provide.

It was Jenna's creative mind, which she was blessed to keep with all the trauma, that soon brought forth another brilliant idea. On one of her many in-stay visits there at their home hospital, Kay and Jenna spent the day talking about all the possibilities she could wish for. Trying to give Jenna something to fight for, they took a rare moment of being nausea-free and headed outside to get some fresh air.

Just down the hall was a door that led to a world filled with imagination. Really, it was a steel door that led to the rooftop of the building, but for Jenna, that rooftop was a place where her imagination could run freely. As she looked around at all the steel pipes and vents protruding from the building, she saw it.

The pipes and vents had created unique shapes that outlined the center of the rooftop. The tiny rocks were perfectly manicured to generate the picture floating around in Jenna's head. It was the shape of a mermaid lagoon. Beautiful waterfalls, with large rocks bulging from beneath the crystal blue waters, were part of the picturesque, Peter Pan view in front of Jenna. She had it! She knew exactly what she wanted for her wish; an in-ground pool shaped just like a mermaid's lagoon. Jenna knew a pool would last forever and was something her brothers and Hannah could enjoy too.

She pictured the day when she would have no lines projecting from her chest and she could swim and play Sharks and Minnows, Marco Polo, and Categories in the pool in their backyard. But as magical blue waters filled her head, the rain clouds quickly scattered above, and lightning struck. She was swiftly ordered out of her imaginary pool with a whopping no from Make-A-Wish. Once again, liability reasons would prevent Jenna from getting her wish. But leave it to the man on the white horse, Jenna thought. Her dad also promised her a pool. That time, he was able to keep his promise when their great Aunt Ethel left money to build it. After fighting cancer herself, she wanted to give Jenna something to look forward to when the sun would finally shine down on her face again.

Now, after four years of battling that horrific disease and everything that came with it, those ladies from Make-A-Wish were back to grant her wish. Although she had to be re-approved by her medical team at Duke, a resounding yes from Make-A-Wish and Dr. K meant Jenna and her family were off to a fun-filled week at Disney World.

Everything was all so magically decorated. A large red mushroom-topped carousel, an ice cream stand with a gigantic banana split hovering over the ordering window, and, of course, a putt-putt course. The one there was even better than the one in Myrtle Beach; it had Jurassic Park-sized dinosaurs hovering over the players. There were also 96 colorful storybook cottages straight out of the fairytale *Hansel and Gretel* for Make-A-Wish recipients and their families to stay in at the *Give Kids the World Village* in Orlando, Florida.

Their family spent four days gallivanting around Disney's park, visiting and enjoying MGM Studios, Epcot, Animal Kingdom,

Magic Kingdom, Universal Studios, and Islands of Adventure. There was a lot of walking, and Jenna's knees did bother her at times, but nothing would stop her from taking in the entirety of that magical place. The 4D shows, with vibrating seats and water spraying from the ceilings, made her feel like an actor in the movies she had once watched while lying in a hospital bed. Jenna did not get to spin the wheel on their Wheel of Fortune show, which she watched every night while in the hospital, but her family did get to play Who Wants to Be a Millionaire.

The mock-up set was packed with contestants. The lights went dim, and the show's music played as over 300 people sat in their chairs with an answer keypad placed in front of them. A sports question popped on the screen. Everyone frantically punched the lettered keys for the correct response, each hoping they would be one of the top ten who answered with the fastest time. Everyone wanted that coveted Hot Seat so they could play for prizes. That was, everyone except for the person who won it.

The correct answer was posted: B, C, A, D. Immediately, out of basic instinct, Hannah pumped her fists in the air. "I got it right!" she exclaimed. But a few seconds later, Hannah began sliding down in her seat when she saw her seat number at the top of the screen. She won.

Hannah's face turned pale white after realizing she had to walk down to the stage in front of hundreds of people to play the game. She desperately looked at Zachary and pleaded with him. "You go!" Zachary was not having any of that and said, "This is all you, Hannah." There was no going back now. All the lights and cameras were now on her. "Maybe this will make up for all those rescheduled birthdays," Jenna thought as her smile widened.

A bashful Hannah hesitantly walked down to the center of the auditorium. The host tried to calm her down because he could tell she was so nervous. The sweat pellets gathering on her forehead were a dead giveaway. Seeing how young she was, only 13, and knowing the play-in question was a sports question, the host asked how she knew the answer.

Nervous and about to faint, Hannah told him, "I had a set answer I was going to punch in even before the question was asked." Little did she know, the combination was the correct answer. The host chuckled in amazement and told her their family should play the lottery. "Oh, how little did he know about their family history," Jenna thought. Hannah eventually made it to the $8,000 question and was never so thrilled to get out.

50

WAR STORIES

When Jenna went down to Duke for her four-year post-transplant studies, Andre, the surfer-style nurse Hannah gushed over, could not believe all she was accomplishing. The transplant team was often concerned about how much the radiation and chemotherapy would affect the children's everyday learning functions later in life. The total body irradiation she endured meant her brain could have been damaged, causing learning difficulties.

Jenna did have concentration problems with studying. It would take her twice as long to do her homework as her siblings, as her mind constantly bounced from one thing to the next. She still had days when her hands hurt so badly she couldn't even grip a pencil and had to dictate her homework answers to her mom. It certainly made keyboarding class all the more difficult. When the teacher wasn't looking, Jenna would use the single fingernail poking method to complete the assignment, putting the least amount of pressure on her fingers.

Kay wanted to stick a hand warmer in Jenna's backpack because the heat seemed to help her bones at times, but there was no way she was pulling that out in the middle of class. There were still little things she had to overcome and pain she had to live with, but Jenna was now on the mend. She felt like she could be normal and do normal things.

Jenna blew out the sixteen candles on her birthday cake and said, "yes," to an 18-year-old boy who asked her to be his girlfriend. She was inducted into the National BETA Club, National Honor Society, and later chosen to be a representative for her high school to attend Girls State. Only four girls out of the entire 580-something students in her class were chosen, and Jenna was selected for her leadership abilities and character. She attended Longwood University for a week with about 400 other girls from around Virginia, participating in seminars and workshops on the objectives and ideals of democracy. To top it off, she was vice president of an after-school group called Christian Youth Fellowship. Jenna took advantage of any opportunity that came her way.

After hearing her adventures, Andre looked at Jenna and said, "I guess the radiation sure didn't affect you much, did it?"

That day, more of her infant immunizations were given, two shots in each arm, all four given simultaneously. Jenna had to be re-immunized as her childhood vaccinations were wiped out due to the transplant. Priscilla, Jenna's phlebotomist, took 22 tubes of blood, but her vein collapsed. Throughout Jenna's treatment, Priscilla had learned different tricks, figuring out ways to use some blood from other tubes to fill the empty ones. She knew how difficult it was to find a suitable vein in Jenna's arms. The chemotherapy had all but destroyed any she had.

Needles terrified Jenna. It was no surprise because of all the horrible experiences with her port. Priscilla knew that. So, every time Jenna came down to Duke for testing, she was called up from other floors to take her blood. As soon as Jenna walked into the room and sat down in the awful chair with the extra armrest on the side, Priscilla prayed. She prayed for a good vein and ordered any bystanders in the room to entertain Jenna with dancing or singing while she searched for one. If Priscilla didn't find one, she would not fish for one. She would tell Jenna, "I think I have one, but it's up to you." Jenna would give her the go-ahead.

The needle pierced her skin. Jenna did not hear a rejoicing comment, so she knew something had gone wrong. Jenna whispered, "You didn't get it, did you?"

Priscilla would reassure her to keep breathing and give her a minute. With the needle still inside, she worked her magic, knowing every stick was torture for Jenna. Priscilla's motto was one and done, and Jenna certainly didn't argue with it.

Jenna would run out of pages if she tried to name the people at Duke who made her life more manageable because of their gentleness, compassion, and full-out empathy for what she was going through. Just knowing that, made all the sticks, surgeries, and painful sponge baths more tolerable.

Although Jenna was surrounded by many people who had been with her throughout her journey, for the first time, it did not feel like her home anymore. Kay no longer packed an overnight bag when they visited in anticipation of a sudden hospital stay due to her daughter's counts being too low.

A video presentation of past patients covered the screens at a Duke staff Christmas party. One by one, the kids' faces would pop up on the screen. A rather large, bald, Michelin man-looking girl with shiny cheeks appeared. No one had to think hard. "That's Jenna," one nurse said. Jenna was one of a kind, and they had seen many children walk through those doors, but she was no match for those steroids. A current picture of Jenna came up shortly after. Only a select few who had recently seen her could identify her. That picture was a wealth of encouragement to them. The doctors and nurses would say meeting someone who had a transplant, survived it, and looked good caused them to just stare at those kids like they were royalty. Those stares were not like the ones Jenna got on the streets from strangers; they were different. It was a gaze of hope and thankfulness.

Jenna left that day and knew Duke would always be a part of her, but she was moving on. Cancer would always be a part of her life, but it was no longer taking over it.

In celebration, Jenna was invited to the Silver Lining Ranch in Aspen, Colorado, a special camp for children battling cancer. The luscious green mountaintops reached the clouds, and the most vibrant leaves filled the trees like those after a fresh rainfall. One by one, kids who had endured the trials of cancer stepped out of the transport van. There was no denying God at that moment. The sight of human life coming off the van brought a sense of wonder to her heart and more proof of a living God than she had ever known before.

It was the first time Jenna had ever been on her own. No family, no nurses, no doctors. None of the kids underwent a transplant like she had, but all of them were either going through or had completed cancer treatments. Jenna could not believe how well those kids looked. They were physically strong, more so than she was, and she was further out than anyone from their diagnosis date.

They did not sit there listening to each other's war stories, even though some of their battle scars told the story for them. The group rushed across the field to fish in Kevin Costner's ranch pond, a man who had donated much to the camp they were all enjoying. They just wanted to ride the horses down the mountains, white water raft down the Colorado River, and swim in the lodge's pool. No one dwelled on their problems. One boy had lost his leg to cancer, but it did not stop him as he dribbled a basketball past the other boys with two legs, looking like he would give Michael Jordan a run for his money. He never complained.

At times, Jenna would catch one boy staring at her. She could tell he had so much running through his mind. She walked over and sat down beside him. After a short exchange, he opened up. He looked down at himself, then back at her and said, "I have never seen another person with stretch marks like mine." At that moment, Jenna realized her appearance had helped ease his many insecurities.

The truth was that boy would face some challenges in the future. Jenna knew it because she had experienced it. Yes, there would be girls who would not be able to handle his scars. Jenna's 18-year-old boyfriend had just broken up with her months before *bear season* came in, a nickname one of the transplant moms gave the springtime as winter clothes would no longer hide the battle scars. But Jenna knew. She knew her boyfriend could not handle being with a girl who was not the norm. But what he did not know was just as time fades, so do the scars. So do the memories of all the pain. So do the stares, and so do the days when you were only considered a cancer patient.

Just like the name of that camp, there were silver linings amongst the gray clouds. Jenna gave that young, timid boy a moment of hope, one most people would never be able to give him. There was hope and comfort in knowing he was not the only one whose outward appearance would be the only attribute some people would ever see in them.

Later that year, Jenna's group was invited back to enjoy the camp again in December. The van made its way up the snow-covered brick driveway, giving Jenna a glimpse of the tallest, fully-decorated Christmas tree she had ever seen standing in the lodge's great room. That night, the kids took a horse-drawn carriage ride down the main street of Aspen where they would be let off just outside quaint stores for shopping.

The following day, Jenna sat behind a team of eight sled dogs as she traversed down the mountain. She reveled in the experience of getting as close as she could to living out the courageous cross-country marathon in *Iron Will*.

Jenna was given the green light from her orthopedic surgeon just days before the trip, allowing her to carve the freshly-fallen snow down the mountain. Well, maybe not like that, but she did get to do a sit-down ski run with an instructor behind her, gliding her down the slopes. Only one other guy and Jenna could make it to the top of the mountain because the other kids were able to try real skiing and never made it off the bunny slopes. They all rode a gondola to the top of the mountain to join Jenna and the other boy for lunch. One by one, as they stepped off the gondola, Jenna noticed a shaggy-haired blond in the distance. It was Owen Wilson. After a brief conversation with their hosts, he took the time to get a picture with them.

Only for a Moment:

A CARD OF ENCOURAGEMENT

Never judge a book by its cover. Everyone has a story and everyone has a purpose. Perhaps Jenna understood that boy at the camp more than most could. She knew he was struggling because he looked different than the normal. But whoever defined normal? It doesn't matter how outwardly beautiful or handsome you are, everyone can always use a compliment. Pass this along to someone who may need a little pick-me-up.

Take a breath, keep breathing, and keep going.

You are fearfully and
wonderfully made...

~ Psalm 139:14 (The Bible)

51

THE CLOCK STRIKES MIDNIGHT

During her final year of high school, Jenna did not feel like a senior, only completing two full school years since fifth grade. Even so, those years were full of missed days as her body had a tough time keeping up with the life she was living. Jenna felt as if she had so many more years to complete before going to college. To even say the word college seemed so unreal to her. She did not feel old enough. Jenna had missed out on so much of her adolescent and teenage years she didn't feel ready to be done at Manchester. But there she was, standing in the hallway after class ended, staring at one of the many corkboards that filled the walls with pictures and advertisements of upcoming school events, the ones she would never attend.

"Hey, Jenna," Rhonda called as she turned the corner.

Jenna closed her locker door and turned to join Rhonda on the way to lunch. She took one step, and a loud pop resounded through the hall. She could not straighten her knee; a piece of bone fragment had broken off and lodged in her joint. Jenna hobbled on her one good leg over to a chair a few feet away and slowly massaged the broken bone back into place.

A concerned crowd started to form around her. Jenna looked at them and started explaining quickly, "Oh, this is normal. My bones always break off. I just work them back in place." But the looks on their faces were not reassuring, and neither was the thought in the back of Jenna's mind.

Sitting in the local physician's office later that afternoon, Jenna and Kay were startled by the look on the doctor's face. His eyes were as wide and glazed as fresh Krispy Kreme donuts when he examined the X-ray. He had no idea what to say. Before he began calling a Rolodex full of oncologists, Kay realized he was a new doctor, and he had never seen Jenna before. She quickly intervened and explained to him Jenna had leukemia, a transplant, and they knew AVN had settled in her knees.

The doctor gasped as if she had just relieved the weight of the world from his chest. He looked at her and thankfully said, "I am so glad you told me that. I was afraid I was going to have to tell you your daughter might have bone cancer because it looked so bad." He was obviously overwhelmed and a little out of his comfort zone.

Jenna quietly sat there as tears began streaming down her face. It meant more surgeries. "How could this be?" Jenna thought to herself. "I'm finally normal now."

In her eyes, it was starting all over again. With the mention of her other knee going at any time, she thought, "I am going to be in a wheelchair again."

After many X-rays, MRIs, and DEXA scan of her knees, it was determined Jenna had multiple dead bone fragments lodged in her joint.

As they waited on a second opinion from Duke, praying some type of better news would be on the horizon, Jenna began homebound schooling once again. She had missed being around people for so long that being alone at home became depressing. An orthopedic specialist down at Duke said both of her knees were in very bad shape. That specialist, someone who had seen patients from all over the world, reinforced the original diagnosis and Jenna knew it was bad. Yet again, it was a complicated case, the doctor explained. She had heard the words complicated case or rare phenomenon so much it was almost like a bad joke turned into a complete roast.

Three different names for her condition were given: AVN, osteochondritis dissecans, and osteonecrosis. The doctor placed the X-rays on the screen and pointed out all the dead bones. He estimated 35 percent of her bone structure was no longer alive. Her options were given, but no matter how they tried to slice it, Jenna would only really have one choice, just like with leukemia.

Her bones could not be drilled and cored to enable blood flow like what they had done with her hip. Also, Jenna was not old enough to receive a total knee replacement. It would only last 10 to 15 years, and they had to use new bone from her knees each time that procedure was done. She would run out of bone if she lived to be 50. An allograft was her only opportunity to walk again.

An allograft surgery was tricky and complex. They would have to use donor bone. A fresh cadaver who matched Jenna's measurements and age as closely as possible would be obtained from a bone bank to transplant into her knee. However, Duke did not do those surgeries.

The thought of more surgery was anxiety-ridden enough. But the news Jenna would be unable to have them at the place she was most comfortable scared her more than anything. She trusted the doctors at Duke. Duke had become her number one, her go-to. Nothing in her life was given a solid yes until it went through Duke's approval, and that time they were telling her a solid no.

Before Jenna could undergo the allograft, she would have an arthroscopic surgery at Duke to remove the dead bone fragments from her joint. The surgery was completed a couple weeks later, and the pieces of dead bone were removed.

"How pitiful is this?" Jenna asked as she sat sideways in the backseat of the minivan, her new boyfriend propping up her leg and pumping a cooler full of ice through the leg brace that would stabilize her on the three-hour ride home from Durham following surgery. She was given a nerve block from her groin down to the bottom of her calf on her left leg to release some of the pain, but unsettledness overwhelmed her as she saw her parents' faces in the rear-view mirror.

When they arrived home, Jenna braced herself before asking her mom, "So, what did the doctors really say?" Kay explained she would need the allograft in three months. Her right knee was now in worse shape and would need an allograft immediately after the left one. She wanted to enjoy her senior year in school and go to prom with her boyfriend, spending the night dancing away in a beautiful ball gown just like Cinderella until the clock struck midnight. But Jenna sat there with her leg propped in the air as tears silently streamed down her cheeks. She would not be losing a glass slipper anytime soon.

In the coming weeks, Jenna returned to school hobbling around on crutches. She was forced to drop two elective classes and add two new ones, keeping just three out of the original seven classes she had started with. However, Jenna wouldn't only be bound to taking tests inside a classroom for the remainder of her senior year, as very different tests on her knees were run inside a hospital examining room. Those tests would determine whether she would travel to San

Diego, California, or Boston, Massachusetts, the only two hospitals in the US that could do that specific allograft.

As she sat on top of the examining table, one of the doctor's looked up at the scans on the X-ray viewer. Somehow trying to reassure her, he said, "Well, Jenna, you are not the only one in the world with this problem." He then paused for a moment, shook his head, and finished with, "But almost; there aren't many."

Jenna wanted to look at him and say, "And the reassuring part of that was?" But she knew he was just trying to ease some of the tension in the room, and in a way, she needed the humor. Jenna could see the questions running through his head. He was stumped. But just like every other doctor she had seen at Duke, she knew he cared.

The doctor wanted a second opinion, which was rare. Doctors did not usually search for other points of view, especially from people outside their practices. It was up to the patients to get a second or third opinion. But he knew this was an area he was not specialized in. Just like going to a hospital that specialized in transplants gave Jenna the best chance to live, seeing someone who specialized in that specific surgery would give 17-year-old Jenna, the best chance to walk normally for the rest of her life. So, after much deliberation, the doctors explained Jenna's best option would be found in San Diego. Kay began planning the next day.

While on the phone speaking with hospitality staff at different hotels in San Diego, the call waiting tone sounded. She clicked over and heard, "Hi Kay, this is David!" Even though they had not talked to him in over a year, Kay knew who it was. Jenna had spoken with him periodically over the past six years. Each time they started a conversation, it was as if she was picking up where she left off with an old friend.

David was shooting scenes for *JAG*, and he told them to come on over, hang out, and have lunch with him on the set while they were in San Diego. Jenna had not seen David since her 12th birthday, and boy was he in for a surprise.

52

SAN DIEGO

Staring at the view outside the examination room, Jenna waited. Palm trees were slowly waving in the gentle, salty breeze. She could see the ocean, and golfers were teeing off less than a hundred yards from the piercing blue waters.

Thoughts raced through her head as she sat atop the examining room table. She had sat there many times before, but perhaps more than any other time, she felt more scared than she had ever felt going into a surgery. Maybe because she was older, that experience became more real, more serious. Jenna had felt the fresh air of normalcy on her face by attending school, joining activities, and trying to live the life she once thought she would never have. She wasn't ready to let it go.

"Does this hurt?" the doctor asked her. He was twisting, turning, and pressing on her knees in ways she did not even know they could move. "No," Jenna shook her head. Yet, the cowering faces and flinches told a different story. It was clear she couldn't hide the pain anymore.

Seeing her reaction, the doctor said, "I have a feeling you're not telling me how much this hurts, and you hold a lot in." He summed her up pretty well in only a matter of minutes. If Jenna could just hide the pain, then maybe, just maybe, he would tell her she did not need the surgery, and life would go back to normal. But as his prognosis continued and more facts about the surgeries ahead were shared with her, she felt its weight.

The first allograft had only been performed about 20 years prior. The doctor in San Diego completed about 50 allografts a year and explained the success rate was 75 percent. Hearing that, Jenna thought, "Hmm, not the highest number, but certainly not the less than one percent chance I've gotten before."

She had to be put on a waiting list because she needed fresh, not preserved, bone and cartilage. When a close enough match became available, Jenna had two-to-three days to fly out to San Diego for the surgery. Afterward, Jenna could not bear any weight on her knee for at least eight weeks. Resting even her big toe on the ground was not an option.

On a one-to-ten scale, the difficulty of the surgery would be a seven, the doctor said. Jenna thought he lowered that number because he could see her getting more and more upset. But it would be a tough procedure since he was dealing with dead bone. Most allograft surgeries were performed on live bone, either crushed or crumbled because of an accident. The numbers were alarming, but when he said he only operated on about two patients a year similar to Jenna's case, loud sirens and huge red flashing lights went off in her head.

"Are you kidding me? You do the most a year in the United States, and you only do two?" she thought. Jenna could see her 75 percent chance of success plummeting right there in front of her. She hated people seeing her cry, but Jenna's eyes began to well up with tears. Her eyelids could no longer hold the tears, and they painted her face in fear. Jenna would have given anything not to come back to a beautiful yet disparaging San Diego, but it was inevitable.

The doctor gave Jenna until the end of the summer to decide and begin the surgeries. If she were an adult, he would have insisted they be done right away. But knowing she was a senior in high school, he understood how graduating with her class would be such an accomplishment for her. He was familiar with her medical history and knew Jenna had beaten the odds more than once. At the end of the summer, Jenna would be placed on the transplant list. It then could take a few days to six months to find a viable donor, but there was no way of knowing how long.

Jenna remained quiet as he finished the examination. There was only one question remaining at the end of that appointment; operate on one or both knees at the same time. Two knees at the same time would be much more complicated. Only Jenna could decide.

At the end of that two-hour long visit, oh how ready she was to see David. After a drive up the Pacific Coast Highway into the Los Angeles area, Jenna and Kay arrived at a large parking lot behind a warehouse that looked like a massive airplane hangar. Staring at the large building, Jenna was about to live out a dream of being on the set of her favorite TV show *JAG*. Well, living out her dream would have actually been to be on an episode, but this was the next best thing.

David escorted Kay and Jenna in. Surrounding her was an oval-shaped room filled with the offices where most of the show's filming took place. Everything looked just like they did on TV. One by one, Mac, then Bud, and then a few other cast members walked by and introduced themselves to her as she sat in David's casting chair. Everything was like a dream. But that dream was soon tarnished as they walked into the neighboring warehouse where Jenna saw the ship at sea and the jets that soared in the sky all in one room. Her childlike fantasies of actual jets flying in the sky and huge Navy ships sailing in the ocean proved that it was Hollywood, and everything on TV was not always as it appeared to be.

Kay and Jenna headed back to Virginia after the visit, hoping a little more magic would be just what Jenna needed to forget what lie ahead. After missing almost the entire first semester of her senior year and much of her second, it was time for her own Prince Charming to arrive and take her to the ball, or prom as it was better known.

Friends and family gathered on the front lawn as if a beautiful princess was to be announced to the public. All smiled and waved as she walked by, not royalty, but a walking miracle, a nickname Aunt Cindy had given her. Jenna's gorgeous, white, sparkly ball gown swished back and forth like a bell in a church steeple. With camera flashes shimmering against her dress, she made her way towards her prince standing next to the horse-drawn, pumpkin-turned carriage. Actually, it was her boyfriend in a black and white tuxedo beside a white limousine. But to Jenna, it felt the same.

Jenna's fairy godmother, her mom, had worked her magic. A limo company and one of the best restaurants in the area wanted to make Jenna's night as memorable as possible, so they offered their services for free. They made it so Jenna could feel like a princess for a night, and it worked. As she danced a couple of slow dances with her boyfriend, there was nothing that could take that special moment from her. Jenna was about to graduate high school, missing so many years of school, but still actually graduating on time.

53

FROM WHEELS TO BEYOND

*B*rring-brrring-brrring-brrring!

Although the phone on the wall in the kitchen was replaced by a cordless one in the den, it seemed every time it rang, Jenna would just stare at it. Over the years, so much bad news had come from the other end of the line. Yet, it was January 20, 2006, and Jenna was at home sitting on the couch. She could not attend college or even have a job. There was not enough room on an application for her to write, "I won't be able to walk for at least six months after returning from a sudden sick leave. Will this be a problem?"

When Kay answered the phone, it was the call their family had been waiting for, the one that would bring life back into Jenna's knees. For another family, however, it meant an irreparable loss.

As Jenna thought about that, she realized that possibly a 17-year-old girl had just passed away. Jenna knew it was the harsh reality of life, but even throughout the whole cancer process, no one had to die for her to live.

Jenna had received cord blood from the umbilical cord of a living baby. No mom or dad had to suffer the loss of their child so she could live. She knew this surgery was imperative for her to walk normally, but at the cost of someone else's life, it hit her hard. Jenna felt guilty and extremely humbled.

After a long plane ride across the country, check-in at a hotel, and a lot of praying throughout it all, the next thing Jenna remembered was lying on a gurney waiting to be taken back to surgery.

"I will be back shortly to start the epidural," the anesthesiologist said to Jenna. Her eyebrows rose as she looked over at her mom. Jenna looked back at the doctor and said, "I was told this would be done once I was put to sleep."

The anesthesiologist firmly responded, "No, that's not going to happen," as if whoever told Jenna that had lost their mind. Tension in Jenna's voice shot up as she explained Duke had always done it like that due to her past horrific needle experiences. But there was more chance of hitting a nerve in an adult, which is why they wanted her awake. Jenna pleaded, telling her she had not grown any or gained any weight since the last time she had an epidural.

Without hesitation, the anesthesiologist looked down at Jenna and bluntly declared, "You're 18 now, and you're an adult. You need to grow up and realize this is going to hurt and just deal with the pain."

The male nurse who had accompanied the anesthesiologist into the room looked mortified.

Jenna looked back up at her mom and dad. Kay saw the fury building inside Jenna, and before she could fire back at that know-it-all doctor, Kay quickly grabbed Jenna's arm. The anesthesiologist pulled back the curtain and walked out of the room. Not even a second passed, and Jenna looked at her parents and said, "I want a new anesthesiologist!"

Needless to say, it was a battle Jenna must have won in the end because the last thing she remembered was getting wheeled into the operating room. The epidural had to have been placed while she was asleep.

After a five-hour operation and a three-turned-seven-day hospital stay, Jenna was never so glad to feel the California air on her face as she was rolled to the rented minivan parked outside the hospital. The brakes on the wheelchair were pushed forward, and her mom, a nurse, and Aunt Vonnie, who had come out to take her dad's place, devised a plan to get her transferred into the vehicle.

Jenna had opted to have both knees operated on at the same time, knowing she would not want to put her life on hold again for another trip to San Diego. She could not bend either leg. Two braces from her ankles to her hips were locked straight. As her mom held one leg and Aunt Vonnie held the other, Jenna slowly lifted up out of the wheelchair with the nurse's help. With a sudden movement in her knee as she pivoted towards the back seat, it sounded like a gun was fired.

Bang!

A terrifying scream alerted everyone in the parking lot. Her screams were so frightening that she attracted a crowd. Innocent bystanders and nurses stopped to see what was happening. The nurses ran back into the hospital for more help. Jenna's only thought was, "This knee surgery was just done for nothing."

Jenna sat sideways in the middle section of the van while an orthopedic doctor was called. After almost two hours of waiting, they were assured that only if they had dropped her on the knee would they have damaged what was done on the inside.

Jenna continued with as much therapy as her knees would allow for the next week while living in two different hotel rooms. The doctor advised them to stay in the area for at least a week for healing and possible complications. She learned how to move around more easily using a transfer board, sliding to the edge of a seat with the board underneath her, and then shimmied down the board into the wheelchair seat while someone held her legs completely straight. That process became quite handy as they finally reached the point to fly home.

She moved carefully from her wheelchair to an even smaller transfer chair that would fit down the airplane aisles. With no footrest on the chair, Kay held her legs in front of her while the wheelchair was pushed from behind. Then, the fun part started. Jenna had to move out of the transfer chair into the airplane seat. Those who fly know just how tight spaces are in a plane. Trying to turn the transfer chair while keeping her legs fully extended was not an easy task. On top of all that, they had an upcoming layover with no time at all between flights.

Many times people wanted to help, as Jenna did look quite pitiful with her legs extended in the air and multiple pillows and bags underneath them to keep them as elevated as possible. But they made it. They made it home, and the recovery process began.

The braces could not come off except for bath time. The only time she could bear weight on her knees was to stand for a transfer. Her life was bound to her bed in the family room, a wheelchair, or the couch. No privacy. Jenna never left the house except for unexpected visits to the doctor, like when a puss-filled abscess on one of her knees led to a bumpy red rash that covered her body and itched like crazy. That visit gave local doctors the chance to examine pictures of Jenna's surgeries. There were very few, if any doctors, who had done that surgery in Richmond.

After a few months, Jenna slowly made her way out into the public in a wheelchair. It was not until then she realized many places were not equipped to accommodate someone like her. As she bumped into merchandise and pieces of clothing came tumbling down on the floor, many people would stare.

Four months after surgery, nearing the end of her wheeled escapades, someone told Jenna they liked her purse. She thought to herself, "Wow, she noticed me for me. No one ever looks at a person in a wheelchair and comments on their style." That lady saw Jenna as a person, not just some rolling object. So did another that day when a lady walked up to Jenna and asked, "Are you Miss Wheelchair Virginia?"

"Ma'am?" Jenna asked in confusion. The lady sincerely thought Jenna was being modest and replied, "You look just like Miss Wheelchair Virginia." Jenna needed that compliment.

After learning gate walking—right crutch forward, left foot forward, left crutch forward, right foot forward, repeat—Jenna probably looked like a newborn giraffe. Still, after four months, she was up out of the wheelchair and just two months away from needing no mechanical help to walk at all. After those two months, Jenna was on her own two legs and complication-free. She was able to start school at a local community college and got her first real job at a local law firm, Cravens and Noll.

Life was moving forward once again, Jenna's knees were continuing to get stronger, and life around her was not slowing down. A year after her surgeries, Gabriel got into a bad go-cart accident. He had been racing go-carts for some time, and while in Maryland, he crashed into the wall, dislocating all five major bones on the top of his foot, breaking the main one, and tearing all the ligaments and capillaries. It looked like his heel had moved from the bottom backside of his foot to the top. Immediate surgery was required, or he could have lost his foot.

Just two months later, Kay was diagnosed with stage three colon cancer. After almost a year of chemotherapy, radiation, and surgery, she was in remission.

Jenna's family continued to face many trials, with multiple people now referring to them as the Kennedy family.

As life does, regardless of her family's trials, Jenna's life continued. Now 20 years old, she was playing softball again. Their church had joined a local league, and after nine long years, Jenna was finally back on that pitcher's mound. Her competitive side would get frustrated because her will to win was much stronger than her body. She could not run very well or move as quickly as everyone else.

Jenna's high school boyfriend kindly reminded her of her lack of movement skills when he said she ran like a person in a scary movie. When Jenna looked confused, he explained, "You know, like when the person being chased is running away from the bad person, and it's all in slow motion." Her feelings might have been hurt if he wasn't so right. None of that mattered, though. Jenna was playing the game she loved. She was working, driving, and was now about to live away on her own for the first time as she went off to attend Liberty University for the spring semester of 2008.

It was a fun two years at Liberty. Now in the fall semester of 2009, senioritis was setting in. After a year off for rare knee surgeries, a year and a half at a community college, and two years at Liberty, Jenna was only a few classes and exams short of graduating. It was a miracle, to say the least. She would walk across the stage down on the football field at Williams Stadium to receive her college degree, despite all her major setbacks.

With all the stress of final exams and the excitement of Christmas, there was no wonder Jenna was experiencing headaches. They followed her home on Christmas break, but nothing would stop Jenna from enjoying the most wonderful time of the year.

54

IT'S THE MOST WONDERFUL TIME OF THE YEAR

Dashing through the snow, in a one-horse open sleigh. O'er the fields we go . . .

The same music Jenna listened to in her parents' house as a child played through the car stereo in the background as she gingerly made her way through the parking lot filled with determined shoppers making last-minute shopping runs to the stores. She sang aloud and danced in the driver's seat trying to drown out the pounding in her head as she waited patiently for a parking spot to open.

"Jingle bells, jingle bells, jingle all the way. Oh, what fun . . . "

There was nothing but wide smiles on children's faces as they waved to Santa ringing his gold-plated bell on the sidewalk, adding one more Barbie playhouse and Lego set to their Christmas lists.

Jenna loved all the hustle and bustle, racing from one store to the next, going to Christmas parties, and, more importantly, spending time with family.

She finally found an open spot and pulled in. With her car in park, Jenna rummaged around in her glove box, popped a few Advil, and got out of the car to wade through shopping traffic. The over-the-counter pills, however, had stopped working as they should. They failed to relieve any pain, but she kept pushing forward and with a slight eye roll, thought, "Oh great, I'm going to start having migraines now."

Christmas morning, 2009, arrived like so many years before. Zachary, Gabriel, Jenna, and Hannah, all a little older now, casually made their way down the stairs and rounded the corner into the den. They opened presents around the warm stone fireplace, with hundreds of multi-colored lights covering the mantle above.

Ray was in his recliner watching as Kay started breakfast in the kitchen, and Jenna quickly retired to the couch away from the chaotic scene of unwrapped gifts scattering their den floor. It was all she could do to keep her head up as another migraine swept through like a Category 4 hurricane. Her head hurt so badly she could hardly mingle with Mema and Papa who had come to visit just like every Christmas afternoon in the past. She fell asleep right there on the couch amidst all the chatter in the room.

Jenna barely mustered up the strength to make it to the dinner feast at her grandma and grandpa's later that day. She could not stand the thought of not being there, even though the echoes of the train chugging around the Christmas tree sounded much like beating drums.

Aunt Vonnie and Aunt Jeannie, typically labeled the Lucy and Ethel of the bunch, were not cackling and rambling on as usual, as their smiles turned to faces of concern as Jenna walked into the room. She was not sporting her typical fashionista style, but rather a Liberty hoodie and jeans. She also arrived empty-handed without her famous jalapeno deviled eggs and cheese-filled crab dip because she had been asleep all afternoon. Something was wrong.

Jenna tried visiting and speaking with everyone, but she couldn't concentrate on the conversations happening around her. Trying to escape some of the noise, she moved to the stairs just behind her crowded family in the den and leaned over with her head in her hands.

Typically, she was the one who led the Chinese Auction gift exchange and the games following dinner. Go figure, as games had become her niche over the last 11 years. Something was not right, but she would push through anything to avoid the dreaded, capital *H* sign.

Three days later, Kay's family headed down from Pennsylvania for their last family get-together of the year. At Aunt Cindy's house, dinner was served, and the conversations began. But the throbbing pain in Jenna's head denied her any comprehension of the words being said to her.

The room started to spin. With her head resting on her mother's shoulder, Jenna looked up at her mom and whispered, "Tell Aunt Renee I like her shoes."

"What did she say?" Aunt Renee asked in confusion.

Kay looked at her with a motherly concern and said, "Jenna has not been feeling well lately. Horrible headaches. She just cannot seem to shake them."

Aunt Renee replied, "Oh, I am so sorry you are not feeling well," completely unaware of the pain it caused Jenna to engage in a conversation.

In all actuality, both Jenna and Kay were not feeling well. Kay headed home earlier in the evening due to side effects from the colon cancer she had a few years prior, but Jenna would not be far behind.

"I think I need to leave. I am not feeling right," Jenna said to Hannah. So, they said their quick goodbyes to family and departed for home. But in the seven minutes it took to drive home from Aunt Cindy's house, Jenna's migraine surged. She barely made it out of the car and into the house before the vomiting began.

For hours, Jenna and Kay rotated in and out of the bathroom, each throwing up. "I don't think we can put it off any longer," Kay said as she entered the bathroom. It was nearing midnight, and the sickness and headaches were worsening. Jenna knew what that meant, but she would do anything to avoid going to the hospital.

Jenna knew she didn't just make two-hour visits to the hospital. Often confusing the hospital as a nice oceanfront resort, she decided to make it at least a two-week long vacation stay. If the weather was nice, she'd get the extended package and stick around for an extra month or so. But thoughts of graduating in just a few short months flashed through her mind; no way that was getting postponed.

Knowing she would be unable to convince Jenna, Kay called in for reinforcements, AKA Aunt Jeannie.

Aunt Jeannie walked into the den, and with her blunt, nurse-concerned tone she declared Jenna was out of time. The headaches had lasted too long, and the vomiting was only exacerbating the underlying issue. Jenna needed to get to the hospital.

As Kay's pains in her stomach worsened, she hopped in the front seat and Ray drove the minivan while Hannah held Jenna's hair back as she aimed her projectile vomiting into plastic shopping bags. In the 20-minute desperate drive to the emergency room, Aunt Jeannie followed behind them. Later on, she commented how fun it was to dodge puke-filled bags as Hannah chucked them out the window like a child flinging shovels of sand over their shoulder at the beach.

Kay and Jenna hobbled into the building under the neon-red letters. The receptionist behind the check-in counter began with the standard question: "And who are we here for tonight?" Kay and Jenna slowly turned to each other, and with bated breaths, said, "Both of us." After a look of alarming confusion, the paperwork was started just as Ray and Aunt Jeannie came running in.

Jenna didn't remember much of what happened from the time they sat at the check-in desk until the next day when she woke up in the ICU. Zachary and Gabriel were standing at the foot of her hospital bed, with pale faces and a look of pure fear in their eyes, much like her parents' faces when she watched them from across the McDonald's booth 11 years ago. Slowly, Jenna began dozing off as Gabriel and Zachary stood there by her bedside, machines beeping, surrounded again by nothing but four white walls.

55

JUST ANOTHER BALL DROP

The hours were ticking away, and the minute hand was just a few numbers away from twelve. As Jenna peeked out her hospital room window with a clear view of the nurses' station, she could see her mom walking towards her room. All decked out in her hospital gown and yellow adhesive-bottomed socks, Kay slowly pushed the wheeled, stainless-steel IV pole across the cold, tile floor. Hannah followed closely beside. Just four days after Christmas, Kay and Jenna walked into an emergency room, sat behind a check-in counter, and now there they were. Jenna was lying in an intensive care unit hospital bed, and Kay was sitting next to her in her hospital gown alongside Hannah, ready to watch the ball drop to bring in the New Year. To say it was a pitiful sight would not quite describe the scene of pure helplessness occurring in that moment. Even one of the doctors said he had never seen two family members admitted on the same night, both with serious conditions but not having been in an accident together.

Bringing in the New Year was supposed to be a joyous occasion, a night filled with friends and family, laughter, midnight kisses with that special someone, and an opportunity for fresh beginnings. But that was not the Hallmark movie scene playing that day in the hospital.

When Kay and Hannah entered the room, they stood there in the dark for a moment, bathed in the red glow from the Exit sign down the hall. Beeping machines and monitors harmonizing within the four white walls brought them back to a past they thought they had left behind. Both of them looked empty.

Hannah took the remote off the bedside table, clicked the TV on, and searched the channels to find the ball drop.

"Ten . . . Nine . . . Eight . . ."

The sounds of live coverage from Times Square were the only voices they could hear. Kay stared at her daughter with tears in her eyes.

"Seven . . . Six . . . Five . . . "

Jenna, staring at the TV screen, thought, "Eleven years of fighting should be enough."

"Four . . . Three . . . Two . . . "

The three of them thought, "None of this even matters. It's just another ball drop."

"One . . . Happy New Year!"

The televised crowd shouted and celebrated as the glittering ball dropped to the ground in the middle of Times Square.

Kay and Hannah could hear the commotion of the nurses down the hall. They were cheering, launching confetti in the air, and toasting cups of apple juice with smiles on their faces, celebrating a new year and wishing each other a great 2010. Kay and Hannah were just happy Jenna wasn't writhing in pain.

The next day, the new year brought on more tests and scans to find the source of Jenna's headaches. There had to be a reason for them, and the doctors were hell-bent on figuring it out, by any means necessary. This became apparent when one of Jenna's doctors walked into her ICU room. With little formalities given, he began explaining he wanted to do an angiogram to better understand the nature of the headaches. As he rambled on, spitting out medical jargon that alone would have been difficult to understand, his thick foreign accent made it nearly impossible to comprehend what exactly he wanted to do.

From her understanding, he wanted to take a needle, stick it in her upper thigh near her groin, and thread a dye-filled tube upward towards her heart, all of this to find out if drugs were the root of the problem. The frustration Jenna was feeling quickly turned to defiance. Slurring her words, she cried, "No, I do not need this procedure because I am telling you now, I am not on drugs!"

Jenna had been through so many surgeries she knew he could not do the procedure if she didn't consent. She forcibly declared she was not having any procedure without Aunt Vonnie or her dad explaining it, as both were on their way to the hospital.

56

22

Jenna woke up the next day in a step-down unit. Kay was out of her hospital gown and in civilian clothes. She looked over at Jenna lying in bed and explained what had gone on. The angiogram had been completed along with a CAT scan. The CAT scan had revealed two bleeds slightly smaller than a golf ball on the right frontal lobe of her brain.

The doctors explained Jenna technically had a stroke but showed no symptoms so far. As Jenna looked over to her mom, her eyes were quickly covered by a hazy film of tears. Jenna leaned back, gently laying her head on that flat, definitely not feathered, hospital pillow, and whispered, "I just can't believe it. How crazy is this? I am 22, and I just had a stroke. Why?"

Not fully understanding the severity of what was just told to her due to the narcotics she was taking for pain, Jenna thought she needed to let her employer know why she wouldn't be coming back to work.

"Hello Kim, may I speak to Donna?"

Donna, the office manager at Cravens and Noll, wasn't expecting Jenna to come into work until the next day. She casually answered, "Hi, Jenna."

"Hey Donna!" Jenna belted into the phone with a perky tone in her voice. "I just want to let you know I am not sure when I will be able to come back to work. I am in the hospital right now with a brain bleed," Jenna said, completely unconcerned.

Donna was speechless. Jenna sounded so calm on the phone, because she was.

For some reason, the words brain bleed from her mother's mouth had not registered with her as a bad ordeal. Jenna knew from the look on her mom's face, but like a small child being told they have leukemia, it flew right over her head like a hard-hit ball over the left-field wall. Jenna did not feel bad, so how could it be bad? All she had was a headache, and even that was partially subdued by the vast amounts of narcotics she was receiving.

"This is just a fluke," Jenna thought. All she would have to do is wait it out. It would dissipate on its own. At least, that was the hope of the doctors who sat around in confusion.

The lights were turned off in Jenna's room, and the blinds were closed shut. The door to her hospital room remained shut to eliminate the noise from the hallway. Any stressful stimulus was erased as Kay did her part to keep Jenna as mellow as possible. Her headaches were so intense Kay worried another stroke could happen at any time. So, Jenna lay in a silent room with only a muted television in the background to offer any break in the day.

With her headaches continuing to worsen, large amounts of steroids were administered to reduce the swelling in Jenna's brain. Well, at least the nurses tried giving them. After countless needle sticks throughout the night, Jenna's veins, damaged by years of chemotherapy and radiation, proved to be another setback. Surgery was mentioned, but it was too risky at that point. So the doctors waited and hoped for the bleeding to go away on its own.

Kay was never so thrilled when much-needed visitors broke up the heaviness of those days.

With a little gift bag swinging back and forth from his fingertips, a friend of Jenna's sauntered down the hallway on his way to her room. He confidently strolled up to Jenna's bed, handed her a present, and smiled from ear to ear. Jenna reached in and pulled out a brown knit beanie. She wanted to smile and say thank you, but the puzzled look on her face quickly led to an explanation from him. He told her how another friend who had visited her just a couple of days prior warned him before coming up there.

The friend said, "Man, um, I'm just warning you she doesn't look like she normally does. Her hair is, uh, well, I don't know how to describe it, but, uh, it's not fixed."

Jenna's hair was matted in the back from lying in bed for well over a week. Frizzy, curled strands of dark hair stuck out, surrounding her face. Jenna was sporting the beehive hairdo from one of the many 1960s movies she watched lying in her hospital bed many years ago. Needless to say, she was not the normal fashion statement her friends and family were accustomed to. So, the only logical gift for him to bring Jenna was a beanie so she could cover up her unfixed hair.

It was the comic relief needed at that point. He and Jenna even had her nurse thinking he had proposed to her right there in the hospital room. The nurse was so upset when she found out she was mistaken. She thought that would have been the most romantic proposal ever. For Jenna, not so much.

Two of Liberty University's vice presidents came to visit Jenna. Both assured her no matter what, she would get to graduate in May.

They brought T-shirts, blankets, and other Liberty memorabilia to cheer her up. However, it was the intangible gift they brought that was perhaps the most needed medicine of all.

While visiting, one of the vice presidents pulled out his cell phone and dialed a number. Handing Jenna the phone, he said, "I hear this guy is your favorite speaker, and he wanted to say something to you."

"Hello?" Jenna said with a confused look on her face.

"Hello Jenna, this is Clayton King." A smile from ear to ear stretched across her face when she heard his voice.

Clayton King had spoken in Liberty's convocation chapel gatherings many times, and his life resonated with Jenna. He talked to her for a little while, telling her how he was on vacation with his wife in Aruba but wanted to pray with her because he had heard she was going through a hard time.

After Clayton prayed, they said their goodbyes, and Jenna fought back the tears. They were not tears of pain, but rather tears of complete gratitude. She lay there and thought to herself, "What other university would do this for one of their students?" Two of the highest people on staff took time out of their winter break to come see her. Not only that, but they also arranged for her favorite evangelist to call and pray for her, and on his vacation, nonetheless.

With every rock overturned, the doctors said it could take two or three months before the bleeds in Jenna's brain would reabsorb. There was no denying more headaches in the future, but maybe they would be more manageable. Jenna was sent home. The only thing to do now, was wait.

57

JENNA, JENNA

Jenna's last semester at Liberty University had started, but she was nowhere to be found on campus. No matter how much her will persisted to graduate, her body just simply would not allow it. The headaches were growing much more unbearable, and now severe pain had lodged in her knees due to the extreme amount of steroids Jenna was taking for her brain. With no improvements, Jenna's records were sent to Duke, and a neurosurgeon confirmed he could see something concerning. Jenna had not even been out of the hospital for two days, and she and Kay headed down to Duke to hear the inevitable.

After multiple tests, the neurosurgeon believed the bleed was a cavernoma, a benign tumor of weakened blood vessels that had ruptured. The suspected cause was the total body irradiation she had 11 years ago pre-transplant. As Jenna heard those words, she wanted so badly to unthread that Peter Pan transplant shadow that continued to linger behind her. Surgery was out of the question, for now, so she was sent back to Virginia, and the days of waiting continued.

"Jenna, hurry up. Get dressed." Kay exclaimed as she scurried around the upstairs of the house, putting extra shirts, pants, and socks into overnight bags. Additional tests at Duke had been ordered for Jenna.

"Jenna, Jenna. We don't have time to play around," Kay declared loudly, wondering what was taking so long as she entered the den. Kay froze. The pile of clothes in her hands fell into a crumpled heap on the floor. Jenna had no reaction. Motionless, she sat there on the couch, with only an inert stare off in the distance. Jenna was seizing.

Upon arrival, Jenna was admitted. Over the next few days, she lay in the ICU bed at Duke and rarely spoke a word. Occasionally, she would give one-word answers and follow the doctor's commands, only to doze in and out during the examination. Aggravatingly, the doctors tried pulling complete-sentence responses from her. She struggled to say one word back. But it wasn't like Jenna during her transplant days, with her typical defiance attitude of, I don't want to be here, so I'm just not going to talk to you. It was different. Her arms and legs were frozen still like twigs that had fallen after a cold winter storm. They never moved; they could not move. Her eyes were completely shut, but not like she did while playing possum; it was completely involuntary.

The doctors would yell at her to open her eyes. At times they would open, but only when the doctors lifted them with their cold, latex-covered fingertips. Blank stares were her only response. Jenna's body was there, but her mind was not.

The doctors and nurses continued neurological testing every day, trying to get Jenna to open her eyes, move her toes, push and pull back on their hands, anything to show she could follow commands. Sometimes Jenna could hear and see the words coming out of their mouths, but it was like they were talking to her in a foreign language.

No matter how hard Jenna concentrated, nothing would leave her lips. Ray and Kay could only watch as Jenna slowly deteriorated in front of them. There were no more sassy comebacks when the doctors asked rhetorical questions. Jenna just lay there, motionless.

58

SNOWMAGEDDON

It was now Friday, just four days since Jenna had been admitted, and she suddenly sat up in her bed for hours and answered all the questions and comments the shocked doctors asked. Riding that unexpected burst of energy that filled her body, her mom prodded Jenna a bit. "How long do you think you've been at Duke?" Kay asked. Without hesitation, Jenna confidently said, "A month." Although her brain functions were not totally linked with reality, she was at least sitting up and now eating. But as Jenna and her family had learned over the past 11 years, never breathe in too deeply for a sigh of relief. As refreshing as the exhale might be, there was usually something lurking in the next moment.

The sun did not rise the next morning on that cold winter's day, Saturday, January 30, 2010. Instead, smoky, gray, snow-filled clouds covered the skies. As the minutes passed, the clouds could no longer hold the weight of the snow aching to fall to the streets below. Snow dusted the brown bark of trees and began to mound over the vehicles packed neatly in the asphalt parking lot outside. Fluffy flakes rustled against the window of Jenna's hospital room.

Jenna's eyelids slowly opened as if she had magnets attached to both sets of eyelashes. There was no number on the pain scale that could amount to the immense pounding hammering inside her head. As much as she fought to keep her eyes open, time had run out.

Within minutes, Jenna was unresponsive. She would no longer respond to any commands. She was breathing, but everything else showed signs of lifelessness. Jenna had slipped into a coma-like state, and the neurosurgeon was called immediately.

It was the biggest snowstorm Virginia and North Carolina had seen in years. With the Armageddon of all snowstorms wreaking havoc outside the hospital walls, everyone inside panicked. They all knew the surgeon's home driveway was on a steep hill, which could make it nearly impossible for him to make it on time.

Kay called the home phone.

Brrring-brrring-brrring-brrring-brrring-brrring-brrring!

No one answered.

On the other end of the receiving line, Gabriel's girlfriend held the ringing phone in her hand. Gabriel was outside feeding his hunting dogs, and she was unsure whether or not to pick up their home phone.

Brrring-brrring-brrring-brrring-brrring-brrring!

Realizing it was Kay's number, she fearfully answered the phone.

"Hello," she answered.

"Hello, please give the phone to Gabriel," Kay asked with urgency.

She ran out to Gabriel.

As the phone reached his ear, he heard, "Jenna's going into surgery. Get everyone to pray."

Gabriel dropped the hose he was using to fill the water bowls and made the calls. His first was to Natalie, their cousin who had rode that terrifying ride with Jenna for far too long. As she answered, she could tell he was crying and broken up on the other end as he asked her to pray and spread the word. Knowing tears were a rare phenomenon for Gabriel, fear arose, and Natalie knew prayer was all they could hold on to. After another call, Zachary rushed home from a friend's house to wait for the post-surgery news with Gabriel and his girlfriend.

Moments later, Kay made another call. That time, it was to Hannah.

Sitting atop her dorm room bunk bed, finishing up her last bit of homework before the weekend, Hannah heard the news Jenna was no longer responding. After sending one text to a friend, it only took minutes for her friends to send mass texts and Facebook posts urging people to come out to the Prayer Chapel in the center of Liberty University's campus to pray for Jenna's healing.

By that time, Jenna was not some random student. The entire campus had been praying for her in every convocation, three times a week since the spring semester had reconvened at the beginning of January.

Hannah clothed herself in as many sweaters and jackets and as much winter gear as she could wear to make the trek towards the Prayer Chapel in one of Virginia's top five winter storms, that would be forever known as "Snowmageddon." She scurried down the hallway of the dorm to the exit. Hannah pushed the metal bar to unlatch the door, but it barely moved. There were multiple feet of snow on the ground in Lynchburg at that point. It was falling so fast maintenance crews couldn't keep up with shoveling the sidewalks. She shouldered every ounce of her body weight against the steel-framed, wooden door in an attempt to push back the snow piled on the other side. Frigid air filled the hallway as Hannah pushed with all her might and the door screeched open just enough for her to squeeze through the opening.

A feeling of apprehension came over Hannah as she thought there was no way anyone would venture out into knee-high snow to get to the Prayer Chapel. But after everything that had taken place over the past 11 years, unforeseen obstacles were always a piece of the puzzle of miracles. Those miracles had always kept their family together. So, Hannah put her head down to avoid the torrent of the blizzard angling towards her face and made her way, ever so slowly, across campus.

Back at Duke, it was now 5:30 p.m., and the nurses were trying to hide the look of panic on their faces as they followed the neurosurgeon into Jenna's room. After a little examination and still no response from Jenna, there was no hesitation in the surgeon's voice. "She needs surgery, now."

The breaks were lifted, and Jenna's bed was rolled away. As they were leaving the room, the surgeon stuck out his hand to Ray and said, "By the way, my name is Dr. Freidman. I am Jenna's neurosurgeon." Her parents had never met him before, but there was no time for questions.

Within 30 minutes, Jenna was prepped and ready for surgery, many people down on their knees praying to the ultimate Healer. Weathering the storm, Jenna's old youth pastor and his wife had come to pray and sit with Ray and Kay as they watched their daughter being rolled away. Kay took one last look at Jenna. Watching her lifeless body rushed into surgery, Kay clung to her only hope.

Just a couple weeks prior, Kay had flipped through her Bible and uncommonly turned to a passage in Isaiah. Shortly into her read, an overwhelming feeling of comfort fell over her as she believed God, in His unfailing mercy, had led her to that scripture for one purpose, to give her hope in a time where she had very little. With Jenna's life hanging in the balance, Kay desperately clung to every word of Hezekiah's story in Isaiah chapter 38. She fervently prayed, "Dear God, let my daughter live to praise You, and not die to praise You."

As the operating room doors flung open, it was as if the massive brass gates of the Beast's castle once again had opened. Belle was fleeing the castle, braving the haunted, dark woods, winds blowing, owls hooting, and a full moon casting shadows on the snow-filled grounds surrounded her. The howling wolves were beginning to circle, her fairytale coming to an end.

Jenna had undergone many surgeries and procedures before, so why should this one be any different?

But it would be.

The doctors would take a drill to her skull and crack it open to save her life. That surgery would not compare to the others. It would be in a category all on its own. And no one could prepare them for it, the surgery that would change their lives forever.

59

SLEEPING BEAUTY

Tick, tock, tick, tock.

The phone rang in the den.

Gabriel looked at his girlfriend; his throat tightened as fear set over him. It had only been two hours since the surgery began, a surgery that was supposed to last three to four. Gabriel yelled and threw a pillow across the room at Zachary, who had fallen asleep on the couch. "Zach, wake up. It's Mom!"

Gabriel did not want to answer the phone. The surgery had not lasted long enough. Something terrible must have happened. Panic filled his mind as he struggled to say, "Hello?"

A mentally and emotionally exhausted Kay said, "She is out of surgery, and the doctor said she did well."

The next phone call was to Hannah. As her phone rang, the prayers echoing from the Prayer Chapel walls fell silent. "She's out of surgery," were the only words Hannah heard from her mom as joyous tears fell from her eyes. The comfort of friends from home who had been through that scenario with them before during Jenna's cancer days surrounded Hannah as she fell to her knees, overcome with emotional exhaustion.

Gathered around Hannah were hundreds of students, risen from their knees with their hands raised high, singing praises to God for protecting Jenna through surgery. Songs of gratitude and prayers for complete healing continued for many hours after that phone call. No one wanted to leave the chapel after feeling the most powerful presence of God and His answered prayers.

It was suspected Jenna had an arteriovenous malformation (AVM). The surgeon removed two intracranial hematomas from the right frontal lobe of Jenna's brain, one of which was the size of a golf ball. Smaller ones were cauterized to hopefully prevent other bleeds from occurring. Nearly 25 percent of her brain had been covered by the bleeds. The swelling in Jenna's brain had become so massive the right hemisphere had purged over to the left hemisphere of her brain. It was a miracle she had survived.

Jenna was rolled back to the ICU to recover. At that point, there was no determining the ultimate damage done. Her mom and dad prayed, unprepared for what they would see when she entered the room. Their prayers were simple, "Dear God, just let her wake up."

With both hands strategically placed on Jenna's chest and their body weight leaning over her, the doctors began forcibly pushing down on her. They needed a response from Jenna. A wiggle in her toes, a blink in her eyes, or a punch to the jaw after nearly cracking her chest in half. But there was none. No matter how hard they tried, the doctors and nurses in that ICU room could not hide the growing concerns on their faces. Jenna had been asleep for far too long post-surgery.

Kay made the desperate phone calls to her other children. "You need to get down here fast," was all she could muster up the strength to say.

It did not matter that the snow was falling hard like freshly shaken snow inside a snow globe. Zachary and Gabriel hopped in Zachary's truck, and he put the pedal to the floor. Zachary passed a policeman flashing his lights as if to warn him to slow down, but there was no option of slowing down.

Headed to Duke in the opposite direction, a lifelong friend of Jenna's, Justin, drove Hannah from Liberty. Weathering the storm, he knew time was not in their favor.

As the elevator doors latched shut, Hannah and Justin began walking down the cold, never-ending hallway of the ICU. Hannah's heart began falling slowly into her stomach as she passed by each room. Walking by one room there was a man raised high in the hospital bed lying completely still, lifeless, with only the sounds of a ventilator in the background. Then she passed by the next room. A young man was lying hooked up to five different machines. His family was waiting to find out if their son would make it off that unit after a gunshot wound to the head during a freak hunting accident.

Hannah did not want to walk forward. Jenna's room was next. She peered around the curtain and saw Jenna lying there, completely still. Her eyes were purple and swollen shut, and she had multiple wires protruding from her. She looked like an alien. For Hannah, it was as if she was experiencing life in a war-afflicted country. Families had gathered around their loved ones who looked lifeless and on the brink of death. Her sister was one of those.

Justin walked to Jenna's beside and grabbed her hand. He began talking to her just like it was any other Sunday night sitting around the family's kitchen table playing card games at Ray and Kay's house.

There was no response from Jenna. Justin and Hannah walked back out to the waiting area and sat down with the rest of the family. It was the waiting, the not knowing that was the hardest. But Justin brought a piece of home and comfort in a time when their family had very little.

Then, almost 24 hours later, the family stood around her bed, and Jenna let out a weak, muffled moan. There was life inside. It was not much, but to her mom sitting there holding Jenna's lifeless hand, it was the sound of the entire Mighty Ducks hockey rink standing to their feet and beginning to shout, "Quack, quack, quack, quack!" as everyone waited for the final goal to win the game. An unbelievable victory was about to occur.

Jenna had hardly uttered a word for a week. Her dad continued to pester her to talk and interact with him, and at that moment, Jenna put her first three words together since she had left home. "Leave me alone," she said. Over the next few days, the throbbing pain in Jenna's head and lower back caused her to slip in and out of consciousness. Afraid heavy narcotics would cause her to fall into a deep comatose sleep, doctors explained her only option for pain relief was Tylenol. Therefore, the immense pain persisted.

With her eyes still swollen shut, nurses placed shiny, round, adhesive discs on Jenna's scalp to run an electroencephalogram (EEG) overnight. They needed to know if she had any abnormalities in her brain waves or was having seizures. Jenna moaned in misery as the nurses placed the leads on her head. The pressure from pressing and pasting the leads brought on an even more massive headache. There was a camera facing Jenna to see how she changed throughout the night.

Her hemoglobin and platelets were low, and two units of blood were given. Not to mention, Jenna's veins were giving out yet again, and the possibility of having to put in a PICC line made recovery all the more heart-wrenching.

Despite all of that, Jenna was able to gobble down a couple Chick-fil-A chicken nuggets, the only food she had eaten in over a week. Jenna had not been able to stay awake long enough to eat, much less swallow, so she battled as much as possible to not have a feeding tube, which was the next step.

Back at Liberty, during convocation, the crowd cheered as news of Jenna eating a Chick-fil-A sandwich filled the auditorium. Hannah just thought to herself, "It was only a chicken nugget."

Jenna needed a break, she needed a moment, and that moment would enter her room the next morning. She woke up to the confusing sounds of a tall, built man standing in the doorway.

"Wow, girl, you looked like you need to be diffused," the man said. There was nothing but a blank stare from Jenna.

"You have a lot of pretty colors coming out of your head," he continued.

Referring to the kaleidoscope of colored EEG wires protruding from her head, Jenna looked like a bomb that needed to be diffused. Unaware of what had occurred since the surgery, the half-smile and slight chuckle was the first positive expression anyone had seen. Jenna barely talked, let alone smiled or laughed since she had been at Duke, but leave it to her youth pastor to bring out that first smile.

Making their morning rounds, the doctors and nurses stepped into Jenna's room with amazement on their faces.

"Your eyes. It's so good to see your eyes," Dr. Freidman said. He asked if she knew who he was. Jenna timidly shook her head from side to side. "I'm the doctor who operated on your brain," he replied.

Jenna softly whispered, "Oh." The words the doctor had just spoken had not completely registered with her.

"We nicknamed you Sleeping Beauty," one nurse added. "You've been asleep for five days."

Jenna had only had her eyes open for a few hours. She was experiencing everything for the first time since going unresponsive. Unable to grasp everything, Jenna looked over at her mom as the doctors and nurses all moved on to finish their rounds.

With deep concern on her face, Jenna asked, "Did they cut my hair?" Her mom responded, "Yes."

"Did they cut my head?" Jenna asked. She didn't fully comprehend the diagnosis or remember the table full of loud drills and shiny utensils placed beside her before surgery. Holding back tears, her mom softly said, "Yes."

Jenna asked where the scar was, only concerned the number of scars on her body had now increased. With her fingertip, Kay motioned the L-shaped path the surgeon's scalpel took from the top center of her forehead to the top of her right ear.

"That big?" was Jenna's only response. In that moment, it was as if the wind had just been knocked out of her chest. The tears slowly began to fall.

It had been five days since surgery, but Jenna had no memory of at least the past ten. To her, it had felt like a lifetime.

Jenna was prodded with hundreds of questions about her memory, the current president, the day of the week, and how old she was. The doctors needed to know if she was experiencing any changes, vision impairment, tingling, numbness, thinking, or anything that seemed abnormal. But 11 years of medical adventures proved abnormal was normal for her.

Jenna felt a trickling down her face from her forehead below her eye. She thought to herself, "No, you're just imagining this, Jenna.

There is nothing on your face." The feeling continued further down her face, now extending past her nose.

"If you tell them you feel something on your face, they will think you're going crazy, and then you'll have to go through more tests," Jenna reasoned with herself.

The doctors sternly explained to her any change in normalcy could mean something was off in her brain. But Jenna wouldn't let them know she was losing her mind, so she lay there, thinking, "Just wait it out; it'll go away."

Not even a minute had gone by, and with hesitation in her voice, she whispered, "Is it weird to feel like I have water dripping down my head?" At that moment, Jenna noticed a bitter, metallic taste on the tip of her tongue.

Kay and the nurse turned towards Jenna and saw a slow purge of blood running down her face and onto the pillow she was holding. A staple had fallen out of her head. The nurse rushed to grab gauze pads. Not caring about the blood, all Jenna could think was, "I am not crazy."

Jenna's progression continued. Her brain was waking up after all the swelling, bleeding, and surgical trauma. She had been moved to a step-down unit, free from all IV lines, the last of the four sites on her hands and arms, all removed after failing. Now, only six days post-surgery, the doctors gave her the green light to go home.

"Home? Am I ready to go home?" she thought to herself. It wasn't that long ago she had weakness on one side of her body, unable to even speak her name. She would ask to use the bathroom, only to stare in the distance for the moments to follow. Unable to communicate any longer, she'd just lie there in her own pee, all while feeling like Barry Bonds was having batting practice inside her head.

But there was no denying going home as Jenna noticed the large red heart embellished in the middle of the Virginia is for lovers' sign on the side of Interstate 85. She did not know it at that moment, but something was left behind, and there was no guarantee she would ever get it back.

60

WHAT'S THAT?

About a week and a half after surgery, Jenna was only now beginning to bend her stiffened twig legs to a 90-degree angle while lying in her bed that was once again, positioned in the corner of their family's den. The once comforting fetal position where she had found her only comfort while sleeping for many years, now proved to be some grueling task that showed just how weak she had become. With little progress, Jenna was set to go back to Duke for an overview of her healing process. That day would prove to be one of complete torment, starting with the ride down to Duke.

Gabriel had taken the day off work to drive Kay and Jenna down there. Knowing the fragile state she remained in, an extra pair of hands was warranted, especially a pair of male hands.

The entire three hours down to Duke, Gabriel dodged the snowstorm aftermath. Potholes were scattered across Interstate 85, and he did whatever he could to avoid any bumps in the road. Any sudden impacts or loud noises would send Jenna's brain into overdrive. Pulsating pains would shatter any relief from the constant headache that had now become her new norm since surgery.

First, an X-ray was ordered for her knees, but it was not a typical X-ray. Gabriel rolled Jenna in a wheelchair into the room because she had no strength in her arms. The physician's assistant observed Jenna's condition and quickly realized those particular X-rays were out of the question. He told Jenna she had to stand on a box to do them.

Jenna sat there. She slightly leaned forward as the strength it took to sit up dwindled quickly. Jenna looked at the physician's assistant and thought, "I can't even say a complete sentence because I don't have enough strength. Do you really think I can step up on a four-inch-high block?" She couldn't stand alone without assistance, let alone put all her body weight on one leg to step up. The X-ray was out of the question. Jenna had to regain her strength before the doctors could even discuss the issues with the pain in her knees.

The next stop was physical therapy. Once again, Jenna was rolled to another part of the hospital. Gabriel pushed her wheelchair into a large room filled with medicine balls, elastic stretch bands, and parallel bars resembling the ones gymnasts compete on at the Olympics. Seeing the gym equipment filled her with feelings of defeat. She knew she could barely transfer from the wheelchair to the front seat of the car. There was no way she would be able to do anything physical for quite some time. It did not take long for the physical therapist to come to the same conclusion, one look at Jenna to be exact. She would need a physical therapist to come to their house before more extensive recovery could begin.

As Gabriel wheeled Jenna back over to the clinic for more tests and her transplant doctors to evaluate her condition, Jenna did not really think about what was to come or what she had been told down in physical therapy. The truth was, she was so weak that thinking was too much of a chore to even try and accomplish it.

The day was half over, and much like a mix between the Hunchback of Notre Dame and Barney, Jenna's slightly deformed, purple-bruised face and her slouched-over body completed her pitiful picture of total exhaustion. Like a newborn baby nestled in a carrier pressed up against their parents' chest, Jenna could no longer hold herself up. The feet and armrests of the wheelchair were the only barriers holding her in. Jenna sat in torture, trying so hard not to tumble forward out of the wheelchair as Gabriel quickly rolled her to the clinic.

The elevator doors glided from side to side as they opened, and Jenna, her mom, and Gabriel squished in alongside a young boy and his father.

She must have looked like a monster out of a horror movie. Jenna's face was colored in shades of blacks, blues, purples, and greens. She was bloated from all the steroids, her head resembling that of a large, overgrown, rotten blueberry. Jenna's eyes were still swollen, not swollen shut anymore, but swollen just the same. Her hair was matted on the sides and in the back, with traces of blood still left behind from the surgery. An L-shaped, three-inch wide area of hair from the top of her forehead to the back of her right ear had been shaven. A line of staples gathered in the center like a centipede that had rested on the top of her head, with its 100 legs clamped into her scalp.

Before the elevator doors opened, Jenna's head was almost lying in her own lap because her strength had all but left her fragile body. Just as the wheelchair crossed over the elevator threshold, she overheard the little boy innocently ask his father a simple question as he harmlessly pointed in her direction.

"What's that?"

At that moment, Jenna did not need a mirror to tell her how terrifying she looked. A small boy could not even identify she was human. As the doors closed behind them, Jenna motioned for her mom to come near.

"Did you hear what that little boy said?" she questioned her. With sadness in her mom's eyes, she replied, "I was hoping you didn't hear that."

Jenna lifted her head barely enough to see Gabriel's face. She felt so horrible for him as she knew he was so out of his element. He would have rather been any other place but there. He was doing all he could to be supportive, but Jenna knew it was more than he bargained for. His sister had just been referred to as a *that*. She could see everything in him ready to flee, but he stood next to her with a weakened, stoic look.

As they entered the clinic, it did not take long for the nurses to realize Jenna needed a bed. She was in so much pain from trying to hold herself up, and her body was fading fast.

Soon, Dr. K came into her room and explained all Jenna had been through. It was as if she was hearing all of it for the first time, and it would not be the last time she felt that way. Jenna had been so out of it during the whole ordeal she had yet to comprehend she had brain bleeds, massive swelling in her brain, major surgery, was bed-ridden for weeks, and had been on a vast number of steroids for almost a month and a half. Dr. K explained the steroids were extremely harmful, eight times stronger than those she was on during the transplant. No wonder she had blown up so quickly, and her knees were now crumbling beneath her.

Dr. K could not stress how imperative it was Jenna move around. Her knees would not allow for much movement, but even if she could just sit in a chair all day, that would be something.

As Jenna lay there completely energy-free, she could not help but think to herself, "Can you not see me? This is what happened after half of a day in a wheelchair." But just like every time before, Jenna knew she had no choice. She had to do what the doctors said, or else she would be left as a shriveled up, decaying blueberry.

Later in the afternoon, while waiting for more test results to come in, Jenna overheard Sue quietly talking to her mom as she slipped in and out of catnaps. Jenna saw a concerned look on Sue's face as she took the few steps towards her bed. With a crooked half frown, she said, "Jenna, we have to take your staples out today."

"What! Are you kidding me? After everything that has gone on today, you want to pry this metal centipede out of my head? You have to be joking," she thought.

After gaining her composure, Jenna looked at Sue and said, "Ok, but I want you to do it." Jenna trusted her.

Jenna knew Sue would stop when she needed her to. Sue would put Jenna first, as she always had, so she would be the one chosen to conquer the task.

Sue's crooked frown quickly turned into a complete sullen look of sadness as she said, "I can't take out staples, only stitches." Jenna's only comfort was knowing Sue would be the one removing them, and now that was gone. She tried comforting Jenna, explaining she would get someone from the neurosurgical team to take them out. Knowing she had no other choice, Jenna waited for the inevitable.

It did not matter how sick and out of it Jenna was, she could still see out the glass-sliding door at the entrance of her room. She watched as a very young-looking guy walked around in what seemed like circles, completely lost as to where he was.

Jenna looked over at her mom, and they both knew what the other was thinking, "This guy better not come into Jenna's room."

Sure enough, he bounced into Jenna's room as if he was a five-year-old boy skipping into class on his first day of kindergarten. He looked old enough to be Gabriel's age. They were sending a kid to take metal staples out of her head.

Jenna's head was pounding from all the commotions earlier in the day. Yet, after asking the kid-like medical technician, "Are you any good?" the staple removing began.

Before the first clip of the plyers, Jenna asked if she could keep her staples, and he looked at her like she was crazy. Jenna told him she and her brother would want to compare battle scars, how many staples from his back surgery compared to her brain surgery.

"Sure," the technician said.

He took the pliers to Jenna's head and snipped the first one. "Owwww!" she screamed.

Blood started streaming down her face, and he joyfully claimed, "I got two!"

Jenna, with a scowl on her face, said, "Don't do that again!"

Then, one by one, he removed nearly 100 staples from her head.

She was never so happy for that day to be over. As they left Duke, there was in a way less hope than when they had arrived. Jenna was in extreme pain from her shoulders down her arms, to her wrists, and from her knees to her ankles. The culprit was the steroids. They were attacking her joints, and her bones were once again dying. Jenna's knees had recovered well from the knee surgeries she had just four years previous, but the steroids were now compromising the progress she had made. Jenna could not comprehend another surgery so soon after brain surgery, but that was where she was headed if a miracle did not happen.

Only for a Moment:

PET THERAPY

If there was something Jenna could use at that point, it was a break from the harsh reality that surrounded her. With her brain vastly compromised and her body exceptionally weak, she was extremely limited in activities that could mentally remove her from the pain she endured. But it was in those mundane moments, when one fluffy ball of joy would jump into her lap, knowing Jenna needed the comfort.

Sugar had been Jenna's cat for seven years at that point, but like most cats, Sugar did what she wanted, when she wanted. She spent most of her days outside, bringing her prey to the back door as if she were a mail carrier dropping off an important package. Maggie had passed away a couple of years prior, and somewhat like human instinct, Sugar knew her role had changed. It was now Sugar who lay by Jenna in her bed as she reverted back to binge-watching her favorite shows while stroking the long, snow-white locks of her new therapy companion. Sugar knew Jenna needed comfort. If you have not gotten a pet, get a cat, and pet it.

Just breathe, keep breathing, and keep going.

61

WHAC-A-MOLE

To say time moved slowly was a vast understatement. Jenna had been doing nothing but lying in bed, not moving her arms or legs without help from someone close by. She lay completely still because she simply did not have the strength to lift any part of her body. One day, Kay walked in, looked at a miserable Jenna, and told her, "You should turn over and lay on your side to give your back a break."

With a smirk and a slight eye roll, Jenna stared back at her and said, "Really?" Her mom knew instantly. Jenna didn't have enough strength in her abs to roll over by herself. So in complete frustration, Jenna just lay there, day in and day out.

As each day passed, Jenna began showing minor signs of improvement. The swelling in her brain began to decrease. She only asked for assistance when her elbows felt like they were on fire, as the steroids were not only attacking Jenna's knees but also her shoulders, elbows, and wrists.

Physical therapy was ordered. Jenna desperately needed to build her muscles. Yet, the AVN in her knees and now possibly in her elbows and shoulders meant any weight pressing down on them would cause more harm than good. Jenna used a wheelchair and had to take extreme caution when operating her arms as leverage to sit down. Pain medicines were given around the clock, and they helped at times, but her only slight relief was from heating pads turned to the highest setting around the clock.

As if the pain was not a big enough obstacle, nausea made it more challenging to get out of bed. All of those things may have seemed small compared to what she had experienced, but at that stage, it was critical Jenna moved around. Regardless, at nearly three weeks post-surgery, she was lying in bed throwing up with a fever slowly taking over her body.

Blood work was needed, but Jenna only had one good vein left, and that one was healing from being overused. But the steroids had compromised her immune system and could cause more severe complications if the fever went on for too long.

"Mommmm," Jenna moaned and moaned from her bed. Her fever was 102 degrees Fahrenheit, and an excruciating headache had also set in. Jenna's immune system was suppressed, and since she was not far out of surgery, red flags were popping up everywhere like a Whac-A-Mole trying to miss the next hammer to the head.

As Jenna tossed and turned to find some sort of relief from the pain, she could not help but wonder why she never seemed to go through surgery without complications. Jenna had infections the doctors could never identify, those referred to as the *Jenna Bug*. Her middle name had become Rare. Rare leukemia, rare DNA, and rare reactions to chemotherapy drugs, all of which were before her transplant.

The week before, Jenna's parents asked Dr. K, who performed the most cord blood transplants in the world, if her brain hemorrhage, AVM, or anything close to that had happened in one of her other transplant patients. Dr. K's answer was a simple, "No." The cause of the bleed had not been determined, but the doctors were taking an educated guess the bleed was the result of the radiation she had before transplant.

At 4:00 a.m., Kay once again sat watching Jenna struggling to breathe as her chest moved erratically up and down. With her fever still so high and gasping for air, there was no other option than to rush her to Duke. Just 20 days after surgery, doctors ordered a barrage of tests, including checking for pneumonia. The quick, shallow breaths she was taking were concerning. Even though the X-ray showed the bottom of her lung was compromised, pneumonia was ruled out. The doctors explained because Jenna could not walk, she was not taking in enough oxygen. Fitting her with a breathing device, they hoped Jenna could begin to take deeper breaths to alleviate her symptoms.

A CAT scan with a contrast dye was also ordered for her brain. The last obstacle anyone wanted was for there to be an infection where they had just operated. That meant an IV line had to be started. A simple needle stick may have seemed trivial at that point, but with Jenna's veins continuing to collapse, actually getting one would be a miracle. Back home, people were praying, and God answered in a very peculiar and miraculous way.

A young male nurse walked into Jenna's room. Kay, Sue, and Jenna all looked at each other simultaneously with an uh-oh-like concern. Sue had been at Duke for over 15 years and had never seen that guy before. To top it off, he even said he was good at finding veins. Jenna had heard that many times before. Countless nurses claimed to be good at finding a vein, but they always seemed to meet their match with her. Sue knew that nearly as well as Jenna and her mom. As he picked up the needle, all three held their breath, stunned by what would occur.

That young guy lived up to his word. With no useable veins in sight, he found a vein no one had ever used before. He got it on the first try.

The scan was given, and nothing concerning was found. Precautionary antibiotics were started through her IV. With no real answers, Kay and Jenna were sent home that Friday afternoon.

Over the weekend Jenna progressively worsened. Her fevers rose. The pain and swelling in her head felt like an over-filled balloon about to pop. Jenna rarely asked for prayers during her years of battling illnesses, but that day she told her mom she wanted prayers around the clock.

Kay continued to watch as Jenna's chest slowly moved up and down. When her sounds became fainter, she would get up from the couch and walk over to Jenna's bed to check if she was still breathing. Although not the least bit normal, this was something Kay had done many times since Jenna was diagnosed with leukemia. No one could deny it was physically painful for Jenna to endure the trials she faced, and many words could be used to describe that pain. But honestly, there are no words to describe being a parent watching your child suffer continuously, always wondering if you were going to walk into their room and find them no longer breathing.

As the hours passed by, Kay wrestled with the choice of whether she needed to take Jenna to the emergency room, knowing she didn't have any more veins to use, and the ER was not the best stick. So, she waited. A couple of days later, Jenna's designated chauffeur, Gabriel, their mom, and she all headed to Duke again.

That day was a long one full of tests, each one scheduled to try and find the root of the fevers and breathing problems. After an inconclusive morning X-ray of her chest, an IV was placed, and blood was drawn. Then, a Spiral CT was ordered to check for a blood clot in Jenna's lungs.

The start of the CT was taking much longer than average, which usually was not a good sign. Sue slowly walked through Jenna's door with pure exhaustion written on her face. She and Jenna's doctors had just spent over an hour arguing with the CT technicians, which was not uncommon for her transplant team. The immense pressure they faced as they held countless children's lives in their hands identified them each as Davids who conquered giants as they worked tirelessly to lay waste to all kinds of diseases and ailments. And that day was no different.

Sue explained another IV would have to be placed, but Jenna's veins were barely usable. Between the countless sticks and high doses of steroids, she thought there was no way another vein would be found. Not only did they have to find one, but a larger needle also had to be placed because a certain contrast needed for the CT would not flow through the existing smaller needle protruding from Jenna's arm.

As Jenna rolled into a small examination room, a nurse entered and investigated her butchered arms.

"Her veins are just so tiny. I'm not sure they will take a needle this size," she said. The nurse was as sweet and comforting as she could be, considering the dilemma she faced. She looked at Jenna, seeing the tears flowing down her cheeks. "I will try one time. If I can't get it, I won't try again," she explained in calming words.

That test was imperative; Jenna had to have it. She would need a surgical procedure to place a line if the nurse missed it. All three nurses now standing around Jenna, Kay, and Sue, prayed and begged God for a clean stick.

He answered.

But be *careful* what you pray for.

Little did Jenna know that CT would not bring the usual warm sensations and sudden urges to use the bathroom. It would be nothing like what she had experienced in the past.

The technician began twisting and turning Jenna's body, getting scans from all different directions. Jenna was so weak and worn down from all the day's activities that merely holding her arm in the air was like bench pressing a hundred-pound weight. Her body was just not equipped to do it. After the positioning, the technician informed Jenna she was ready to administer the dye into her vein.

She told Jenna, "This is going to be uncomfortable." Jenna understood, as she was prepared for the warm sensation and to hold in her bladder.

"On the count of three, I am going to push," the technician said, holding the syringe in her hand. "One, two, three."

Jenna screamed.

As soon as the dye was pushed into Jenna's veins, it felt as though the inside of her arm had burst, just like a paintball after it had hit its target. Jenna thought her veins had splattered inside.

Seeing Jenna shaking in pain, the technician tried to calm her down. "I know, it's not a good feeling," she said.

"Not a good feeling," Jenna thought to herself. "Are you kidding me? Do I still have an arm after that?"

Later that day, when Sue checked on Jenna, Jenna told her about her CT experience. All she had to do was take one look at Sue's face, and she knew.

"You knew it would do that, didn't you?" Jenna questioned her. Jenna had learned so much about Sue by that time, and Sue had about Jenna, also. Sue told Jenna she knew she wouldn't have done the test if she knew that was going to be her experience. But Sue understood how imperative the test was.

After a few hours, the CT results were in. Jenna had atypical pneumonia in both lungs, an infection, and the sacs (alveoli) at the bottom of her lungs were closed, and they needed to be opened. So back into the hospital she went, just a few short weeks after her craniotomy.

Antibiotics and other medications were prescribed, covering anything they may not have been able to see on the scans. Jenna was on three breathing treatments a day, using a spirometer as much as possible. She was placed on oxygen because when she arrived at Duke, her oxygen level was at 83. There was no wonder she was having such a hard time breathing the last few days.

The nausea, throwing up, elevated heart rate, and excruciating headaches were hard to cope with, but nothing compared to the frustration of not being able to use her arms. Jenna had IVs on the insides of both elbows, making it nearly impossible to do simple, everyday tasks like feeding herself, her breathing treatment, taking medicines, and scratching any itch above her waist.

Her mom was now her hands, something she had been many times before. That may have been a small hurdle for what she had been through, but now at 22 years old, Jenna just wanted her independence. She wanted normalcy. Yet again, normalcy was something she would be reminded she didn't have as Andre entered her room.

Kay had slipped into the restroom while Jenna fought off nausea as she lay in the hospital bed watching reruns of *I Love Lucy*. Andre had not made it two steps into the room, and all she could say to him was, "Bucket!"

He raced over to grab Jenna's all-too-familiar chuck bucket, and into it, Jenna's head went as Andre held it in front of her unmovable arms. Kay opened the bathroom door and realized what had happened, and her nurse mom instincts kicked in, assuming the position of holding the bucket for Jenna. In all the commotion, Andre slipped out the door.

At that moment, Jenna began to realize that time at Duke was different. She was older now. Andre, her previous nurse, who she and Hannah used to have a schoolgirl crush on, was now a nurse practitioner in the dating range of Jenna. Her peers were now administering all the tests and procedures once administered by adults on a small child.

After about a week, Jenna was off the oxygen and breathing independently. It seemed as though she was on the mend enough to be discharged, but Jenna had so many mixed feelings about being released. She knew what she faced if she had to come back. Jenna couldn't stand the thought of being stuck anymore, fearing if she went home, something would go wrong, and she would have to head back down to Duke for more sticks. However, her fear was not a good enough reason for the doctors to give her more inpatient care, so she was sent home.

Give a Moment

THE GIFT OF ENCOURAGEMENT

It's crazy how God works. He brings people and experiences into our lives in the most unexpected ways. The night before Jenna's brain surgery, two guys from Liberty who did not personally know her, came to pray with Kay and Jenna. They had come to know Jenna through hearing her story in convocation. Weathering that treacherous winter blizzard, and at nine o'clock at night, they walked into Jenna's ICU room and handed Kay flowers. Two strangers drove in a dangerous storm three hours one way to sit, visit, and pray with her for all of fifteen minutes, only to get back in the car and drive three hours back to Liberty. They were called by God to be the encouragement Kay needed in those dire hours.

It was visits from those boys and so many others, like Chantel, who brought so much hope in such a desperate time. A friend of Jenna's who had just recently undergone a double lung transplant, Chantel was a fighter in every sense of the word. Only a month after her transplant, she walked the long distance from the parking lot to the hospital halls of Duke with her oxygen machine in her hand, because she knew the importance of encouraging people in their time of need. If two strangers can face a treacherous storm and a double lung transplant survivor can walk a mile to give a mother encouragement as she watches her daughter lay there unresponsive in a hospital bed, then surely, there are countless ways for you to encourage and bring joy to someone else's life. A meal, flowers, a visit, a card, a cup of coffee, a compliment, the options are endless.

Don't waste a breath, get out there and be the joy in someone's life!

62

WHERE HAS MY DAUGHTER GONE?

Jenna placed one hand on the wheelchair armrest as she pivoted her hips and scooted into the chair, and her mom slowly began pushing her towards the house. As she reached the bottom of the ramp, she looked at it as though it was a mountain. Jenna had survived surgery and the countless complications, but the mountain ahead would only prove to test her body both physically and mentally. Reaching the summit meant year 22 would be behind her, so she started up that ramp, she started up that mountain.

Over the next couple of months, Jenna struggled to regain a sense of normalcy as the pounding in her head became so severe volts of nausea would strike her body, making it nearly impossible to do anything other than stare at the television screen. The frustration of her siblings would fill the room as they exclaimed, "Oh no, not *Bonanza* again!"

In all honesty though, it was the shows like *Bonanza, The Big Valley, Survivor, I Love Lucy, Full House, Family Matters,* and *JAG* that brought Jenna comfort as they had so many years ago while she battled cancer. Her brothers, completely annoyed watching reruns Jenna had now started quoting, could not understand those shows were the only constant that ever remained in Jenna's life. It was the only positive that would never change to a negative. So, she watched as her brain slowly began to strengthen.

As the days and weeks passed, she began new stimulating brain activities by playing card games and doing crafts and puzzles. Jenna was once the girl who would think two moves ahead, but now she could only visualize the move in her head, unable to communicate with her hands to play the right card.

Frustration sank in, and a feeling of defeat would overtake Jenna. But in between those feelings, sounds of laughter began filling the family's house again as people started coming over after months of everyone sitting around in silence. Only the random sounds of whispered conversations had been echoing from the walls of their den for the past couple of months.

Any noise felt like a bomb had just been set off right beside her ear. Noises that would have never bothered Jenna before had become like terrible nails on a chalkboard that sent Jenna into an annoyed and angry state. The deep, scary bark from their black lab, the mechanical chopping sounds of chewing food, and the rhythmic shriek of a phone ringing sent Jenna into a crazed, anxious state. Even the soft cries of her cat, Sugar, created throbbing pains pounding inside her head.

The concentration it took to look at pictures in a magazine would send her head into a whirlwind. There was absolutely no way she could read. As Jenna began to focus on the words covering the page, they would quickly combine into the world's longest word, only to end up causing her vision to blur.

After almost three months, Jenna asked for her phone to text a friend for the first time. Before that, the concentration it took for her to form a text had been too much. Between pneumonia, headaches, nausea, constant joint pain, and certain brain functions returning at what seemed like a race between a sloth and a snail, Jenna's entire body was trying to salvage any remnants of the life she had before. But her old life was being stripped from her body. Like rose petals after the first winter's freeze, once beautifully colored and vibrant, they were now falling to the frost-bitten ground, crumbling and withering away. Remnants of who Jenna was had begun to disintegrate as she started talking and talking and talking and talking.

Jenna went from barely forming sentences, as it was physically and mentally painful to talk, to rambling about how the sky was blue and the grass was green. A near-college graduate was now speaking with the words and phrases of a child. Heaven forbid if her words were not acknowledged, because she would repeat them over and over again until someone did. Jenna had to learn how to process conversations, completely oblivious there needed to be two people involved to have a conversation. Jenna could never turn on her listening skills as she began talking over everyone in the room.

Just weeks before, when asked a question, Jenna would look at her family with a blank stare. Little did they know, she was trying to speak, but could only see the word flashing in her head like a hotel vacancy sign, unable for the words to ever leave her lips. The empty stares soon turned into words, but words no one had ever heard before and certainly would never be found in the dictionary. She described tornadoes as *rampid* and her life battle as *tremulturous*, only to have her mom explain maybe she meant rampant and trembling or tumultuous. Jenna would snap back, arguing they were real words and made complete sense in how she was using them.

During a trip to OfficeMax one day, Kay and Jenna stood at the checkout line paying for the items in their cart. Trying to make light of the conversation, the girl behind the cash register said, "No worries, we print dollar bills here." As Jenna walked out of the store, she looked at her mom and, in all seriousness, questioned, "I didn't realize that Office Max printed money." It was like she had the mental comprehension of a kindergartener, believing conversational jokes and irony as actual facts.

Jenna had not only acquired the new gift of gab but a quick wit, with a side of vulgarity added in. While watching television with her family, a commercial would appear on the screen, and Jenna would blurt out some obscene comment relating to the scene. Much like the cast on *Who's Line Is It Anyway?*, Jenna was quick-witted with comebacks, but she never ceased to mix in a little *Two and a Half Men* by adding in some type of sexual innuendo. While her mom and Hannah would look at her as if she had lost her mind, the guys in the room could not help themselves from laughing, knowing it should not have come out of Jenna's mouth.

Along with her newly-formed personality, Jenna now had unnatural, animated facial expressions that resembled Lucille Ball's. She had always been fascinated with Lucy's ability to do crazy facials, and in Jenna's eyes, she could now replicate that phenomenal talent. The only difference, Lucy's facials were on command, and Jenna's were not. Kay would look at Hannah with a concerned question forming in her mind. "Where has my daughter gone?" she thought.

As family members watched Jenna have conversations with herself, Kay's brother looked at her and said, "This is some rollercoaster ride you're on, isn't it?"

Jenna's life had been a roller coaster for as long as she could remember, but that new track was not one anyone in their family was prepared for. If Jenna knew all the twists and turns, all the hills and flips, and that one piece of the unfinished track her roller coaster car was headed towards at warped speed, she never would have chosen to get on that ride. But with so many lingering physical trials ahead, there was nothing to do but sit back and watch as Rapunzel had just been freed from the tower, and Flynn Rider, or in other words, anyone who came to visit Jenna had to sit there and listen to the ramblings of a newly-freed girl who had just seen the world for the first time.

63

A MANE LIKE SAMSON

The old saying, from your head down to your toes, never meant so much as it did when everything from Jenna's brain to her elbows, lungs, knees, bones, and emotions needed rebuilding. It would become even more apparent on their next trip to Duke as Jenna had more follow-up appointments.

Orthopedic doctors had confirmed the graft in Jenna's right knee from the surgery four years prior had started to fail. When it completely failed, her knee would collapse. The surgeries to correct it were very complicated and cutting edge, as the doctors explained what was to come. First, they would look inside her knee arthroscopically to determine the damage. After evaluating, they would choose between two types of knee surgeries.

One option, an osteochondral graft, would use transplanted bone and cartilage from a frozen cadaver, which was similar to what Jenna had been through before. If the area needed a more extensive repair or was much more damaged, the second option would be a Carticel surgery, which would take bone from her hip. That was much more extensive, lasting about five hours, and of course, that was the surgery the doctors believed she would need. But the devastating news continued to pile on.

Jenna's femur bone, which connected her hip to her knee, was out of alignment. Before even thinking about operating on the knee, Jenna would need her femur repaired, or her knees would fail again. Not one, not two, but three surgeries to fix her knee, and that was just one knee.

After hearing the news, Jenna wanted to be strong, but she had no strength left inside her. She still had not even grasped the uphill battle she would face healing mentally from brain surgery, and now she was headed towards three more surgeries. Jenna sat there in her wheelchair, exasperated. She thought to herself, "I just don't think my body can take anymore."

She wanted to laugh at the doctor and say, "Do you know what my body has been through? I can't do this! Like, you don't understand, I'm physically and mentally destroyed."

Jenna was always the easy target in a rousing game of chase. Remember, she was the slow-motion runner in the scary movies. But in real life, she was tired of being tagged as it. Sure, she would have a little time to go hide before being chased again, three months to be exact, but Jenna couldn't even entertain that thought.

With the trauma from the brain hemorrhage, craniotomy, double pneumonia, and now knee surgeries that prowled around her like a lion circling a pack of zebras in an African safari, Jenna steadily began losing her hair. Globs of hair covered her purple, Grandma's hand-sewn, silk pillowcase. She knew something was not right, and a dermatologist confirmed it. Jenna's body had gone into protection mode, saving all her vital organs, her brain, heart, lungs, and stopped working on others like her hair and fingernails. The doctor explained it like chemo. Chemo was so harsh on the body, the body naturally fought to save the most important organs first.

Jenna held back the tears as best she could as she said in unbelief, "Wow, I've already lost my hair once. Who loses their hair twice and at only 22 years old?"

Gabriel and Zachary came riding in on their white horses in a gallant effort to make the loss of her hair easier. Gabriel said, "If you shave your head by next Friday, I'll shave mine." With her eyes as big as saucers, Jenna couldn't believe what she was hearing. There was no wonder Gabriel had received the senior superlative award for best hair. He had thick, dark brown tight ringlets that he had grown out since his back surgery five years prior, and cutting it all off was definitely out of his comfort zone. Zachary, with his senior superlative best smile, grinned from ear to ear and said, "I'll take that bet too!" Neither of them thought Jenna would do it, as the joking quickly turned to nervous apprehension when they thought, "She actually may go through with it."

Friday had arrived, and Jenna decided she might as well not be the only one with no hair, so she took the bet.

A friend came over, and Zachary eagerly jumped into the hot seat first.

Bzzzzzzzzzzzz, zzzzzm, zzzzzm, zzzzzm.

It did not take long, and Zachary's dirty blond, crew-cut fade had fallen to the floor of their back deck. In true Gabriel form, he demanded Jenna go next, unsure she would really shave her head.

Scissors began snipping away, as the doctors did not want a razor near Jenna's incision. Inch by inch, layers of Jenna's long black hair fell to the ground once again. Just like Samson's strength was robbed from the cutting of his hair, each strand of Jenna's fallen hair symbolized her becoming weaker as her identity eroded away.

Shortly after Jenna's turn, hundreds of tiny curls piled on the deck around them as all of Gabriel's curls were shaved off.

While Jenna was appreciative of what they did, she thought, "Great, now Mom has three boys and a girl," as she wrestled with new feelings of a lack of feminism as all her hair lay on the ground.

With the loss of her hair, Jenna would have been fine nestling inside the cocoon of her home for the next six months while it grew back, but that would not be the case as her friends and family had other ideas. Close family friends who had endured many battles with Jenna throughout the last 11 years thought it most fitting to hold a praise and worship party to give thanks to God for all He had done in Jenna's life. There was no denying the countless miracles they and many others had witnessed God complete in Jenna's life. Although Jenna understood the intent behind the idea, she wanted no part of it, and she made that abundantly clear as detest spewed from her mouth one weekend getaway to her aunt and uncle's house in Pennsylvania.

"I do not want to praise God! I am tired of being the sick girl. I am tired of being the poster girl for cancer. God could have prevented this from happening, but He did not, and I do not feel like praising Him!"

As Jenna's family in Pennsylvania heard those words, they knew something was different about her. Aunt Renee had not seen Jenna often since her brain surgery. She had been told by Kay about some of the changes in Jenna but had not witnessed them for herself until that moment.

Jenna was the girl who stood up in front of their church there in Pennsylvania and Jenna's home church after her battle with cancer. She thanked everyone for the many prayers said on her behalf. Jenna told them she knew she would not have survived cancer if it were not for their prayers. That girl sitting on the couch that day after the heated exchange was not Jenna. Her family understood Jenna's feelings of anger because they knew she had suffered greatly. She had endured so much in her short 22 years of life, and she had hit her limit. She didn't know how to cope. While Jenna may have questioned God in the past, she never blamed Him. But that time was different. With only the faint pleas from the song *Say Something (extended)* by A Great Big World echoing in the far-off distance of her mind, Jenna pushed back on the one who was easiest to push back on. Her heavenly Father who held her life in His hands would never stop loving her, no matter who she had become or how she had changed, and boy had she.

For the rest of the warmer months, Jenna spent her time barking at dogs and carrying dog bones in her mouth while on all fours. She swam with girls ten years old and younger, playing Marco Polo and running around the house with them as if they were all schoolyard friends during recess. The problem was, Jenna, at 22 years old, fit in with them laughing, imagining, and playing as if she was ten years old again. Jenna's brain was complicated. She was like a child but could also accomplish adult tasks.

An occupational therapist was coming to the house to help Jenna re-learn age-appropriate activities. During one of those visits, Kay spoke with the therapist out of earshot of Jenna. She described the disturbing changes she was seeing in Jenna's personality.

After hearing the concerns, the therapist sadly explained, "Her brain has been injured. This may be your new daughter. You may have to get used to this."

Kay's only gut-wrenching thoughts were, "I don't want a new daughter. I want my daughter."

Kay would have done anything to freeze time, or better yet, reverse it. But time, as well as Jenna's unfamiliarity, seemed to be slipping away as Jenna's new-found freedom from the wheels beneath her were lifted. She had been given the green light from her doctor in San Diego to begin walking again, as she had been wheelchair-bound due to her knees for the previous eight months. Her doctor understood why Duke thought her knees were in such terrible condition but assured Jenna they looked very normal for the surgeries he had performed four years prior. So with that unexpected blessing and answer to many prayers after a long and arduous eight months, she ditched the crutches and broke loose.

After almost a year of no driving, she put her foot to the floor, looked back at her mom, and said, "I've never been able to experience life. I've missed most of high school, and my college experience was cut short. I just want to live life!" So that's what she did.

With her hair now just slightly below her jawline, she embraced her early 2000s-style, mom-flip bob, and prepared for the upcoming semester at Liberty in January. Just one year after surgery, Jenna would finish her final semester of college. And with fear in her eyes, Kay let her go, knowing Jenna was no longer the daughter she had raised for the past 22 years, only clinging to the prayer that one day, maybe she would get back the daughter she once had.

64

KID IN A CANDY STORE

The start of the spring semester in 2011 felt like a total reset. New classes. New jobs. New scenery. New faces. Everything seemed new to Jenna, but was it? It was impossible to distinguish between the past and the present. It was as if her professors had just taken the whiteboard eraser and cleared the memories of Jenna's last two years of life. She could not remember which classes she had taken the year before brain surgery. There was no recollection of the many individuals who would wave and say "hi" to her as they passed in the hallways. Often, she questioned, "Am I actually friends with this person, or do they just know me because of the Facebook page started for me, *Desperate Prayer Needed For Jenna*?"

There was one girl who passed Jenna on the sidewalks often, always smiling, waving, and engaging in small talk as if they had been friends for years. Each time, Jenna would oblige in the conversation, each time walking away never knowing the girl's name or how she knew her. It was not until later in the semester Jenna found out she had eaten lunch with that girl almost every day the semester before her brain surgery. Jenna had no memories of those lunches with that girl.

It was moments like that when small light bulbs would flash in Jenna's head. Much like yellow flashing caution lights, she began recognizing that maybe, just maybe, there was something off. Also, key indicators were the faces her mom and Hannah made the entire year.

Jenna carried her newly-talkative personality to Liberty with a hint of locker- room talk on the side. Frequently, Hannah, completely embarrassed, knew Jenna was not getting the social cues from her peers that she needed to stop talking. Hannah's free-spirited, never met a stranger, crowned Prom Queen personality, struggled as she would watch as friends would make faces, knowing Jenna had done or said something not in the social norm. She wanted to be there for Jenna, but she didn't know how to protect Jenna from herself.

Immediately following brain surgery, nothing registered to Jenna as being off, but slowly as the months passed, Jenna began to understand there were reasons people would give her funny looks as she talked. As soon as comments left her mouth, she knew she shouldn't have said it, but it was too late to take it back. The looks she would receive from her mom and Hannah would now only infuriate her more, slowly creating distance between Jenna, her mom and Hannah. She no longer needed them telling her she wasn't acting right because she knew it. She just couldn't tell her brain to stop. So, she just embraced her new life, with only the sounds of her new ringtone playing in the background. *Smack that, all on the floor, smack that . . .*

The changes from brain surgery controlled more than just her mouth and what she listened to. They also governed her impulses. Like a kid in a candy store, Jenna's childlike mind told her anything she saw, she could have. She dated, flirted, and played with many people's emotions over the next year. Usually, the guys would look at her in complete disbelief as many of them knew her or at least of her reputation before brain surgery. They could not understand how she could hint at certain things and be so forward. It was only because of her virtuous character before surgery those guys never took her down a path, they knew she would regret.

As the months passed, Jenna's brain continued to heal. Before long she was walking across the Williams Stadium stage to receive her college diploma. While most would never understand what it took to reach that milestone, Jenna was just beginning to. Slowly, she was starting to see brain surgery had changed her.

Jenna knew she said things she would have never normally said, like one of her favorite remarks, "Freakin' A!" She knew she talked enough to hold conversations with herself. She knew the impulses she had were more like a high school jock rather than a girl who grew up in church and followed Jesus.

The thought of getting a job after graduation was daunting, knowing Jenna could not remember one minute to the next. In her head, Jenna knew if she left the morals and integrity encompassing Liberty's campus, there was no telling which direction her life may go. So, she stayed and did the only logical next step. She decided to pursue her master's degree.

When Jenna started her master's in human services with a concentration in executive leadership, the classes interested her. But she honestly chose the degree because she thought it would be the easiest to obtain after undergoing brain surgery. Little did she know, she did not choose that degree, but rather, that degree chose her. God had led her to that degree for one reason, and one reason only—to wake Sleeping Beauty. That wake-up call would happen in a very unsuspecting way as she walked into a class entitled interpersonal communications.

65

WAKING SLEEPING BEAUTY

The teacher had strategically designed the class to dig deep into each student's personality, to decipher the exchange of information passed from person to person. Students would begin to better understand themselves so that ultimately, they could better understand the people around them. The objective of the class was relatively straightforward. Complete the project due at the end of the semester, and the student would pass.

Throughout the semester, the teacher would give brilliant but subtle hints for the requirements of the final project. However, the perfectionists in the class wanted a point-by-point outline of the specific requirements, something they would never get. As more and more of the class became anxious during the semester, not knowing exactly how to complete their final project, Jenna, along with a friend, sat in the back row with smirks across their faces.

They had figured out the class. The teacher was toying with the students' minds to bring out certain personality traits built up in them. He was trying to frustrate them. If the student knew what made them tick, then they could learn how to deal with it and work through it, the essential key to interpersonal communication. As he watched the smirks on Jenna and her friend's faces, he knew they had caught on. The project was simple. Dissect a personality trait that the student did or did not like about themselves, find the source, and ways to change or enhance it.

However, as the assignment grew closer, Jenna had a bigger problem than even the teacher was prepared for. Jenna was fighting a battle within; one she had been battling for almost two years. Her personality had changed so drastically. She wrestled with thoughts of who she was and the inability to get those traits back. After explaining her *split-personality* dilemma, the teacher told her to concentrate on the here and now. And there was no questioning about it; she knew exactly what she wanted to change about her new personality.

Jenna had turned into Toby Keith's song, *I Wanna Talk about Me*, and could not control her yearning to be heard. Jenna knew the sign of people walking away was her cue to stop talking, but she just could not get her brain to do so. If there was anything she wanted to change about her new life, it was that. But to complete the project fully, she had to find out why she had the need to talk endlessly.

Sitting there atop her college dorm room bed, Jenna began reading the countless websites that explained what the right frontal lobe controlled. As she scrolled the pages, words like excessive talking, working memory, impulse control, attention and concentration, social and sexual behaviors, reasoning and judgment, mood changes, and many more personality traits flooded the screen. Those words were like sharp daggers through her soul as she began to realize almost every aspect of her personality had been altered. As tears streamed down her face that day, she was seeing and reading for herself what her brain had endured for the first time. She was waking up from a nightmare.

I was waking up from that nightmare.

66

FOREVER MOMENT

Just before undergoing brain surgery, a TV show neurosurgeon stated, "When you're going into surgery, you worry you won't wake up. But with brain surgery, you worry you will wake up, *but you won't be there when you do.*"[3]

As I sat on top of my bed that day, I woke up to the realization my identity had been stripped from me. The confidence I had in my abilities, my looks, and my personality had been stolen. Everything had changed. No longer was I the person I was before brain surgery. That girl . . . was gone.

The emptiness was overwhelming. Issues I had never struggled with were now like the walls of Jericho that seemed nearly impossible to make fall. As I kept reading through pages upon pages of medical journals, I learned that the frontal lobes were the emotional control center and the home to my personality. It was no wonder the security in the way I spoke, acted, and lived no longer offered me any moment of relief from this new life I was facing. But I read on and studied those pages. And I came to the realization of something far greater than any medical journal could ever teach me.

The excessive talking, memory loss, lack of social behavior, impulse control, and so forth, were only small issues in the grand scheme of life. As a result of the brain surgery, I had personally and relationally disconnected with everything and everyone around me.

I was once the girl everyone called, Dear Jenna. My friends would come to me for support or sound counseling advice, but after brain surgery, I struggled to even care about a close friend who had undergone a serious surgery themselves. I knew in my head I should offer him a meal and an ear to listen, but I felt not one ounce of care for what he had just endured.

Hannah, who had brought the most joy into my life even while I was in the most excruciating pain during the transplant, now only brought on an internal struggle for me. I wrestled with the thought that we may no longer have the same relationship. No longer was I the sister she had known her entire life. While my head understood nothing could ever break that deeply rooted sisterly bond that had been forged together so long ago, the relational aspect of my brain had been severed. Like a thief in the night, it had carried away my precious relationship with Hannah.

And my mom. She was the woman who had literally fought side by side with me for my entire life. After holding my hand through fibromyalgia, leukemia, a radical transplant, surgery after surgery, and the loss of many precious lives, she was now watching her daughter become someone she barely knew. My mom was my rock, my constant. I knew in my head I loved her, but the ongoing battle to be the daughter I was before brain surgery, only left feelings of bitterness and ultimately emotional isolation from her. The bond that was unbreakable, broke. Our relationship was severed and there was no guarantee it would ever be complete again.

But it was the lack of those relationships that brought me to a piercing reality. There was an even larger chasm that seemed to separate me from a love far greater than any of my friends, siblings, or parents could offer me in those moments of healing. It was the love and relationship with Jesus Christ, who I had accepted into my life as a young girl.

The day I realized Jesus Christ died on the cross for my sins, asked Him into my life, and I turned from those sins, was the day I started a relationship with Him and became a follower of Christ. However, due to the trauma my brain had endured, there was a disconnect in that relationship, or at least, that is what it felt like.

I wanted so desperately to feel something, anything. With frustration setting in, I knew in my head even though this was not the journey I would have chosen for myself, it was God's plan, and I had the *knowledge* that His plan was perfect—Jeremiah 29:11.

Remembering all the stories in the Bible I had learned my entire life growing up in church was not an issue for me. That part of my memory wasn't erased. But just the mere knowledge and memory of who God is, was not helping me surpass the utter disappointment and downright anger I was feeling being disconnected from everything and everyone. For years after the brain surgery, those same hopeless feelings of failure continued as my impulses rebelled. My brain could not switch from religion, or the knowledge I had of Jesus Christ, to the relationship I had with Him. But that is the difference between religion and faith.

What I had in those moments was my religion. I knew about God. I believed that Jesus Christ died for me. So, in turn, I knew what I was supposed to do. I went to convocation, listened to the speakers, and joined in with my fellow classmates singing praises to God. But none of that mattered. I wanted to do the right things. So, that should have been enough, right.

Wrong.

There was nothing I could do to earn a relationship with Jesus Christ; that's religion.

For someone to truly know Jesus, it is not simply a prayer, going to church, or being a good person. You see, God accepted me as His child the day I asked Jesus into my heart and never left my side, no matter how far I had run from Him and what my brain was telling me. I didn't need to do more because Jesus Christ did it all—Ephesians 2:8–9. He took on all my sins, insecurities, and all of my good works on the cross—Titus 3:4–7. It wasn't about what I could do for Christ, but all about what Christ did for me.

For me, salvation is like the cord blood transplant I had at 11 years old. Death was eminent until that day when I was offered a special gift. It came in a small bag filled with tiny, life-altering cells. But that's all it would have been had I not chosen to receive the transplant. Just a gift of a bag of cells. When I chose to have the transplant and take those new cells as my own, I was given another chance at life here on earth.

But God, in His unconditional love, has offered each one of you and me an even greater, life-altering gift, one for here on earth and for an eternity in heaven. It is one we all have to choose whether to receive or not.

For my mom, she truly grasped the depths of God's love when she watched me suffer at Duke during the treacherous days of transplant. She talked to God in complete brokenness and said, "I know that I have four children. But . . . I am not willing to give up one." At that moment, she realized how much God loves us because

He willingly gave up His *only* Son to suffer and be crucified on the cross for everyone—John 3:16.

For me, it was *my brain injury* mentally stripping me from my identity in myself, everyone around me, and my relationship with Christ, including the feeling of being loved by God. It was the lack of love that allowed me to see how vast His love was for me. Often in life, we do not realize what we have until it is gone. In my brain, the sense of God being absent brought me to a greater understanding of who He is and had been in my life over the past 22 years.

It took cancer at age 11, and a craniotomy at age 22 to realize the only thing in life that truly matters is a relationship with Jesus Christ. I cannot express how much the activities of drawing horses and cars, playing games, the company of Maggie and Sugar, visits from people who loved me, and so many other blessings brought me many moments of happiness and freedom from the pain that surrounded me. That was what they were, moments to pass by the moments.

You see, moments come and go. Good moments, bad moments, and all the in-between moments will always come to an end. Don't build your life on moments that will not last.

It is Jesus Christ and the unwavering joy of spending an eternity in heaven with Him that gave me the peace and strength to endure this crazy thing called life. While I began a relationship with Christ before age 11, it was through cancer and brain surgery, and the aftermath of both that I experienced God's love in a much deeper way than I ever could have imagined.

If there is one thing I pray you gain from reading this book, it's this. My story isn't about an 11-year-old girl who cheated death numerous times. It's not about a 22-year-old young woman who lost her identity and regained a new one all because of brain surgery.

It's not about the helpful moments I used to get through multiple hardships in my life, and it's most certainly not about religion.

My story is about experiencing God. When you truly experience something, it changes your perception of everything. It's the difference between having the knowledge a fire is hot and actually feeling and understanding what it is to be burned by the flames that engulf you.

God was and is my Healer, my ultimate hope, my Savior. He is my firm foundation to lean on when moments of relief are just not enough. He was and is the miracle maker of my story.

Before my brain surgery, I remember having a conversation with God as I watched a family friend undergo brain surgery while he was still awake. I said, "God, you can mess with any part of my body, please just don't touch my head." I laugh now for two reasons.

First, never tell God what to do because He knows far more than you do.

Second, I learned without brain surgery stripping me of the security I placed in my own strength and ability, I would have never seen God's glorious power throughout my life and given Him complete glory in it. I had to be erased so He could be seen.

Many people throughout my life ask me, "How do you smile through this? Why do you still want God after all you have been through? How do you still have faith?"

My answer, "How can I not?"

I smile because I cannot deny God even if I wanted to. He was and is all over my story. He was in the random police officer's sirens, the ones sounding the charge in getting me to the hospital on time when my lungs collapsed. He was in the less than one percent of a collapsed lung. He was in the worst case of mouth sores those doctors had ever witnessed. Without those sores, I would not have discovered drawing, which offered me many moments of relief over the span of my lifetime. He was the fighting spirit in Joe, the doubting donor coordinator, the two sons of Mary, and the kindness of almost 10,000 donors. He was in those Dr.'s words, "There is no match for your daughter." Without those words, without the news of no hope and no chance of survival, and without that random, *Better Homes and Gardens* magazine article, we would have never been led to the best transplant hospital and my only chance of survival. He was the creator of the brilliant minds of the transplant team at Duke. He was my protector when my numbers dropped below survival levels on those helicopter and plane rides. He was in the thousands upon thousands of prayers all over the world received on my behalf during the transplant process, and then years later at Liberty University as over 10,000 students and faculty prayed consistently for me. Each season of my life specifically covered in prayer by loved ones, friends, and strangers alike. And God was with me, even through the loss of all my friends.

I may not get all my questions answered of why so many kids suffered and lost their lives. Oftentimes, we just don't get the *why's* answered. But I do know this. I had to draw closer to Him for the strength to get through those times. One day, I will know why that was a part of His greater plan, and on that day, I will not only smile, but I will stand face to face with Jesus Christ, knowing He always saw the greater picture, while I only had an in-the-moment view.

The God moments go on and on. I should not be alive. Miracle after miracle, moment after moment, God spared my life, physically and mentally, while battling the leukemia and the transplant. But God wasn't done with performing miracles. After a horrific brain bleed and craniotomy, I should have remained in the state I was in right after brain surgery. But I went on to receive both a master of human services and a master of business administration degree, all while the makings of my former identity were being rebuilt. Only for His glory, He restored me and healed my brain completely, allowing me, *Jenna Anne Sailsbury*, to write my story for you. This is Him working everything out for His purpose and not my own.

So, what is your Eleven, 22? When did God change from a religion to a relationship with Jesus Christ? Or have you even had a moment in life where you realized God loves you so much, He sent His only Son to die for you? Do you *know* without a shadow of doubt where you will spend eternity, in Heaven or in Hell? Because you can!

What are you waiting for? Don't let this moment pass you by. God loves you! Jesus Christ died for your sins and was raised to life three days later! Turn from your sins and accept Jesus into your life. When you make this decision, it is a moment that will last forever here on earth and as you live an eternity in heaven with Him, receiving everlasting peace and joy, instead of, *only for a moment.*

Do you want a relationship with Christ? Just talk to God in prayer; something like this.

> "Dear God, I know there is nothing I could ever do to earn a relationship with You. I am a sinner, and I am asking You to forgive me. I believe Jesus Christ is Your Son, that He died on the cross to take away my sins, and that You raised Him to life. I don't know everything there is to know about You, all I know is, I trust Jesus as my Savior and want to spend my life getting to know You more. Guide me and teach me to represent You to everyone around me. There is nothing greater than Your love. I pray this in Jesus' precious and Holy name, Amen.

If you have just accepted Christ as your Savior or have more questions, scan the QR code to let me know!

Only for a Moment:

IT'S TIME TO CELEBRATE!

"You love Him even though you have never seen Him.
Though you do not see Him now, you trust Him; and
you rejoice with a glorious, inexpressible joy. The reward
for trusting Him will be the salvation of your souls."
— 1 Peter 1:8-9

Let's celebrate your journey, the good, the bad, and the ugly!

Celebrate your new relationship with Jesus Christ! It is the best decision you have ever made!

Listening to Christian music was instrumental to my recovery after brain surgery. It was one of the very few things that triggered the relationship with Christ that had been severed. It pointed me back to Him. Despite what our circumstances tell us, God is and will always be in control, and loves us unconditionally! Scan the QR code below and let's celebrate who God is.

ACKNOWLEDGEMENTS

I hope after reading this book, you are encouraged to know God is alive, moving, and performing miracles. My story would have never reached you without His sovereign grace and protection over my life, so I must start with giving God all the praise and honor for allowing me to live through everything this crazy life threw at me.

God also specifically placed so, so many people to encourage, strengthen, and fight alongside me and my family during my journey. There is no way to list the multitude of people that have made a lasting impact on my life. Please know that even if I miss thanking you publicly, God knows, and if you are a child of His, there are crowns in heaven waiting for you! But here we go from the beginning!

To all my home doctors, nurses, and caregivers: Dr. Abernathy and the entire practice, Angus Dentistry, Dr. Metts and staff, everyone at my home hospitals, and to Dr. Bugbee and all the medical personnel at the University of California San Diego Medical Center. Thank you for caring for me and my family for so many years during our journey. Words cannot express how your kindness made such a hard process a little easier to bear.

If there is one thing I have learned through my journey, it is that life is precious. There are not many people who know that better than Dr. Kurtzberg, Sue Wood, the doctors, nurses, and medical staff who have served and serve now in the Duke University Pediatric

Transplant Program. There are no adequate words to express the gratitude I have for you. Without the endless hours you pour into others' lives, many children would not have the blessing of living another day. You all are truly heroes.

To my Liberty University family: you loved me before I had any affiliation to Liberty at all, holding the second largest Bone Marrow Drive the state of Virginia had ever seen. Then, the love continued as countless students and faculty prayed that God would yet again spare my life during brain surgery. Wow! You all are extremely special people, and I cannot wait to see how God shines down upon the university. Thank you!

Anyone who has ever written a book, knows the arduous journey it can be. For everyone who has walked this long road with me, you all will be rewarded for your patience! Without the countless hours poured into editing, reading, design, marketing, etc., this book would have never reached publication. It was a hard road, but your faithfulness to the mission allowed this project to keep going until completion. Thank you from the bottom of my heart.

I am not really sure how you adequately thank someone for their constant sacrifice, financial support, and selfless prayers, but I do. I would not be who I am today if it weren't for all my aunts and uncles, grandparents on both sides, so many other family members, and many, many friends that are more like family to me. I hope you remember the countless prayers you asked on my behalf and continue to pray and go after God with all you have! Let's celebrate Him as He continues to move in all of our lives!

And lastly, to my family. Dad, Mom, Zachary, Gabriel, and Hannah thank you for always supporting me. There is nothing like the love of family, and I am forever grateful that I have had such a strong family to walk alongside me. God must think of us as special!

He has allowed us to endure much, and all for His glory alone! I love you and pray you continually live your lives so God is reflected first and foremost!

BIBLIOGRAPHY

1. Folger. "Richard II - Act 5, Scene 5 Folger Shakespeare Library," n.d. https://www.folger.edu/explore/ shakespeares-works/richard-ii/read/5/5/.

2. Education.com. "Word Search Worksheet Generator Education.Com," n.d.https://www. education.com/worksheet-generator/reading/ word-search/?gclid=EAIaIQobChMI4_fzkKr__ AIViUZyCh1WNwUrEAAYASAAEgIfv_D_BwE.

3. Hope, M. writer; Rhimes, S. creator. "Ain't That A Kick In the Head." *Grey's Anatomy*, Season 14, Episode 4. ABC, 2007.

- Illustrations and activities all done by Jenna unless otherwise stated.

- All activity illustration answer keys are located on my website – jasailsbury.com

- All QR codes are generated from qrcode-monkey.com.

ABOUT THE AUTHOR

J. A. Sailsbury is an author and speaker dedicated to uplifting others through telling stories of the impossible made possible. From Chesterfield, Virginia, Sailsbury looks forward to meeting and engaging with readers online and at local, national, and global venues alike. Connect and learn more by scanning the QR code below to visit J. A. Sailsbury's website.

Made in USA - Kendallville, IN
15609_9798989024711
10.10.2023 1348